'An inspiring, powerful book and a clear explanation of the development of modern slavery and the responses to it over the last 20 years. Written with humility and warmth, it demonstrates what an individual can do to really make a difference.'

– Dame Sara Thornton DBE QPM,
the UK's Independent Anti-Slavery Commissioner

'Kate's compelling case studies reveal the agonising decisions survivors and their support workers must face in a system fit for purpose on paper, but that in reality offers very little, and risks re-traumatisation, criminalisation and even in some cases re-trafficking. Her book's recommendations, including from survivors themselves, alongside her message of empathy provide a powerful guide for both the public and policymakers alike.'

– Tamara Barnett, Director of Operations,
Human Trafficking Foundation

'A beautifully written and eye-opening book that draws from the author's unique front-line experience over more than a decade. This is an absolutely essential read, full of engagement with survivors, deep research, and fresh ideas for how we can see, hear, understand, and confront modern slavery in our society.'

– Professor Zoe Trodd, Director of the Rights Lab

'This is a must-read book for anyone who wants to understand one of the gravest problems of contempora─ ─ ─ ' ─ give voice to the unseen, provoke and w as ordinary citizens we are all deeply i king, and slavery, but at the same time sl hink about how to bring about change. E

– Samantha Knights QC, Matrix

'An intelligent and authoritatively written book based on evidence. Every survivor is different, every agency has different thresholds and criteria, and it is no surprise that we have a messy, dysfunctional system tackling modern slavery.

This book should be read by those who know very little, but also maybe more importantly by those who think they know it all. As a former Police and Crime Commissioner and magistrate, I recognise that the author brings clarity to a confused scenario. Solutions are neither clear nor straightforward. Victims have limited choices, or no choice. The least worst choice just reminds us that this is our responsibility to know more. All our agencies and the public need to know the signs, to listen to our gut feeling. The "them" and "us" are clearly articulated. Under different situations, "us" could become "them". This book is not about "do gooding". It's not about telling victims what to do, it's about giving them the power to make choices with knowledge.'

– Sue Mountstevens, Former Police and Crime Commissioner,
Avon & Somerset, 2012–2021

'This is a very personal moving story of the journey of one determined woman who decides that listening to the experiences of the victims of trafficking is not enough. Her response to the harrowing testimonies we read about is to set up the charity UNSEEN and champion the cause of victims to Government. Kate Garbers shows us that she is more than a campaigner, as you will find when you read her book. She cares deeply and hopes that you will as well and then act. The question she is really posing to us all is will we?'

– Lord Coaker House of Lords, Former Co-Chair of
All Party Parliamentary Modern Slavery Group

UNSEEN LIVES

UNSEEN LIVES

THE HIDDEN WORLD OF MODERN SLAVERY

KATE GARBERS

Jessica Kingsley Publishers
London and Philadelphia

First published in Great Britain in 2022 by Jessica Kingsley Publishers
An Hachette Company

1

Copyright © Kate Garbers 2022

A CIP catalogue record for this title is available from the
British Library and the Library of Congress

ISBN 978 1 78592 635 8
eISBN 978 1 78592 636 5

Printed and bound in Great Britain by Clays Ltd

Jessica Kingsley Publishers' policy is to use papers that are natural, renewable and recyclable
products and made from wood grown in sustainable forests. The logging and manufacturing
processes are expected to conform to the environmental regulations of the country of origin.

Jessica Kingsley Publishers
Carmelite House
50 Victoria Embankment
London EC4Y 0DZ

www.jkp.com

To all those who have dedicated their time, energy, and resources supporting people, trying to help, fighting for what is right. Thank you and keep going!

Contents

Disclaimer

All views, thoughts, opinions, and presentation of facts in this book reflect only the author's views. The author has written this book in a personal capacity based upon her own experiences. Consent was sought from those who directly contributed.

Slavery and Me

When I was first exposed to the issue of slavery, or human trafficking as it was then coined, I was a Key Stage 2 primary school teacher, fiercely relearning my times tables to ensure that I would be able to outwit the seven- and eight-year-old bright sparks in my class. As part of my summer holiday one year, I made the decision, along with my husband, to join a team of volunteers heading to Ukraine to work in an orphanage. We wanted to offer something back, to visit a new country, to explore and adventure. This trip was to become a regular feature of the next five summers for me, continuing even after I'd left the world of education.

I enjoyed teaching – I loved seeing children learn, grow, grasp concepts, take risks, and work things out for themselves – but the summer I learned about the issue of trafficking, I began to struggle with the routine of the classroom. I began to resent the education system and what it demanded from teachers, and the sense of entitlement I saw in some of the children. The contrast between the situations children were facing in Ukraine and the UK felt increasingly unfair and frustrated me. It was not long – a matter of months – before I had made the decision to hand in my notice.

I visited the orphanage in Balta, in the south-west of Ukraine, as part of a team of volunteers from a local faith community. Every day was an adventure; we never quite knew what we would find or what we'd be asked to do. One year, we arrived to be told that all the children had gone to summer camp for the week and that we were to drive another four hours to go and be with them; another summer, the police arrived, threatening to arrest us all for proselytising (we weren't!). One August, my husband and I celebrated our wedding anniversary with 100 Ukrainian orphans. On one of our trips, I could be seen early every morning using the dusty field as my running track, in preparation for a half marathon when we got back home. Sometimes children would join me and serve as my motivation to keep going (I hate running!).

Nothing was quite like arriving at the orphanage, after some 15 hours of travel, exhausted, weary, and always a little apprehensive. As we stepped off the mini-bus, little faces would appear at the dormitory windows. Children who knew and recognised us from previous years would excitedly shout out greetings, welcoming us back. Children and volunteers alike would head for bed, excited to see each other the next morning – at this point, it always felt as if we were coming home. But as much as it felt like home, I knew it was always temporary; I knew I'd leave and return to my comfortable Western lifestyle – a glaring difference to the experiences of the children who lived there and what I learned may happen to them when they came to leave the orphanage.

The discovery that children were being preyed upon when they left the orphanage – offered opportunities that would never come to fruition, promised a job, money, a place to live, and because they had no other options, would accept and find themselves in situations of exploitation – made me feel physically ill. The children we'd connected with, played with, kept in contact with, hugged, would be taken advantage of and put at risk.

I learned about trafficking on my first trip to Ukraine. The thought of those I had connected with being bought and sold angered me. I was incensed that people would take advantage of people, of children, who, to my mind, had very little. That adults would promise them the world and then force them to do things they didn't want to do for profit did not sit well with me. It gnawed at my core – a dull ache, a sense of despair and helplessness that would not go away. I felt that I needed to do something, but at this point I had no idea what.

Once I had learned about trafficking and its impact on those I cared for, I felt overwhelmed and convinced that I needed to do something. Initially, my ideas were based upon facilitating adoptions out of the orphanage – this was thwarted early in the thinking process as there was no reciprocal adoption agreement in place between the UK and Ukraine.

At one point, my husband and I considered moving to Ukraine and setting up a second-stage home for those children leaving the orphanage so they would have a safe place to go and continue their education or vocational training. I tried to persuade the faith community I was part of to expand our summer visits by bringing children for respite care in the UK, where they could have new experiences, practise their English, access some basic health care (the children's teeth and eyes tended to be bad), but this was met with resistance from the wider community and commentary that it would not be fair to expose children to something they could not have.

We managed Christmas packages, donations of clothes and various items throughout the year, and the annual visit. As priorities for the faith community and those involved changed, the visits and our support of the orphanage and the children also dwindled.

For several years after we stopped visiting, we tried to keep in touch with some of the children and often hoped that one day we might find one on our doorstep, having turned 18 and managed to secure a visa to visit England – pie-in-the-sky dreams, but we had built strong connections with several of the children and certainly felt somewhat hopeless about what we had not managed to achieve for them. Yes, it would have been a drop in the ocean, but for the individuals we might have helped, it could have made a difference.

Subsequently, my opinion about short-term volunteering trips, such as our trips to the Ukraine, has altered. I am not sure that they always offer lasting benefit to those that we 'go to help', even though they are a practical response that is often welcomed and needed. Although the children enjoyed the games, the crafts, and the music, and our time with them offered them a break from the mundanity of the routine of orphanage life, I am not sure we were able to achieve any beneficial lasting change. I think these brief exposures to and experiences of other cultures, people, and their situations offer far more benefit to the visitors than the visited. It certainly changed the trajectory of my own life.

On my bedside table sits a Barney the Dinosaur toy. It was given to me by a young boy, Alexey, at the orphanage. He got up super early on the morning we were leaving to say goodbye and thrust his prized possession into my hand. I took it back with me each year to try to return it, but he would never take it.

During a conversation with a friend, Andrew, on my return from that first visit to Ukraine, I expressed my frustrations and concerns about the children and the risk of trafficking they faced. He'd heard similar stories previously and posed a challenge to me. *What was I going to do about it?* Being presented with this challenge ultimately resulted in me resigning from my teaching position and starting the anti-slavery charity Unseen.

We started in 2007 as a two-person team, Andrew and I, with me as a volunteer and him working full-time elsewhere. The development and growth of the organisation was like a roller-coaster ride; we had to strap in and enjoy the adventure. Everything we did was uncharted territory; we had to learn everything from scratch. I had never started a charity before, nor had I run support services; funding applications were minefields, and establishing partnerships took diplomacy to the next level. Tirelessly explaining that, yes, trafficking (slavery) was an issue that was prevalent in the UK and dealing with people's and agencies' subsequent disbelief were exhausting. We continually asked, of others and of ourselves, the questions: *What can be done? How can we help?*

Learning about the issue – how it presented, whom it impacted, how it occurred, the legislation in place, the support offered, the lack of services available, the complexities it manifested, and the interplay with other issues – was immense. At times, I felt scared and overwhelmed by it all.

I certainly experienced sleepless nights, overarching dread, anger, and, at the beginning, fear of what on earth I was getting into – the more I read about traffickers, the more worried I became. How risky was this? It was a concern that prompted me to ensure staff teams were supported and protected as best we could over the years, and my natural tendency to assume the worst and work back from there has meant that to date there have been no repercussions. I think, in reality, the risk was always low, but the unknown always feels more daunting than we often like to admit.

I knew I wanted to provide support for those who had been trafficked; I also knew this was a sticking plaster, and that stopping it happening at all was the ultimate aim, but that didn't help those who were already stuck in cycles of exploitation. It needed to be both: the provision of services for those who needed them, as well as challenging the wider systems that allowed for this to happen in the first place. There was work to be done, and Unseen was established as a charity to provide safety, hope, and choice directly to survivors of human trafficking in 2008.

My objective at this stage was to be able to offer women a place of safety, a homely environment in which they were safe and in which they could begin to work out what was next for them. It took me two years of learning, meeting with those in the sector, developing the service, and securing funding before this was achieved, and at multiple points I was ready to walk away. I knew the issue was real; I knew more services were needed, and even once a suitable property had been identified, without funding in place there was no way the necessary members of staff could be employed. I remember walking to the office one day ready to tell my co-founder that I didn't think this was going to work, I had tried my best, sunk numerous hours, late nights, heart, passion, and tears into this – but for some reason it was not meant to be.

At 5.28 p.m. that same day I got a call from a funder who we had met with a few weeks previously. They were willing to take a punt on us (my words, not theirs) with three years' funding that would allow us to employ the initial skeleton team we would need to open the safe-house doors!

In 2011, the first safe house opened for women who had experienced sexual exploitation. The first women through the doors had been exploited for domestic servitude and forced labour. Within 24 hours of our first beneficiaries arriving, I was back to the drawing board, rethinking elements of the service and checking whether the approach developed for victims of sexual exploitation would also be relevant for those who had been forced to work in a domestic setting. Having thought I had dotted all the i's and crossed all the t's, I had already learned that the issue was far wider than I thought.

Other organisations, more established in the field, told us that if we were still around in a few years, they might look to work with us but they did not hold their breath. Twelve years later and we were still there – sitting around tables with governments (both the UK and further afield), being asked for our opinions, influencing the agenda, legislation, and policy frameworks.

Practically, we were training frontline professionals both in the UK and abroad, spotting and filling the gaps in service and support provision as we identified them. Over the next eight years, we offered a longer-term resettlement service (2013), opened a men's safe house (2016), established the UK's Modern Slavery Helpline (2016), and piloted a children's home (2018).

I've supported survivors first-hand and worked with statutory agencies, law enforcement, and governments to work out how the issue of trafficking and slavery can be tackled more effectively.

I left my day-to-day directorship at Unseen in late 2020. For me, it was time to step away from the fast-paced, reactive, solution-focused, sharp end, and work out how I could use all I have learned and seen to attack and influence the issue from another angle, knowing that, as hard as stepping away from the thing I had created would be, both Unseen and I would be able to embark on new chapters of our journeys as we work towards a world without slavery.

I am fiercely proud of all the organisation has achieved and will continue to achieve in the future, and remain an Ambassador for the organisation.

Writing this book has offered me the opportunity to reflect on the whistle-stop nature of being involved in running a charity for the last 12 years and given me the opportunity to share this journey and my discoveries and the people I met. It is my way of honouring what I consider the privilege I had to meet them.

The hidden world of slavery has been my normal, day-to-day life for more than 12 years. As part of my work for Unseen, I've sat on a brothel floor, trying my hardest to listen to the words of the individual in front of me, despite the incredibly overbearing heat and the pungent smell of lubricant and sex in the room.

I've vomited with nerves on numerous occasions prior to presenting thoughts and research to people I know have the power to make a difference.

I've contained my frustration during a government department launch meeting of a new policy that, while looking great on paper, would have inevitable (albeit unintentional) consequences for those needing support.

I've found myself travelling all over the world, talking to inspiring individuals and professionals who've been willing to share their most intimate selves with me.

It can sometimes feel as if the exploitation of people in our society is endemic – just something we accept as par for the course. It's been happening for as long as we can remember; the people have different names, but someone is always being taken advantage of.

I do believe it can be different.

On our last visit to the orphanage, Barney the Dinosaur was packed and ready to be returned, but Alexey, the boy who had given me the toy, was not there – he had been transferred to another orphanage. Over the years, that toy has served as a powerful reminder of what I am fighting for. I am reminded of him often and wonder what he is up to and what he has experienced. Maybe one day we will get the opportunity to grab a beer and I can thank him for the strength he unknowingly passed to me over the last 12 years.

CHAPTER 1

Our Connections to Modern Slavery

> The choices survivors face and the systems that hold them in untenable positions need to be addressed. Until we, as a whole society, believe those at the bottom of the supply chain are worth as much as those at the top, we will continue to have this problem.
>
> **(KARA 2021)**

Slavery is enmeshed with lots of well-known global issues: poverty, climate change and natural disasters, violence against women and girls, war, unstable economies, and lack of employment and educational opportunities.

These global issues directly impact people's lives.

An issue hits. Burdens increase. Options are limited. Exploitative practices appear. Choice decreases and personal freedoms diminish. People get stuck.

Our global society paves the way for exploitation to exist: the children mining in Indonesia and the Democratic Republic of Congo in order to provide the minerals needed for our mobile phones; the Bangladeshi women and girls who cut and sew cloth for the clothes we wear, working 16 hours a day for as little as 12 pence an hour; the Sudanese pickers in Italian fields supplying fruit and vegetables, scared of being reported to officials if they complain about their living conditions or their lack of pay.

What does any of this have to do with you, with us?

The fruit and veg end up in our supermarkets and then our fridges and kitchen cupboards. Those clothes briefly reside in our wardrobes until the next trend comes into fashion. The phones end up in our back pockets and handbags... It is closer than we may like to think.

Very few of us wake up in the morning and decide to participate in the exploitation and enslavement of another person, but we – you and I – are accountable for contributing to its success. We are part of a global system of supply and demand that allows these exploitative practices to exist.

There are truths and realities that lie behind our everyday experience of society. There is a very real and utterly *human* price being paid. The challenge is for us, individually and collectively, to think about the part we play in slavery today. Slavery doesn't only happen in far-flung places, disconnected from our daily lives. It continues around us all the time, hidden in plain sight, unseen.

Slavery is a big issue. It is overwhelming. It has the power to make us feel small and powerless.

But we must work out how we can fight for those who can't fight for themselves right now, figure out what we can do, however small and insignificant it may feel, to work towards a world where there is no place for slavery to exist.

There are many things that are not right in the world. The fact that 'slavery' still exists is one of these things. It is a symptom, an indication that our world is not how it was intended to be, that we are not treating each other right.

I put 'slavery' in quotation marks because it is a term that many, myself included, both in and out of the anti-slavery sector, are not comfortable with. Its definition in legislation (both domestic and international), policy, and guidance is not always clear, and its intersection with other areas, such as migration, prostitution, access to the labour market, exploitative working practices, and immigration controls, means that the term can be misused and misunderstood. Confusion over terminology can leave potential victims unidentified, misrepresented, and not afforded the protections and support they are entitled to. In some instances, even those who are not victims, but who may be experiencing less than ideal employment situations, actively experience discrimination and even criminalisation at the hands of the systems we have put in place to protect them. People who are not victims of slavery fall foul of the systems, and this is only amplified for those who are.

It is both a word and a movement fraught with complications. I will use the term 'slavery' as it is defined under the Modern Slavery Act (2015) and will define and describe it, along with trafficking and exploitation, in more detail in Chapter 2: The Present Reality of Modern Slavery. Chapter 3: What the Law Says about Modern Slavery and Chapter 4: Meeting the People Affected by Modern Slavery will also frame what is meant by the term 'modern slavery' in a UK context, as well as considering how slavery may present itself across the globe – likely in a place not that far from wherever you are reading these words. I will do this by introducing you to people I have met along the way and telling their stories. We can see the realities of modern slavery when we give voice to those whose lives have been shaped by it. We can see them.

Throughout the book, I refer to 'we'. Depending on context, I variously use 'we' to infer you and I, 'we' as a collective of individuals, humanity, the individuals that make up our society, and 'we' in reference to the systems at play that guide and influence us.

I am not a fan of labels, especially not ones that people have had assigned to them through no choice of their own. Labels do, however, afford us the opportunity to understand something in a similar way for an agreed period. For the purpose of your reading of this book, I'll use both 'victim' and 'survivor' to describe those who have experienced slavery, trafficking, and exploitation. 'Victim' will refer to an individual who is still in the situation of exploitation (as I perceive it) and 'survivor' is used when they are no longer in a situation of slavery (again, as I perceive it).

The people you'll meet are far more than the label of 'victim' or 'survivor' that we assign to them. These labels are problematic. They are not the definitions that the individuals I've met would use to describe themselves. They are commonly defined labels that the anti-slavery sector, government, and law enforcement use. Such labels are widely acknowledged as problematic. An individual released from a situation of slavery may not be free, may not feel they'll survive. What they have experienced will remain with them, and part of their journey will be learning how to re-acclimatise and adapt. This means that although they may be technically free from their situation of exploitation it may be some time until they feel they are free and able to embrace this. Exploring the complexity of what it means to be free is not a topic for this book.

What I do know is that the kinds of support, structures, and policies that have been created, which cover what a victim is entitled to, how they should look and/or react, and which elements are required in the accounts they give of their experiences, can in fact restrict their access to freedom and the establishment of their independence. Our systems promote survival while stifling any opportunity for individuals to thrive (see Chapter 5: Support for Victims of Modern Slavery, Chapter 6: Disconnected Systems, Chapter 7: Problems in the Identification Process, Chapter 8: Problems in the Support Process, Chapter 9: The Problem of What Comes Next, and Chapter 10: The Problem of Viable Alternatives). Some potential solutions and approaches that need to be considered are explored in Chapter 11: Can We Fix What Is Broken?, alongside the views, thoughts, and suggestions of those with direct experience of being trafficked and enslaved. Their voices deserve to be heard and their realities seen.

Increasingly, there is the recognition that we have built systems and mechanisms of support to meet our own purposes rather than those of the people we are supporting. We have not always put victims and survivors at the heart of our response to them; too often we are guided by the needs of the system rather than the needs of the individual in front of us. This has to change.

Slavery past and present

There is no denying that slavery is a powerful word – a word with historical connotations that have very real impact on society and people's lives today. It was once an establishment enshrined in law. An establishment that allowed particular groups of people to be treated and viewed as less than others – things, items, objects to be bought and sold. For many of us, it will conjure images of the transatlantic slave trade of the 18th and 19th centuries; of African Americans enslaved in the Deep South; of slave ships, sugar plantations, and cotton picking. Civilisations, trade, wealth, transportation routes, and cities have been built, literally, on the back(s) of trading people. Our version of history tells us that this horrific violation of human rights stopped with the abolition movement of the late 18th century, but although the transatlantic slave trade, thanks to the work done by numerous individuals and groups that took up the cause, is a thing of the past, we are still reliant on violating others' human rights to get access to cheap goods and cheap services. Slave markets, slave ships, and workers in the fields far from home. Once this trade was visible; now it is hidden. Just as embedded in society but maybe no longer quite as overt and obvious. This hidden nature of modern slavery has numerous consequences for the organisations responsible for identifying and supporting those deemed victims of it and for prosecuting those who perpetrate it. Across the world, people are trapped in situations of exploitation, paid nothing for their work or maybe just enough so they return the next day, held in a perpetual cycle of debt. We have continued to commodify our fellow human beings, and until we start to see them as people, real people, people beyond any labels assigned, we will continue to be part of creating the perfect storm in which slavery and exploitation can continue to exist.

The lens through which we view slavery has changed over the years, the parameters of acceptable and unacceptable have been moved and often redefined, terminology has changed, laws have been written, policies put in place, support systems established, and yet it appears it has always been here, woven into the fabric of our society, endemic in our approach towards people who we don't think are like us. I have heard it said that as humans we have an innate need to separate ourselves from people who have experienced things that we fear (Brown 2020). I think slavery is one of those things – we are understandably overwhelmed by it and unsure what to do about it. It is frustrating encountering people who are surprised to hear that slavery still exists and is fundamentally embedded in our society. Increasing news reports, media coverage, legislation, businesses being publicly outed for their practices, and still we remain blind to this issue – it continues around us, hidden in plain sight, unseen.

Once we do know about it, we must battle the tendency to block it out, to turn a blind eye and not see our own connection to it. This is a completely normal reaction, and people often feel weighed down by the enormity of the issue. Thinking about people being abused is not easy; thinking about the role we are potentially playing to keep them trapped in a cycle of exploitation is uncomfortable.

Our internal dialogue kicks in: 'I am a good person... I am sure that if the situation were that bad, they could choose to leave... There are always other options, right? I mean, I don't pay for sex. I know that T-shirt is cheap, but I want it.'

It goes on: 'I need that new phone... Yes, the people that did my drive were super cheap, and no, they didn't speak English, but they seemed OK, I didn't really think about it much – it's all Eastern Europeans that work in manual labour now, right? Are they even here legally?'

And on: 'Anyway, what choice do I have? What other options are there?'

We often have a choice. We could consider if we do truly need what it is we are buying. We tend to think there are no alternative options, the cost of those on offer may feel prohibitive, or we don't know what to do to find out what our options are.

We all have decisions to make when faced with some of these everyday purchasing decisions. Are we going to make ourselves think any further beyond the bargain that T-shirt appears to be? Will we question how it is physically possible that cotton can be picked, spun, transported, and made into a T-shirt thousands of miles away from where it started and now only cost us £3?

While it may seem I'm being somewhat reductive to make my point, I've heard all these justifications, assumptions, and myths. I've witnessed both victims and survivors being blamed for the situation they are in. It's not that people don't care but that slavery is a thorny issue, inextricably linked with our daily lives and the choices we make. It's an issue that often feels so big that it is almost easier to do nothing, frozen in a helpless state. We are often exhausted by compassion fatigue, so worn down by politics and the other issues we are bombarded with that we are unsure what part we can play or how to engage. Subconsciously, we tend to reconcile ourselves to justifying our lack of action on the basis that it seems so distant from us, so far removed from our experiences. And yet that fruit and veg is in our fridge now. Those clothes, however briefly, hang in our wardrobes until the next trend comes along. Those phones end up in our back pockets and handbags. Slavery is closer to us than we like to think.

Once we see it, in the things we buy, the services we commission, the lifestyle choices we make, our connections to slavery are staggering and currently somewhat unavoidable. Slavery isn't just happening in far-flung places, disconnected from our daily lives. Across the world, people are being forced to work in poor conditions for little, if any, money. They have limited choices, are taken advantage of, working to meet our demand for cheap goods and services. Not all these individuals will be completely controlled by another, but they may be somewhere on the ever-expanding spectrum of exploitative practices. Practices that take advantage of those who find themselves in precarious positions. Practices that prey on those for whom there is no good choice. There are just choices that may, in that one point in time, appear to be less bad than the alternative. What do we do when choices are taken away from us or we find ourselves without the capacity, resilience, or resources to make the choice we would want, should everything else be equal?

The issue of trafficking and slavery fundamentally stems from a basis of inequality and discrimination, and we are involved in keeping these systemic wheels turning.

When the realisation that humans hurt other humans, knowingly or otherwise, is so starkly laid bare for us to see, it feels awkward and uncomfortable. We are part of a global system of supply and demand that allows these exploitative practices to exist. Our behaviours encourage the establishment of slavery and allow it to continue. What we do, what we buy, how we approach people and think of them as other, or less than, or only good for, provides fertile ground for slavery to exist. This may not be intentional on our part; we are not actively agreeing with slavery, but we are facilitating its existence. One of the biggest drivers behind slavery is our insatiable desire for cheap – we love a bargain, we love new, we love quick and easy, and we love disposable. All of this comes at a cost – a very real, human cost.

Slavery is an issue we knowingly or otherwise are perpetuating with our day-to-day actions. We are accountable for contributing to its success. We have a desire for cheap and the ability to switch off. We can justify our spending by complaining about a lack of viable alternatives, leaving a large tip, or telling ourselves that at least they have a job and life is better for them here than it could have been.

When we think about trafficking and slavery, it can be hard to imagine ourselves in shoes other than our own. We may find ourselves thinking, 'I work long hours too, I don't get paid much either, my boss is always expecting more of me, I can't just leave if I feel like it – I have bills to pay.' We may feel that our choices are restricted, and they may well be. But it is also most likely that we can choose to leave our overpowering, high-maintenance boss at any given point, and although that will certainly come with consequences that may be hard to navigate, we can most likely deal with the issues that arise from making this choice.

This is not to say that all of those who are enslaved and exploited cannot choose to leave their situations but that for some the stakes of doing so are too high to risk. Some will be experiencing trauma, some will fear threats of (or actual) violence to themselves and their families, some may be physically locked in or restrained (in my experience, this has been rare), and some will be afraid of the authorities and what leaving their situation means for their status and ability to access work in the UK. For some, all these things will combine to create the perfect situation for a trafficker and result in individuals staying in exploitation. They stay because they are scared for themselves and their families, they stay because they fear deportation, they stay because they feel shame. The adage of 'better the devil you know' comes into play. Time and time again, over my years of working in the sector, I have seen and been told about situations where those who do come forward, who do choose to speak up, leave, or seek help are let down. This didn't happen to just one or two individuals, but time and time again, as a recurring theme. Let down by our prejudices and the disbelief inherent in our political, legal, and even our support systems.

Some of us may think any job here in the UK is better than that available to someone in their home country. Our inner soundtrack may ask, 'What's the problem? Coming here, taking our jobs, they knew the score, they took the risk, it's not my fault...' Certainly, the media portrays this attitude loud and clear – the hordes of migrants sweeping our shores, taking the jobs that we are entitled to. Some of us may fall into the trap of blaming victims and survivors and comparing their choices to our own, assuming that we would never find ourselves in the situations they face. We risk perpetuating an 'us and them' narrative, seeing 'them' as people who take job offers we would never accept, people who travel with people they do not know, people who fall in love with the wrong person, people who choose to stay in their situation.

Some of us may find we can empathise with a victim of slavery and trafficking, but only up to a point. Fundamentally, we don't believe it could ever happen to us. I invite you to put on someone else's shoes, understand their situation, consider their options (or lack of), as if they were your own, remembering that when every choice we're faced with is less than ideal, we still need to make one.

> If you can learn a simple trick, Scout, you'll get along a lot better with all kinds of folks. You never really understand a person until you consider things from his point of view, until you climb inside of his skin and walk around in it. (Lee 1960, p.33)

If we do not know about an issue, we do not have the choice or capacity to connect with it, think it through, or, where needed, change our approach to it. We cannot consider our actions, make decisions about how we want to proceed, or challenge not only ourselves but others and the systems that support it. Modern slavery is an ever-growing and ever-changing complex issue that requires a range of different responses and actions at different times and in different situations. This is a journey I am still on; I don't profess to have all of the answers or solutions, but it is an issue that has compelled me to act and to do *something*.

Slavery isn't a historical fact – it's a present reality. It was a present reality for the first person I knowingly met who had been impacted by slavery. His account of his and his mother's experience was my first connection point with slavery.

When I describe the interactions, emotions, and experiences shared, they are my reflections and perceptions of the circumstances, based on my recollections. Where I'm given permission to share the words of an individual, they will be presented in italics and in quotation marks. Every survivor has a unique truth that is not mine to tell. One day, I hope they get the opportunity to tell their stories themselves, in ways they choose. In the meantime, I trust that you will find yourself able to relate to these individuals and their circumstances, even though I do not refer to them by their real names.

The beginning of the journey

For me, it all began with the experience of a boy I'll call Anatolyi. Although it would be inappropriate for me to share his real name, it is imprinted in my memory. To my shame, this is not the case for all those I met.

Anatolyi's experience is an example of an account I've rarely shared publicly. On a personal level, it now feels important to recognise the particular impact meeting him had on me. He'll never know the impact that his sharing had on me. It was a conversation that would change the course of the next 12 years of my life.

On a stifling hot day in the summer of 2008, I got talking to Anatolyi, sitting under the shade of a large tree in the grounds of the orphanage. The tree was nestled between the rooms we slept in and the classrooms, the dining hall, the field, and the imposing shadow of the Ukrainian Orthodox church that stood in the middle of the orphanage grounds.

The difference between the beautiful church building with its gold-leaf detail and the exposed grey breeze-block walls of the orphanage buildings was stark. While unconnected, their proximity made the evident effort and funding put into each of them incomparable. It was the chiming of the bells of this church that, after a couple of days into our visits, had the whole team trained in some strange Pavlovian way. Days started and ended with the clamour of the bells ringing out, were supplemented by smaller handbells rung by the orphanage staff team to indicate when we were to line up for breakfast, lunch, and dinner. Routine was a big part of orphanage life, and it was scary how quickly we fell into this.

We were immersed in orphanage life, sleeping in dorm rooms, on beds with no mattresses to speak of – one year my mattress was flattened cereal boxes on top of the springs. We had showers once a week, a lack of Western toilets, high-carbohydrate and low-protein meals, and nightly football matches and dancing sessions.

We were sitting on the dusty floor under the tree making friendship bracelets – the classic summer club activity – when I asked a question of Anatolyi, via our translator. The general clamour of the orphanage seemed to stop as I sat under the tree and tried to absorb what I was being told. Anatolyi, along with a few other children, had been my shadow for the week – a cheeky boy, with a massively wide grin and hair so blond it was almost white. His English was good and he had dreams of living in America one day. As he told me this, I felt guilt spring up inside me. We were aware another group from the States visited the orphanage, and I was sure that for him and many of the other children our annual arrival stirred in them the hope of one day being selected and taken away from the orphanage. Little did they or we know at this juncture that the UK and Ukraine, unlike Ukraine and the USA, had no reciprocal adoption agreement process and that this would not be something the group visiting from England would ever be able to offer these children. Also with us was Vlad, a boy of seven or eight, who, over the next few years of visiting, I would come to know as a scrapper unable to control his temper and language. He sat quietly during this conversation, taking in what he was hearing, respecting his friend and his recollections, and clearly affected by hearing it. It became apparent that the stories of where the children came from and their dreams of where they might go were not topics regularly discussed or engaged with in the orphanage setting. It was a case of 'Where you come from doesn't matter; you're here now'. Anatolyi was the same as Vlad was the same as the next child.

Via the translator, I'd asked whether Anatolyi would mind telling me how he'd come to be at the orphanage. I had a genuine desire to know, to try to understand, to hear, and to connect.

Anatolyi had arrived at the orphanage at about three or four years old. He'd been dropped off there by the people who had kidnapped his mother. He described how he and his mother been walking down the street in their hometown one day when a car pulled up alongside them. His mother had become engaged in conversation with those in the car, and before he knew it, some men had got out of the car and surrounded him and his mum. He remembered how he'd been approached by one of the men and offered an ice cream. As he turned to show his mum his choice, he saw her being bundled into the back of the car. It was the last time he saw her. He was taken to an orphanage and some years later transferred to the one where we were to meet. When we spoke, Anatolyi had no knowledge of where his mum was or if they would ever see each other again. He seemed reassured that he was better off than other children in the orphanage. At least he'd not been abandoned by choice.

The translator suggested that his mother would have been forced to sell sex for money – that she'd been trafficked for sexual exploitation. At the time, these were words I did not fully comprehend.

Figures now suggest that there are more than 100,000 children living in Ukrainian orphanages (Humanitarian Relief Foundation 2014, p.21). Orphanages in a Ukrainian context are not always for children who have no parents; rather, they are a government response to support children whose parents and families are unable to for a variety of reasons. The state may determine that they are not suitable to parent their children and remove them as a protection mechanism. As a result, children in orphanages in Ukraine are often referred to as 'social orphans'. They may have parents and biological families but are 'cared for' by the state in orphanages.

My brief exposure to orphanage life informed my understanding not only that is life hard while growing up in an orphanage but that hardships often tend to continue once the orphanage has been left behind. Children who grow up in such orphanages are often institutionalised. With restricted access to financial resources, limited education, life skills and opportunities, and no onward support to speak of, either from family or from the state, the system actively makes them vulnerable.

A conversation with the director of the orphanage later in the week confirmed the disturbing fact that there were 'people' who waited outside the orphanage gates when the time came for the children to move on. These people offered places to stay and work and opportunities that would never transpire. Alone, homeless, and with little or no income, the children were at clear risk of exploitation. As director, she was resigned to the fact that, for some, there was little she could ultimately do.

In 2017, Ukraine began a process to re-house orphans in family home settings, disbanding the orphanage system in favour for something more akin to the foster care model (Hope and Homes for Children 2019). This may reflect a positive change of direction, but such a fundamental change in approach to the care and support of children will inevitably take a long time to achieve.

As the boys continued to make friendship bracelets in the shade of the tree, I remember having a hundred and one questions I wanted Anatolyi to answer. Injustice raged inside of me; a sense of unfairness overwhelmed me. I tried my best not to let my emotions show. The bell rang, rudely interrupting my thoughts and telling me it was time to line up outside the dining hall, wash my hands, and try to force down a bulgur wheat and vegetable soup and stewed fruit juice, with everyone else carrying on around me as if everything was normal. This was just one child's experience, but there were 150 children in that dining hall. What if what Anatolyi and the orphanage director described was to be the fate of all of these children? What if many of them were destined to be kidnapped or promised the world at the orphanage gates? They were no longer faceless and nameless children. These were children I knew and cared about.

Over the course of the next 12 years, I would meet so many people who'd experienced situations like Anatolyi's.

Someone I know and admire in the anti-slavery sector says that ethical storytelling is about being introspective and ensuring you remain authentic. The retelling of my interactions with those who have experienced exploitation is just one part of the story, seen only through my lens of 12 years working on the frontline. I can't and don't intend to present all the solutions; those who have been affected by slavery must be given the opportunity to contribute to the conversation as and when they can, are able to and want to. Their experiences help to create an accurate narrative about modern slavery, its impacts on individuals, the systems that allow it to exist, and what we can do about it. Those with lived experience and those with learned experience need to come together and work to break down, rather than perpetuate, unhelpful stereotypes and narratives. The interactions that we, professionals in the sector, have, the dilemmas we face and the cases that keep us up at night are rarely heard, and I think they have a part to play in the conversation, hence the writing of this book. Working together connects us and reminds us to focus on what we share, rather than what divides us. It's hard to have compassion for others if we don't understand what they have been through. It's hard enough to see what needs to change when you've encountered slavery first-hand; it's even harder to feel the reality of the issue if experiences aren't shared and heard.

The 'effective altruism' movement proposed by Peter Singer (2015) and the philosophy it offers provides us with a useful outlook on life. At its simplest, it asserts that in order to make the world better, we must use the resources we have. We determine the most effective ways to benefit others and improve things for them. Our resources equate to our skills, our time, and our money. Effective altruism encourages us to get the best value we can from what we have. In sharing my 12 years' experience of interactions and issues that largely remain misunderstood and unseen, I aim to contribute what I have to give in the hope that it will help to move our conversations forward in ways that lead to positive outcomes. I also invite you to begin, or continue, to discover what doing so might mean for you.

These individual truths expose what is happening every hour of every day within our societies. They challenge us to think about the part we play ourselves in slavery today, knowingly or otherwise.

Those I've met deserve to be believed. What they've faced are realities – the realities of someone's son, daughter, brother, sister, mother, father, friend.

When we talk about poverty or inequality in our societies, we so often do so without interacting with, including, or considering the views of those with lived experience. When we institute policies or design processes to support those affected, we tend to base our conclusions on published theories, on media portrayal, or on the opinions we read voiced on social media.

We lack evidence, and we lack exposure to how real people live the harshly real lives that exist on our very doorsteps yet are beyond our worst imaginings.

If ethical storytelling is about being introspective while remaining authentic, my aim, rather than to perpetuate stereotypes, is to:

- **reveal** the direct (and indirect) impact of modern slavery on those who have themselves been enslaved
- **expose** how systems, policies, and approaches designed to support in fact allow slavery to continue in the 21st century
- **suggest** some of the ways in which modern slavery can be reframed and the systems that aim to support survivors reimagined.

My unique access to the truths of lives of survivors may not make for a comfortable read. What follows certainly does not profess to offer complete solutions to the issues.

This is a book of challenge. This is a book of discovery and journeying.

This is a book of insights about trafficking, about the systems that cause harm while trying to help, about the people it impacts, and about the ways it pervades our society. A book of discovery about what it is like to work to support and advocate for victims and survivors day to day, month to month. A book that challenges us to be better and to look for ways to fix what has been broken.

CHAPTER 2

The Present Reality of Modern Slavery

It feeds on social instability, economic turbulence, chaos.
We've had plenty of this in the last two decades.
(DIAS 2017, P.673)

S lavery is the illicit trade in human beings for profit. The true scale of modern slavery within the UK, and indeed globally, is unknown at this point. The numbers used are flawed and inaccurate. Today, in my country and yours, wherever you live, men, women, and children continue to be bought and sold. Humans are being treated as commodities and exploited for someone else's gain.

Modern slavery, while increasingly becoming part of our everyday language, is a term fraught with difficulties. Slavery is an economic system in which the principles of property law are applied to people – people own people, and people are used as commodities for the profit of other people – but it is a term that does not have a universally agreed definition.

'Modern slavery' is *not*:

- a static term
- a term used widely around the world
- an easily quantifiable phenomenon.

Every individual's experience of being exploited and forced to do something against their will is inevitably different. Today, victims of modern slavery are coerced to work in car washes and in nail bars on our UK high streets, in the hospitality sector at the restaurants we frequent and the hotels we stay at, on farms that supply our food deliveries, and in factories that produce the everyday goods we need and want. They may be forced into criminal activity. They may be forced to sell sex. The workforce in these sectors is largely unregulated, and this makes workers especially vulnerable. We do not just see slavery in small-scale enterprises, though. Global corporations are increasingly being challenged to look forensically at their supply chains to understand who supplies their labour, where their products come from, the environments in which these are made, and the conditions under which employees are put to work.

Modern slavery, trafficking, and the exploitation of people are complex. They are cogs in a wheel of interrelating actions that mean slavery is rarely a one-off event that fits neatly into one or other definition of human exploitation. The person who has initially offered the job, the person who helps arrange transport and accommodation, and then the person you work for on a daily basis may all be different people – it is a complex and intricate web of false promises, lies, and abuse.

Modern slavery may be found in every industry, in every sector today.

No individual account of exploitation is ever the same.

Not one of us can be immune from its ever-extending reach.

In his book *Development as Freedom*, Amartya Sen (1999, p.8) talks about his experience as a young boy witnessing a worker being killed in a fight. The worker was a Muslim having to get to work in a known Hindu area at a time of riots. All things being equal, it can be assumed that this worker was not likely to have opted to be in an area where unrest directed towards his religion and culture was a known risk. If he had been able to get work closer to home, he probably would have chosen this option. He had to work, his wife and children needed to eat, and this was the 'best' option available to him. Yes, he made a choice. But was it a free choice that he made? His lack of economic freedom ended up costing him his life. The position of poverty he was in reduced his options and the freedoms available to him.

We see similar today, closer to home. The issue of the media portrayal in the UK of those crossing the English Channel in dinghies has been misunderstood and classified as smugglers taking advantage or organised criminals trafficking vulnerable people who should be taking other safe routes available to them or staying in the first safe country they arrive at. In fact, some of the people on those boats will have paid an agent to get them into the UK (considered smuggling[1] in law, a crime against the state, not the person); some will have paid but on arrival will be exploited (considered modern slavery or human trafficking, a crime against the individual). They will be told that the deal has changed, the journey cost more, and they need to pay it off by working (considered forced labour). Those people in those dinghies will be presented with a range of options on arrival in the UK, none of them ideal, all exploitative. For some of them, the crossing will be the last leg of their overall journey, as they may have been forced against their will to provide services and labour along the way, and have already been trafficked and exploited when they enter the UK.

Some will not make it that far.

But we often won't hear those stories; it doesn't fit how the UK wants to frame and position migrants. The positioning in the media and in political rhetoric of the migrant influx and the hostile environment it creates prompts polarisation of opinion.

We aren't encouraged to remember what it is that people are trying to escape from. Nor are we persuaded to look too deeply at the lack of choices people have, the lack of safe routes on offer, or the fact that often no option on offer is a good one.

Some of us view those travelling as having made 'bad' or 'poor' choices. Some of us assume that they are coming to take jobs from us; others that they will take advantage of health care, education, and the benefits system, and should go back to where they came from. The

---

[1]   For a definition of smuggling refer to the Glossary of Terms.

public portrayal of those travelling, often referred to as illegal migrants, as outsiders, as somehow sub-human, adds continuously to the hostile environment I increasingly witness.

Some of us assume they will not contribute. Some of us assume that we know and understand their motivations.

Often, we do not think the best of each other. We rarely take a moment to try to understand. We do not tend to see the ways in which we connect with people, people who, at first glance, appear to be fundamentally different to us.

The connections will be there if we look for them. The questions we might ask ourselves begin to become obvious if we take that moment to consider what we might do if faced with a similar situation.

It seems we tend to get lost in our assumptions that those we see travelling had other, more attractive choices they might have made. We often fail to see how we may act in similar situations.

Yes, they are appearing to make a choice, like the man in Sen's book did. He chose to put himself at risk for the benefit of his family. He had to work to feed them. He died to provide them with food. These are individuals who chose to travel to the UK, to take dangerous journeys, putting themselves and their families at risk for the promise, the hope, and the dream of a different, a better, a safer life...

This may have been their only choice. Choice between war and peace. Choice between having income or not. Choice between protecting their children or not. A choice between life and death. A choice about survival when all the options available are equally as poor, but there is often still hope that things will be different, that you can make them different, and that you need to take the opportunities as they present. While we may not have ever had to make decisions on such a scale as those made by people we see travelling across oceans in dinghies or going into hostile areas for work with no protection, we all understand the sense of hope, the belief that things can be and will be different.

At times, we may fail to appreciate that the lives that we have led afford us different choices. If we ourselves had started life with similar freedoms, experienced the world with different options, and/or made different choices, we too might make the decision to try to reach the shores of a different nation for opportunities we do not currently have access to. We could so very easily be one of 'these people' ourselves.

The trafficked people that I've met often have not known that they were coming to the UK. None of them arrived on a dinghy. Some entered the UK via clandestine means on the back of lorries into various ports. The vast majority of those I have worked with entered the UK via legal routes, using their EU citizenship or visas that allowed them to enter. For some, being trafficked started in their hometown, village, or city. For others, it began once they reached the shores of the UK and realised that the systems here were not stacked in their favour and that their options in reality were less than limited. Their exploitation might also have occurred on the course of their journeys to the UK. When modern slavery and trafficking happens, it is not a one-time event; it occurs as part of a continuum. Control mechanisms, violence, threat, the treatment of workers and recognition of their rights, payment for employment, and the influence of isolation are all subject to change during a person's journey, whoever they are. Being passed between different individuals or gangs during different parts of a trafficking 'operation' succeeds in keeping those orchestrating it reaping the benefits but protected from exposure.

Every single individual victim and survivor of modern slavery I have met has, without exception, shared how their motivation has been economic, driven by opportunity and the chance to provide for others, or by a dream of being able to live a different life.

Most of us feel a connection to the dad who wants a better life for his children, to the young woman who wants to earn her own money and to find work to support her family at home, to the family unit that decides it is best to stick together, come what may. Yes, they are making choices, just as we would, based on the options available to them, on the social, economic, and political freedoms they have had access to and the systems in place that have helped or hindered them – all the elements of life that lie beyond their control. Their choices have come as a result of all that has gone before, and, like any choice we make, they are not made in isolation.

If modern slavery were to be thought of as an equation it could be simplified to:

(life circumstances + limited and less than ideal options) + (people willing to take advantage + the prospect of economic gain + control) = modern slavery and practices on the exploitative spectrum

CHAPTER 3

What the Law Says about Modern Slavery and Trafficking[1]

> The various incarnations of modern slavery continually morph and evolve, as do the complex nuanced environments within which they exist. We must understand the particularities of modern slavery in order to determine and evolve appropriate responses to it. We must also understand how to develop and secure support for appropriately responsive, proactive and exacting legislation that does as much to incapacitate the supply of slaves as it does to eliminate the demand for it.
>
> **(BHOOLA 2018, P.3)**

S lavery is no longer a socially accepted phenomenon, a legal institution whereby the ownership of another is allowed. Slavery has been abolished. Today, worldwide, slavery is prohibited in both international and domestic law, but in practice it continues to thrive globally and within the UK.

---

1   Please refer to the Legal Appendix for a basic overview of what legislative instruments state in relation to slavery. For an understanding of how the definitions have arisen and a full exposé of the law in relation to trafficking, refer to Anne Gallagher's book *The International Law of Human Trafficking* (2010).

Slavery and trafficking in international law

The United Nations (UN) Universal Declaration of Human Rights (1948) states the rights and freedoms to which 'all persons are entitled'.

All means *all*. The declaration is clear that it exists to uphold the rights of all, irrespective of gender, ethnicity, sexual orientation, religion, or any other societal or personal label. It stands for equality in the form of ten basic human rights.

When we fail to see others, whoever those others are, as equal, we risk taking away their basic human rights and we put them in danger.

As a matter of international law, slavery and human trafficking are defined within distinct legislative tools and instruments, with human trafficking being covered by the international instruments which prohibit slavery. There are a range of international, regional, and domestic instruments, legislation, conventions, directives, and treaties that apply to slavery. The initial international treaty prohibiting slavery was the Convention to Suppress the Slave Trade and Slavery 1926 (The Slavery Convention 1926). Slavery is also expressly prohibited in numerous key international and regional human rights instruments. Article 4 of the Universal Declaration of Human Rights 1948, Article 8 of the International Covenant on Civil and Political Rights 1966, Article 6(1) and Article 7 of the International Covenant on Economic, Social and Cultural Rights 1966, Article 4 of the European Convention on Human Rights 1950, and Article 5 of the African Charter 1981 are examples of instruments that prohibit slavery globally.

Forced labour is considered a form of slavery and is defined internationally in the International Labour Organization Forced Labour Convention 1930 (No. 29) as:

> all work or service which is exacted from any person under the menace of any penalty and for which the said person has not offered himself voluntarily.

The UN's specialist agency, the International Labour Organization (ILO), offers instruments and establishes labour standards, conditions, and protections for workers at an international level. These instruments include a range of treaties, directives, and other international texts that serve as legal sources for the creation of law in individual countries. They provide a set of minimum standards that must be included in any domestic law.

The ILO presents expected and minimum labour standards within international conventions, which include the International Labour Organization Forced Labour Convention 1930 (No. 29), the International Labour Organization Abolition of Forced Labour Convention 1957 (No. 105), and the International Labour Organization Worst Forms of Child Labour 1999 Convention (No. 182).

The main international instrument that addresses human trafficking is the Protocol to Prevent, Suppress and Punish Trafficking in Persons, Especially Women and Children, Supplementing the United Nations Convention against Transnational Organised Crime (United Nations 2000). Agreed and named after the Italian conference at which it was created, the Palermo Protocol provides the first global legally binding instrument with an agreed definition on trafficking in persons. Article 3(a) of the Convention defines 'human trafficking' as:

> the recruitment, transportation, transfer, harbouring or receipt of persons, by means of the threat or use of force or other forms of coercion, of abduction, of fraud, of deception, of the abuse of power or of a position of vulnerability or of the giving or receiving of payments or benefits to achieve the consent of a person having control over another person, for the purpose of exploitation. Exploitation shall include, at a minimum, the exploitation of the prostitution of others or other forms of sexual exploitation, forced labour or services, slavery or practices similar to slavery, servitude or the removal of organs.

European law on human trafficking and modern slavery

Both Article 4 of the European Convention on Human Rights (ECHR 1950) and Article 5 of the EU Charter on Fundamental Rights (Official

Journal of the European Union 2012) address the 'Prohibition of slavery and forced labour', stating that 'no one shall be held in slavery or servitude and no one shall be required to perform forced or compulsory labour'. The EU Charter further adds that trafficking in human beings is prohibited.

In addition to the Convention and the Charter, both the Council of Europe and the European Union have legislated in this area. The principal instruments are the Council of European Convention on Action against Trafficking in Human Beings (ECAT) (2005) and the European Anti-Trafficking Directive 2011/36/EU (Official Journal of the European Union 2011). Both the Convention and the Directive focus on what countries need to do to effectively offer protection and assistance to victims, as well as providing parameters for prevention and prosecution. As per the Council of Europe Convention definition, for human trafficking to have occurred, three basic components must be identifiable: action, means, and purpose. Children are considered unable to consent to exploitation and therefore the means element of the definition of trafficking does not need to be evidenced as it is assumed that they have been forced into the position they are in.

In human trafficking cases, exploitation can take many forms, including sexual exploitation, forced labour, slavery, servitude, forced criminality, and removal of organs.

Table 3.1: Human trafficking constituent parts

Act	The recruitment, transportation, transfer, harbouring, or receipt of an individual, which includes an element of movement (whether national or cross-border), which is achieved by a **means**.
Means (physical and psychological)	The threat or use of force, coercion, abduction, fraud, deception, abuse of power, or vulnerability for a **purpose**.
Purpose	For example, sexual exploitation, forced labour or domestic servitude, slavery, financial exploitation, removal of organs.

Table based on information from Statutory Guidance under the Modern Slavery Act 2015 (Home Office 2021), p.16

The UK context

Since the early 1800s, a range of domestic legislation has been enacted against slavery including the Slave Trade Act (1807), Slave Trade Felony Act (1811), and the Slavery Abolition Act (1833). Following the aftermath of World War 2 and its atrocities, the European Convention on Human Rights was signed. However, Article 4 of this convention was rarely used or cited in the domestic context. It was also not directly applicable in law until October 2000 when the Human Rights Act (1998) came into force.

The UK also has ratified the previously referred to ILO Conventions (No. 29 and No. 182), confirming a commitment to ensure minimum labour standards are set and adhered to as part of the response to reduce forced labour and child labour.

The UK ratified the ECAT in 2008 and began its implementation in 2009. In addition to ensuring international cooperation to tackling trafficking, the main purposes of the ECAT were to prevent and combat trafficking and protect the human rights of those identified as victims, offering them protection and assistance. By signing the ECAT, the UK agreed to implement minimum standards in relation to the identification, protection, and support of victims.

As part of its implementation, the UK established the National Referral Mechanism (NRM), a framework for identifying victims of trafficking and ensuring they receive the appropriate support (this mechanism is described further in Chapter 5). In 2011 the UK also opted into the European Anti-Trafficking Directive 2011/36/EU, committing to better protect victims and prosecute criminals involved in facilitating trafficking and exploitation.[2]

Modern Slavery Act (2015)

The Modern Slavery Act came into force in 2015 and now provides

---

2   At the time of writing this book the Nationality and Borders Bill had just been tabled. If this Bill passes as drafted the Directive would cease to apply in the UK.

the UK's domestic legislative framework in relation to modern slavery (HMSO 2015).

Under the Modern Slavery Act, modern slavery is defined as an umbrella term that 'encompasses the offences of human trafficking and slavery, servitude, forced or compulsory labour' (Home Office 2021, p.15).

Prior to enactment of the Modern Slavery Act (2015), several legislative instruments in England and Wales were relied on in relation to human trafficking. These included:

- Section 59 (A) of the Sexual Offences Act (2003)
- Section 4 of the Asylum and Immigration (Treatment of Claimants) Act (2004)
- Section 71 of the Coroners and Justice Act (2009).

The Act consolidated the existing offences of slavery and human trafficking and the associated maximum sentences if convicted of the offence.

If it is not clear that all the elements of human trafficking (act, means, and purpose as outlined in Table 3.1) have occurred, consideration will be given to the other forms of modern slavery in the act. These include:

- slavery
- servitude
- forced or compulsory labour.

While slavery, servitude, and forced or compulsory labour may be present in trafficking cases, not everyone who is exploited has been trafficked. In some cases, there will be no obvious signs of the 'act' – the recruitment, transportation, transfer, harbouring, or receipt of a person. This means that even though someone may have experienced exploitation, the definition of trafficking has not been met. In such cases, the other forms of slavery will then be considered.

To put the legislation in simple terms, for someone (an adult) to be considered a victim of modern slavery, they must have at a minimum been subjected to some form of threat or use of force, coercion, abduction, fraud, deception, abuse of power, or vulnerability, which means that their work/labour has not been freely given by them but has been forced from them. If there is evidence that the individual was actively recruited and moved as part of their exploitation, the human trafficking offence will be used. Alternatively, the absence of movement means the slavery, servitude, or forced or compulsory labour offence will be applied.

The Modern Slavery Act (2015) didn't just consolidate the domestic legal frameworks for slavery and trafficking – it also introduced new civil orders to act as part of a prevention and deterrent strategy (ss.14–34), created the office of Independent Anti-Slavery Commissioner (a role intended to encourage good practice in the prevention, identification, investigation, and prosecution of slavery and human trafficking) (ss.40–44), introduced new measures to better support and protect victims (ss.45–48), including the creation of a statutory defence for those forced to commit crime as part of their trafficking experience (s.45), special measures for victims who are witnesses (s.46), access to legal aid (s.47), and the development of specific child protection measures in the form of Independent Guardians (s.48). The Act also introduced Transparency in Supply Chains regulations (s.54) requiring businesses to disclose activity being taken to identify and prevent slavery from occurring in their own supply chains and to report on this annually. The Act also enacts new maritime enforcement powers (ss.35–38), further protections for overseas domestic workers (s.55), as well as requiring the Government to look at the role of the Gangmasters Licensing Authority (now known as the Gangmasters and Labour Abuse Authority) (s.53).

Although the devolved administrations rely on elements of the Modern Slavery Act (2015), they also have their own legal instruments:

- Human Trafficking and Exploitation (Scotland) Act 2015
- Human Trafficking and Exploitation (Criminal Justice and Support for Victims) Act (Northern Ireland) 2015.

Modern slavery is seen first and foremost as a crime

Theresa May, in her time as Home Secretary and Prime Minister

(2010–2019), viewed modern slavery through a law enforcement and criminal lens, stating: '[The Government] must work collaboratively with law enforcement agencies across the world, to track and stop these pernicious gangs who operate across borders and jurisdictions... These crimes must be stopped and the victims of modern slavery must go free...' (BBC News 2016).

Successive governments have overtly focused on the criminal nature of slavery and trafficking, and how those who are perpetrating this must be identified, disrupted, and prosecuted. This has not worked, and numbers of prosecutions and convictions remain low while numbers of victims identified rise.

The cost of modern slavery is significant

In an attempt to quantify the enormity of the trade in people, the International Labour Organization (ILO 2014, p.44) predicted trafficking, as a global industry, is estimated to make annual profits in the region of $150 billion. This figure refers to the estimated profit, the business side of trafficking, the money the perpetrators are making from the buying and selling of people, the tax-free money in the hands of criminals.

Separately, in 2018, the UK Home Office commissioned a report (Reed et al. 2018) to try to estimate the cost of modern slavery in the UK. Associated costs were put into three brackets – costs associated with anticipating slavery (such as preventative work and actions), costs associated with the consequences of slavery directly (such as victim care services/required health services), and costs associated with the response to slavery (such as law enforcement costs). By splitting costs identified to be related to modern slavery it was predicted that the social and economic cost to the UK of modern slavery was between £3.3 billion and £4.2 billion annually.

Historic anecdotal figures used across the anti-slavery sector, including by me, often refer to slavery as the fastest-growing international crime, stating that it has now surpassed the drugs industry, as people can be bought and sold more than once, and is second only to the international arms trade.

Although it makes sense that the routes used to move drugs and arms illegally out of and into different countries would also be used for the movement of people, it is important to remember that legal routes are also often used – work visas, study permits, and travel documents all in place so that, to the authorities and the unsuspecting victims, all appears as normal as possible, for as long as possible.

Of course, figures, whilst useful to help us gauge the nature and scale of an issue, can be misused, misunderstood, and misquoted.

The number of victims of slavery identified increases year on year in the UK

The figures that are used to try to quantify the number of potential victims are contested and only represent the number of those found. The hidden nature of modern slavery makes producing an accurate prevalence measure difficult. The statistics that are publicly available refer only to those who have (a) been identified and (b) agreed to be assisted. Currently, there is no definitive source of data or suitable method available in the UK (or globally for that matter) to accurately quantify the number of victims of modern slavery. The numbers also don't tell us the stories of the people impacted.

The Modern Slavery Act (2015) does not outline any victim protections

The Act does not, perhaps surprisingly, include support and protection for victims. Instead, Section 49 of the Act requires the Government, via the Secretary of State, to issue guidance. This guidance has to include information on indicators of modern slavery and trafficking, the expected arrangements and standards for support and assistance, and how these are to be delivered. The guidance Government offers and the arrangements contained within it are subject to frequent changes.

Laws, policy, and guidance have evolved, responding to fluctuating views on human rights, greater understanding of appropriate working conditions and practices, fairer labour laws, developing notions of equality, changing patterns in migration, and ever-increasing globalisation. It is yet to be seen if legislative frameworks can remain fit for purpose to tackle an evolving crime that refuses to conform to the parameters we set around it.

Almost two centuries may have passed since the movements to abolish the transatlantic slave trade and yet slavery, one of the greatest violations of human rights, remains part of our culture in the 21st century. Forms of slavery remain. Even with all the international, regional, and domestic legislative frameworks and conventions in place, we continue to see practices similar to slavery exist.

An economic system in which the principles of property law are applied to people endures today; people own people, and people are used as commodities for the profit of others.

CHAPTER 4

Meeting the People Affected by Modern Slavery

> Five years on from the Act, the UK has taken significant strides in tackling modern slavery... But there is much still to do if we are to create a society hostile to trafficking and supportive to survivors.
>
> **(TAMARA BARNETT, QUOTED IN REUTERS 2019)**

There is no definitive definition of modern slavery. Trafficking is defined in international and regional frameworks but modern slavery is not. Identifying its victims can be hard.

Every individual's experience of being exploited and forced to do something against their will is inevitably different. Often a lack of freedom will present as a key feature of victims' narratives and some forms and types of trafficking, modern slavery, and exploitation are better documented and understood than others.

It is an ever-changing and evolving phenomenon, and enslaved people are closer to us than we may think.

General indicators

People who have been trafficked may:

- believe that they must work against their will
- be unable to leave their work environment
- show signs that their movements are being controlled
- feel that they cannot leave
- show fear or anxiety
- be subjected to violence or threats of violence against themselves or against their family members and loved ones
- suffer injuries that appear to be the result of an assault
- suffer injuries or impairments typical of certain jobs or control measures
- suffer injuries that appear to be the result of the application of control measures
- be distrustful of the authorities
- be threatened with being handed over to the authorities
- be afraid of revealing their immigration status
- not be in possession of their passports or other travel or identity documents, as those documents are being held by someone else
- have false identity or travel documents
- be found in or connected to a type of location likely to be used for exploiting people
- be unfamiliar with the local language
- not know their home or work address
- allow others to speak for them when addressed directly
- act as if they were instructed by someone else
- be forced to work under certain conditions
- be disciplined through punishment
- be unable to negotiate working conditions
- receive little or no payment
- have no access to their earnings

- work excessively long hours over long periods
- not have any days off
- live in poor or substandard accommodations
- have no access to medical care
- have limited or no social interaction
- have limited contact with their families or with people outside of their immediate environment
- be unable to communicate freely with others
- be under the perception that they are bonded by debt
- be in a situation of dependence
- come from a place known to be a source of human trafficking
- have had the fees for their transport to the country of destination paid for by facilitators, whom they must pay back by working or providing services in the destination
- have acted on the basis of false promises.

(UNODC 2010)

We live in an age where we believe we are in control; we assume that all individuals have agency. We look to the extreme examples of success, of those who have made it from nothing. We believe we can be who we want to be and do what we want to do, and we teach the next generation anything is possible. This is not to distract from the truly remarkable humans out there who have, against all odds, defied the systems and structures they grew up in or were subjected to. It is a challenge to us to think about how many times we compare the success stories to the poor choices others make. 'Well, he came from a background of poverty and look where he ended up.' Today, we tend to treat the few success stories as the norm and assume those who have ended up in situations of exploitation have made bad or poor choices, that they are somehow to blame. We tend to overlook the fact that systems that exist to enable choice may be unfit for purpose or broken. We tend not to see how they are a part of an eco-system that enables exploitation to occur. It isn't comfortable to know that the systems we may benefit from put others at risk.

I've met individuals who've experienced every type of slavery and trafficking identified in the UK. They have been forced into labour, exploited sexually, coerced into service, threatened into criminality, and had their organs harvested for others' financial gain. Through the people who've lived these lives, I've learned that we need to be careful that we do not compare different experiences and that we must avoid the temptation to consider one form of slavery as worse than any other. We need to keep in the forefront of our minds that some of them will have been held captive, and/or assaulted, and/or violated. Others may have experienced less abuse or physical restriction but may have been controlled psychologically and lived in fear of harm to themselves and/ or their family.

No individual's account of exploitation is ever the same. That said, what they often share is that they trusted the person who exploited them. Often, those who've been through these experiences do not understand that they are being exploited or abused; they may be dependent on their abuser or too scared to tell anyone what is happening. They may even appear to be complicit in their own exploitation. For some, there is no other option in sight; they feel trapped.

The truths of those I have met are harrowing to hear. They reveal the depravity of humanity. They appear unbelievable, far-fetched, but are nonetheless accurate accounts of those with lived experience that may be hard for us to imagine or accept.

The slavery, trafficking, and subsequent exploitation of people is complex. They are cogs in a wheel of interrelating actions that mean slavery is rarely a one-off event that fits neatly into one or other definition of human exploitation.

My interactions with individuals with lived experience of slavery have taken place in prisons, safe houses, detention centres, brothels, on car-wash forecourts, in police stations, and in lawyers' offices. The majority have met the definition of having been trafficked and they have each shared details of the act, means, and purpose of their slavery in what they have shared. Chapters 6–10 explore in greater detail the systems that let these individuals down and the challenges that they (and the professionals supporting them) face in working towards an end to the commodification of people.

First, I'll outline the types of slavery identified in the UK and introduce some of the people I've met who have been affected. When I refer to them again in subsequent chapters their names will be in bold.

Experiences of forced labour

People who have been trafficked for labour exploitation may:

- live in groups in the same place where they work and leave those premises infrequently, if at all
- live in degraded, unsuitable places, such as in agricultural or industrial buildings
- not be dressed adequately for the work they do: for example, they may lack protective equipment or warm clothing
- be given only leftovers to eat
- have no access to their earnings
- have no labour contract
- work excessively long hours
- depend on their employer for a number of services, including work, transportation and accommodation
- have no choice of accommodation
- never leave the work premises without their employer
- be unable to move freely
- be subject to security measures designed to keep them on the work premises
- be disciplined through fines
- be subjected to insults, abuse, threats or violence
- lack basic training and professional licences.

(UNODC 2010)

It could be argued that 'forced labour' should, in fact, be the overarching terminology used instead of 'modern slavery'. As a term, 'forced labour' appears far-reaching enough – 'any work or service extracted', whether this means being forced to sell sexual services, forced to pick cocoa beans, forced to water cannabis plants, forced to transport drugs, forced to wash cars, forced to paint nails, forced to cook food, forced to pick fruit and vegetables, forced to clean homes, forced to look after children. All of these examples are reliant on the individual being *forced* to do a job to make money or save money for those forcing them. Everything that individuals are forced to do is a form of work.

Forced labour (also known as labour exploitation) is the most common type of exploitation seen in the UK (as well as in other countries). Those who experience forced labour may have agreed to carry out a job they were initially offered, giving their consent to undertake the work as it was described at the time. Workers may, in fact, have given consent in a situation in which they felt they had no viable alternative or in a situation where all the choices available to them were as bad as each other. On balance, this job offer may have appeared the best of a bad bunch. Alternatively, the job and opportunity described may never have materialised and the conditions, terms, and pay may have differed greatly in reality from what was initially offered.

It is easy to misunderstand the subtleties of forced labour. Many of the people caught in the forced labour net will have been looking for work, will have wanted to work, and may even have been desperate to take a job. These dynamics create the perfect conditions for people to be exploited. Jobs offered and ostensibly 'freely' agreed to are so often not what they were set out to be: hours are longer, wages are lower, threats are made when questions are asked, and people feel unable to leave without repercussions, especially when they feel trapped and unsure of their rights and entitlements or whether authorities might support them.

Forced labour is not restricted to a particular sector. Trends in certain sectors have begun to emerge in the headlines as exploitation in the form of forced labour has been found in supply chains. States and territories have been accused of funding state-sponsored forced labour and/or subjecting people to concentration-camp-like conditions to extract work from them.

In the UK, those who have been trafficked for the purpose of forced labour have been identified in the service industry, the hospitality sector, agriculture, packing and processing, the sex industry, construction, and manufacturing. This is not an exhaustive list. As restrictions tighten in the UK post-Brexit, we are sure to hear more about workers with fewer and fewer protections across the full range of industries and sectors.

In our day-to-day lives, it appears that gone are the days when we spent weekend afternoons washing, shining, and chammying our prized possessions on our own driveways. Now we drive our cars down the road and get a full valet inside and out for £15. Why would you not? We are time-poor and relatively cash-rich now. We all love a bargain, especially if it saves us a job and means we can get on with something else instead.

The minimum wage is in the region of £9 per hour, and the National Living Wage even higher. Four men spend an hour zooming around our cars to make sure it is spick and span ready for us to collect. How can this only cost us £15? We pay the man at the entrance – you know, the one wearing the bum-bag where all the notes go. He takes all the money. We forget to question *how* this service can come so cheap, and *who* is being paid. We forget to think about whether people had any other choices and why they made the ones they did.

Marios, Riso, Andre, Dung, and Ly (not their real names) experienced exploitation in the service, hospitality, and agricultural industries. In some of the case studies that follow, names are missing where I've been unable to recall them with confidence.[1]

Their accounts are retold from my personal perspective, based on our interactions and drawn from my memory of these. Of course, despite

---

1   Giving these individuals fabricated pseudonyms when I don't remember their real names feels uncomfortably inauthentic, but it would not add any value to their account and risks detracting from it. I've therefore made a policy decision for them to remain nameless in these circumstances. Similarly, all ages are approximate. It should also be noted that all of these interactions occurred prior to Brexit and when EU nationals had the right to work in the UK.

my commitment to representing them accurately, their perceptions of these encounters might differ from my own version of events, but each illustrates aspects of modern slavery and trafficking for the purpose of forced labour.

Name: Marios

Age: 16

Nationality: Albanian. Without a visa, as an Albanian national, Marios was not legally allowed to work in the UK.

Type of modern slavery: Trafficked for the purpose of forced labour at a car wash.

How I came to be involved: I was invited as part of my role to attend a multi-agency welfare visit with police and immigration officials to several car-wash sites where concerns had been raised about worker conditions. I had been asked to engage with workers and help identify any indicators of trafficking, as well as inform the workers about their rights and entitlements, providing them with information that they needed.

This visit was memorable for several reasons: first, the response from the public; second, the response from social services; and third, the journey Marios had been on and the experiences he'd had. Marios, a 16-year-old young man, technically still a child, was working on the forecourt of a busy car wash when I met him. He was at first noticeably quiet and unsure of what was going on – a response often seen when multi-agency visitors arrive on site and hope to speak to people individually. We went to the portacabin at the back of the car wash to speak – it was littered with rubbish and had two plastic school chairs in it. From the outside, it had the façade of a staff room for people walking past to see into; in reality, it was a mess of a room with no running water, no toilet facilities, nowhere to sit down or take a break. A shelter from the British weather, yes. Comfortable? Definitely not. I was working with a police officer and translator, and we began a conversation, reassuring Marios that he was in no trouble at all and that everyone was here to ensure that he and the other workers were OK and all being paid. We outlined and alluded to the fact that sometimes in car washes people were forced to work against their will, that they had been duped, believing work and pay would be forthcoming, and that while the work was done, fair pay was not always provided. In fact, for some workers in car washes, not only was the pay they were expecting non-existent, but the debt they owed seemed forever to be increasing.

Marios nodded along with what was being said, giving the impression he understood the translator, but it quickly became evident that he did not: he was faking it. As we began speaking (via the translator), it was noticable that there was some confusion between the two: they were not speaking a shared language. It became apparent that Marios was not Romanian but Albanian. His reasoning was simple. If he pretended to be Romanian, he could be here and work legally, no problem; Romania is in the European Union and, at the time, he would have been able to exercise his EU treaty rights as a Romanian and work in the UK. Once the translation issue had been identified and an Albanian translator secured, it became clear that transport, accommodation, and a job had all been arranged for Marios while he was still in Albania. He confirmed he was given accommodation, food, weekly cigarettes, and beer money, but although all this was offered in a congenial manner, it was simultaneously being added on to the money he was told he now 'owed' his employer. He was paying off his debt with his labour at the car wash. He was not sure how much he owed, how much he was being paid, or how long it would take him to pay off his debt. What appeared originally to be part of the deal would soon equate to him needing to work for longer in far from ideal conditions, especially for someone who should have still been pursuing his education or starting an apprenticeship.

Suspecting he was a minor, procedure dictated that Marios left the car wash under police protection that day. At the police station, we all hung out in the officers' staff room and made use of the vending machine. Marios was cold and hungry and needed time to decompress. The TV was on, and as he sat on one of the couches, he told us about how he had been woken up in the middle of the night by a disturbance in his family home. That disturbance transpired to be someone attacking and killing his father. He described the noise, his fear, and the amount of blood. Marios had left

Albania with the help of family friends and had needed to leave his village in fear of his life. His father had been murdered in front of him as part of a business deal gone wrong. Marios explained that, in his culture, it was expected that he would defend his family's honour by inflicting the same level of violence on the family who had killed his father. From his perspective, if he did not do this, he too would be at risk of being killed. Not knowing what he should do, he had sought help and found someone who would arrange transport and a job with accommodation for him, for a fee. Marios was out of the situation in Albania but was living precariously in the UK, an illegal minor being taken advantage of and made to wash cars day in and day out for no pay.

We went with Marios to the supported accommodation we found for him in the city centre. This accommodation was the only option available to him according to the out-of-hours team at the local authority. He would be assigned a social worker the following morning.

Names: Unknown – car-wash workers

Ages: Unknown – young adults, all reported to be over 18

Nationality: Slovakian. All able to legally work and reside in the UK as EU citizens.

Type of modern slavery: Trafficked for the purpose of forced labour at a car wash and cleaning business, as well as for the purpose of criminal exploitation in the form of benefit fraud.

How I came to be involved: As part of the Anti-Trafficking Partnership Problem Profile Group (a multi-agency group that organises multi-agency visits to premises where slavery may be taking place). Police, council, and Unseen staff members visited car-wash sites to gather information about those working there and to check on their welfare. I'd been asked to engage with workers to help identify any indicators of trafficking as well as to inform them about their rights and entitlements and provide them with information they might need. The visits included both the car-wash location and the workers' accommodation. The 13 Slovaks (12 young men and one young woman) I met on this car-wash forecourt had all just turned 18 and had all been brought to the UK from a life on the streets in Slovakia. They viewed the man who brought them here as a good person, who had freed them from the lives they would have led. He was also a man who was making massive profits from their work. All of the 13 young people lived in a three-bedroomed house, with one bathroom. The bedrooms were occupied by their boss and his family, and they themselves, all 13 of them, slept on mattresses in the attic space.

Their movement to and from their place of work was controlled, their work days were long and tiring, they worked outside all day every day, regardless of the weather, and their pay was non-existent. Not only did they work at the car wash but they were also employed as cleaners elsewhere every morning and night. At this stage, they were unaware that they were not just being exploited for their labour, but also for their identities. This resulted in the welfare visit leading to further law enforcement investigations into those believed to be responsible for the exploitation.

Names: Riso and unknown female

Ages: 28–35

Nationality: Lithuanian. Able to work legally in the UK as EU citizens.

Type of modern slavery: Trafficked for the purpose of providing labour in the agricultural sector.

How I came to be involved: I was invited in my Unseen role to assist at a multi-agency reception centre (a safe physical space for potential victims) in the south-east of England – to be a presence to accompany people brought in, to introduce them to the different agencies who wanted to speak with them, to explain what was happening, and generally be a friendly face.

It was two weeks before Christmas, and a colleague and I had been invited to attend a multi-agency operation. Evidence and intelligence indicated that men and women were being put to work in a farmer's field in the south-east of England. We were not cited on the operational details but were requested to attend to provide support to individuals found. Those found working there would be taken by law enforcement staff to a reception centre, where other statutory agencies would be waiting to learn more about what was happening to them on the farm. At its most simple, the aim of a reception centre is to provide a safe physical space for the individuals who have been identified as potential victims. A place away from the location in which they are thought to have been abused and exploited. It is a place where other agencies are present and will offer access to clean clothes, food, a hot drink, medical check-ups, immigration checks, interviews to try to understand what has been happening to them.

My interactions with Riso, a tall, slim Lithuanian man, and another young woman stands out in my memory. Although not related to each other, they sat together at the reception centre. What I learned about the young woman's experiences during her exploitation was at best incongruous when sitting around a Formica table with cups of tea and soup in plastic cups. At worst, it was deeply unsettling. She was still in the clothes she had been wearing when brought in from the field, and her fingers showed signs of frostbite. Below her woollen fingerless gloves, the tips of her fingers were shades of blue, purple, and pink, and they were swollen and inflexible. She had gathered clothes to try to keep herself warm while out in the field in the bracing winter weather, but had not been provided with any warm or wet-weather gear by those who were employing her. She had been living in a breeze-block garage attached to the accommodation her fellow workers were housed in. It appeared that a few people were living inside the space, intended for cars, and that it was being used as an overflow space from the house where Riso was sleeping. Like Riso, she was transported every day from the accommodation to the field where they both would work picking vegetables by hand. I am not sure when she became pregnant, or how she made the decision not to keep the baby, but I do know that she felt she would not be able to work if she was pregnant, and that money needed to be sent home, and that she had an abortion in the garage in which she was living. She was given no medical treatment during or after, no support, and the next morning she was picked up from the garage as normal and back working in the field; a day off, sick leave, and access to medical care were not options available to her. After having a cup of tea together, I left her behind at the table with another volunteer. I had been asked to stay with Riso and guide him through the various processes that the reception centre had lined up.

Riso had been offered and promised what he thought was the chance of a better life, an opportunity to earn money, more than he would earn in his home country, a new job, a new start. Everything was arranged for him – his transport, his permit to work, his accommodation and the job. He knew he would be working outdoors and that it would be hard, physical work. What he did not know was that he would be living in a three-bedroom terrace house with more than 30 other workers, or that he would be picked up and transported to and from work in a mini-van that had no windows – a panel van with rows of bench seats inside it. The van would not draw unwanted attention and people would not realise that the goods being transported inside were in fact humans, people being exploited to pick the fruit and vegetables that find their way into our supermarket trolleys, our cupboards, and on to our dinner tables. He worked seven days a week, for up to ten hours every day. When he had arrived in the UK, the people who had brought him had helped him set up a bank account and he had given these details to his employer so he could be paid. What his employer did not realise as they transferred money to multiple accounts on a weekly basis as contractually agreed was that those they were paying did not have access to their accounts. Their cards had been taken – 'for safe keeping', of course. Control of their earnings was not theirs. In the eight months he had worked, Riso had not been paid.

Between the reception centre and the house, we had popped to the local shop when we discovered that the new accommodation was pretty much unfurnished, and some of the essentials were not in place – soap, a toothbrush, toothpaste, bedding, and a fresh basic set of clothes. Riso was so grateful as we handed over a Sainsburys bag full of all the bits we thought he might need for the next couple of days. He had been deprived of access to the most basic of items, things most of us consider essential.

Riso was a fully grown man utterly broken by what he had experienced, physically and mentally exhausted, with physical evidence showing overt signs of the abuse he had been through. I had seen the cigarette burns littering his arms and had seen the doctor's report showing that these continued over his upper chest and across his back. He could not recall the rationale for all the burns or what he had or had not done to incur the wrath of those exploiting him, but the marks were evident to see and the reasons, even if he did know them, were immaterial, did not matter: he had spent the last months of his life under the control of another.

Riso looked at me nervously as he closed the door on the unfurnished, unhomely, terraced house that had been secured as a safe location after his 'rescue' from exploitation. It had an old-fashioned PVC double-glazed front door that we'd told him would 'keep the bad people out'. Riso and two other men had been brought here from the farmer's field earlier that day. It was this door that Riso wanted to check worked and locked properly with us several times before my colleague and I could leave. It was a locking system that required the handle to be lifted first, sending the bolts into position before the key would turn and lock the door. We worked it out together; Riso and I were on one side, my colleague on the other, as we practised shutting the door, lifting the handle, and locking everything – and everyone – out.

When he asked *'They can't find me here, can they?'* I wanted to say 'No,' but I could not. I was unable to promise him safety, that his life would be OK, and that he would find the work he so desperately hoped for. I heard the key turn in the lock on everything he'd come from as I walked away and hoped that he would be all right. Riso was now 'free', but this was just the beginning of his journey.

Names: Unknown

Ages: Three men aged 20–45

Nationalities: British and Eastern European (specific nationalities unknown). Being British and EU citizens, the three men did not require visas or permits of any sort to live and work in the UK.

Type of modern slavery: Trafficked for the purpose of forced labour. Living at a caravan site but being transported around the South-West.

How I came to be involved: A law enforcement reception centre I was involved in setting up as part of the core coordination group established with police and partner agencies was housing people recovered from a caravan site as part of a police investigation and warrant. Its function was to meet the needs of anyone recovered; I was present on site when people arrived.

Months had been spent planning this operational activity, and the intelligence gathered by the police suggested there should have been a significant number of people on the caravan site. When the message came in over the radio that just three men were en route to the centre, it came as a surprise. Later, I was to learn that the individuals who'd been living there just 24 hours previously were no longer anywhere to be found.

The three men arrived at the centre looking dirty and tired. They'd been working and living in awful conditions – tarmacking, gardening, tree felling, doing odd jobs here and there: wherever their boss dropped them and doing whatever they were told. They worked long hours, six days a week, and were paid sporadically. Even though the police found vast amounts of cash on site and hidden in the exploiter's caravan, a caravan that, in comparison to what the men were sleeping in, was described as utterly opulent. The caravans that housed the workers had no running water, no shower or toilet facilities; they housed multiple people and were in a state of disrepair.

One worker told us he slept with his wellies on just in case his boss called him in the night and he needed to get up quickly. He had got up slowly once before and paid the price of being physically beaten; it was a risk he was not willing to take again.

Another had needed immediate medical treatment and had been taken to the local hospital.

I spent the next hours accompanying individuals to go outside for a smoke, made copious amounts of tea, helped people to access showers and clean clothes, and attended various meetings with different agencies involved, police interviews, medical examinations, as the men wished.

The centre had been set up and staffed to house people for up to a week. It was hoped that it would not be needed for this long, and once law enforcement had completed interviews, partner agencies had committed to providing alternative support, accommodation, and employment to those who needed it.

One by one, the men left the centre.

They decided they did not want help; they did not want assistance; they were worried about what might happen to them and their families if they did not get back to the caravan site and be available to work. Maybe they could not accept help. Maybe what we could offer was not enough to break the cycle of exploitation. Maybe it was not a risk worth taking.

Name: Andre

Age: 24

Nationality: Romanian. As an EU citizen, Andre was able to legally seek employment anywhere in the EU.

Type of modern slavery: Trafficked for the purpose of forced labour. Working at a car wash in a small town on the outskirts of a larger city.

How I came to be involved: Andre decided he had had enough when he jumped in the car as it pulled into the car wash and persuaded the driver, a car-wash customer, to leave with him immediately. By some incredible coincidence, the driver whose car he jumped in randomly knew me and called me, asking for my help. Along with a female police officer, who over the years had become a friend, I went to meet Andre to learn about what had happened. As always, the officer wasn't in uniform and her approach, understanding, and kindness went above and beyond the call of duty. Andre described being held by the throat and slammed against the wall. The bruising and finger marks from his attackers were still clear to see around his neck, and he was visibly shaken by what had happened. He told us the reason he had been hurt was that he had asked for the money he was owed. He had worked for some weeks and the pay he was due was always promised to him; there was always one more thing he was expected to pay for, one more reason why he would be paid next week. He didn't like the work conditions, and things weren't what he had expected, but he was willing to put up with this, to hope and believe he would be paid. But when he was beaten up, he knew he had a problem and needed to leave.

Andre explained to us that he had his own accommodation; he travelled to and from work each day. He showed us his employment contract. He didn't understand what it said and he went on to explain that at the place he stayed he shared his room with several others, but that this was OK and better than before. He seemed to accept he had been duped, put to work for no money, presented with a debt for his travel, his food, and a 'finder's fee' for his boss for helping him to find a landlord who wouldn't ask too many questions, wouldn't ask for references or a deposit. He initially was willing to hope he would get paid, but after eight weeks of working and continuously being told he would be paid the following week, he had had enough.

Andre knew it was a risk to ask about being paid. During his time work-ing at the car wash, he had seen people try to leave the work, but they had been forcibly brought back – they would just reappear and quietly get on with the work they had been told to do. Andre was stuck, stuck between collecting the money he was owed and leaving his situation. One linked to the other: he needed the cash if he was going to survive before getting more work. The day we met him, Andre decided enough was enough.

Andre self-identified as wanting help. When the officer and I met him, he was clear he wanted help; he wanted out and he wanted to know what was available for him. We went to meet him. The driver had taken Andre to his office with him and got him a coffee and some food – we were able to speak with him in a private room about what had happened. After explaining what was available to him, we all went back to the police station to take the process further.

Andre was an EU national and, at the time, was able to live and work in the UK, but as someone who had appeared to have experienced exploita-tion, he was eligible for assistance and support. We were aware that we didn't have Andre's full account at this point, but we didn't need it: there were indicators of trafficking for the purpose of forced labour, he had visible injuries, and he was asking for support.

With limited English, limited understanding of his rights and entitlements, and limited options, he needed time and a safe place to be while he worked out what was next. He knew he wanted to work, but he also knew he had been shaken by his experience and wanted some time. We explained what support was on offer – that he may be able to get accommodation, that he would have access to a support worker, help to work out the next steps, and in the meantime, he would have access to financial support, medical care, and legal advice. It would give him time to work out what was next.

Andre agreed this is what he would like to do.

Many of those I've met in situations of forced labour have been male. We might assume that the element of hard graft or tough working conditions means that it is only men who are subjected to forced labour, but this is not the case.

Names: Dung and Ly

Ages: 14–18

Nationality: Vietnamese. Putting their ages aside, Dung and Ly required a visa and work permit to allow them to legally live and work in the UK.

Type of modern slavery: Trafficked for the purpose of providing labour. Working in a high street nail bar in a small town.

How I came to be involved: I was part of the Anti-Slavery Partnership Welfare Team Visits to nail-bar sites with partner agencies including the local council, police, health, and Unseen, and had been tasked with checking on the welfare of staff and giving out information on support services as required. The local authority had observed an increase in nail bars across the area and wanted to understand more about the industry, so planned a day of visits to gather information and understanding to develop community cohesion.

We could see through the shop window that the two girls working were making the most of the quiet and the lull in customers by getting some sleep. Both had their heads resting on towels on their workstations; behind them were their official-looking certificates showing that they were in training as beauticians. Dung and Ly presented as young, timid, and unsure of what was happening and what was expected of them. What transpired was that both girls were under the age of 18, that they had arrived in the UK in the back of a lorry, their journey facilitated from Vietnam to the UK via land, sea, and air. I met them before the horror of the articulated truck in Essex in which 39 Vietnamese nationals lost their lives hit the news in late 2019 (Gentleman 2020); this was the same journey that Dung and Ly had taken.

Both girls said that they were orphans and had been offered the chance for work. What had transpired was a long and dangerous journey ending up in a nail bar in a sleepy town in the South-West of England. Working for no pay (because their travel and accommodation needed to be paid for and they were still in training), long hours, no access to education or friendships, taken to and from the nail bar every day by their boss, who they lived with. On visiting where they lived, we found that the difference between their living conditions and that of their boss was stark. Like the Eastern Europeans from the car wash, mattresses had been slung in the loft space and, bar a framed picture from back home, there were no other personal effects.

Like Marios, Dung and Ly were still children, and because of this local authority children's services were required to step in and lead on the support given.

Experiences of criminal exploitation

People who have been trafficked for criminal exploitation, including for the purpose of begging or committing petty crimes, may:

- be children, elderly persons or disabled migrants who tend to beg in public places and on public transport
- be children carrying and/or selling illicit drugs
- have physical impairments that appear to be the result of mutilation

- be children of the same nationality or ethnicity who move in large groups with only a few adults
- be unaccompanied minors who have been 'found' by an adult of the same nationality or ethnicity
- move in groups while travelling on public transport: for example, they may walk up and down the length of trains
- participate in the activities of organised criminal gangs
- be part of large groups of children who have the same adult guardian
- be punished if they do not collect or steal enough
- live with members of their gang
- travel with members of their gang to the country of destination
- live, as gang members, with adults who are not their parents
- move daily in large groups and over considerable distances.

The following might also indicate that people have been trafficked for begging or for committing petty crimes:

- new forms of gang-related crime appear
- there is evidence that the group of suspected victims has moved, over a period of time, through a number of countries
- there is evidence that suspected victims have been involved in begging or in committing petty crimes in another country.

(UNODC 2010)

Criminal exploitation has only recently been identified in the UK as a distinct category of forced labour. Criminal exploitation refers to the forcing of someone or a group of people to undertake criminal activity. Those acting criminally may not realise that what they are doing is illegal, while those orchestrating it certainly do know. It is hard to identify, hard to evidence, and as a result hard to defend in a court of law. In a UK context, trafficking for the purpose of criminal exploitation has been identified in gang-related criminality – including the movement of drugs (usually crack cocaine and heroin) and the cultivation of them (specifically cannabis), other crimes such as shoplifting or pickpocketing, begging, sham marriages, and financial and benefit fraud where individuals' identities are taken and used to commit the act of fraud, often at the same time as exploiting them in some other way.

The Slovakian car-wash workers had all been registered with the Job Centre and on a weekly basis were dropped off there to claim their benefits. Thirteen people registered at the same address were all linked to the same bank account. They were all working, yet their identities were being illegally used to fraudulently claim housing benefit and Jobseeker's Allowance.

Yes, they were the ones that physically got out of the van and went into the Job Centre and signed the piece of paper they were required to sign, but what choice did they have? Their every move was controlled; they were told what to do and how to do it, transported to where they had to be – yes, they were provided food and accommodation, and it was better than what they had at home, but it was still exploitation. Their lack of awareness of the system was used by those exploiting them to make more money by fraudulently using their identities.

I have also worked on cases where individuals have been registered for multiple National Insurance numbers without their knowledge, or where their name has been used on rental agreements or on utility bills. Often the individuals are completely unaware of this. Not only is it a cunning mechanism of control and a clever way of ensuring that those behind the scenes remain anonymous and untouchable, but it also means that those being exploited are doubted from the very beginning; their names are on documents and their credibility is questioned. For those people whose names are used without their knowledge, this will affect their ability to access the systems they will need in the future once out of their situation of exploitation.

Matt, Pham, and Stephen were all forced into different elements of the drugs trade including cannabis cultivation and criminal activity related to gangs involved in county lines activity. Mihaela was forced into a sham marriage and her EU citizenship used to facilitate someone else's ability to reside in the UK. Their experiences illustrate some of the aspects of modern slavery and trafficking for the purpose of criminal exploitation.

Name: Matt

Age: 20

Nationality: British. As a British national, Matt was not subject to any visa or immigration considerations and had full access to welfare, benefits, and support systems in the UK.

Type of modern slavery: Trafficking for the purpose of criminal exploitation – county lines activity.

How I came to be involved: I was contacted by Matt's legal representative who was concerned he was being treated as a criminal rather than a potential victim. I was asked to provide my opinion on his case.

When I met Matt in 2020, he was facing drug charges for incidents that both his legal team and I felt had happened while Matt was under considerable duress. Matt had not been paid for any of the work he had undertaken, which was ironic as those who offered him the work and recruited him promised he would make money. For family reasons, that was what Matt needed to do: he needed to make money.

Matt would receive a call telling him to go to the local train station where he would be either met and given a ticket or told where to buy a ticket to. Sometimes the destination on the ticket was where he would be going, but this was not always the case – he would be called and told what station to get off at. He would be travelling on his own, to all intents and purposes, to any observer, of his own free will – a young man off on an adventure. Matt had no idea where he would be staying when he left London or what he would do for money – he would always be picked up from the station and accommodated in a house. The house had drugs in it – drugs he was then responsible for ensuring were sold and the right amount of money collected.

He had no idea when he could leave and go home, or when he would be called again.

He was in such a house when he was found by the police, who prosecuted him for being in possession of and distributing a class A drug.

What Matt was experiencing has been termed 'county lines'. Although not legally defined, a 'county line' has a dual meaning: it is the number that people call to take an order for the drugs, and, as a concept, it refers to the drugs (usually crack cocaine and heroin) that are transported from one area to another, often by children or vulnerable people who are coerced into their roles by dealers' gangs.

It is a form of trafficking that has been on the rise in a UK context over recent years. This is contentious, though, because not all county lines activity will always be trafficking, and as with all forms of exploitation, once we think we know what we are looking for and how to disrupt it, the numbers spike. As with other forms of exploitation, those individuals who are involved may not view themselves as victims and therefore can be arrested as criminals. For a county lines case to be considered trafficking, it must, as with all other forms of trafficking, evidence the act, the means, and the purpose.

To reveal what had happened to him and to get the help he needed meant that Matt may have to speak about those he had worked for. Deciding to speak out against those he had worked for was not a decision he was able to take lightly.

Name: Pham

Age: 29

Nationality: British Vietnamese. Pham had a British passport and was not subject to any immigration or visa restrictions.

Type of modern slavery: Trafficked to be criminally exploited via cannabis cultivation.

How I came to be involved: I met Pham in prison as part of research being conducted on perpetrators of modern slavery crimes in conjunction with the police and prison services.

Pham was in prison when we spoke. It was during our conversation in a room on the prison estate that Pham told me he had once been one of the workers locked into a cannabis farm. He had been expected to look after the plants, following a strict regime of watering and adding chemicals to them. The conditions he had survived in were poor: food was delivered once a week, he slept on a mattress with other workers, and he had no access to fresh air. Pham was not free to come and go as he wanted; he and the other workers were locked in and received no payment for the work they did. When the chance to be the person who delivered the food and checked in on the workers was offered, Pham took his opportunity and accepted this 'promotion'. He would no longer be restricted to the bunker, no longer locked in; it was his chance to have more freedom. The officer and I left Pham to return to his cell and spent the journey home discussing the flaws we saw in the system and his case. How had no one noticed or considered the indicators of slavery in his case?

Name: Stephen

Age: 33

Nationality: British. Like Matt, Stephen was not subject to any visa or immigration considerations and had full access to welfare, benefits, and support systems in the UK.

Type of modern slavery: Trafficked for the purpose of transportation of drugs (criminal exploitation).

How I came to be involved: Identified as a victim of trafficking by a housing officer, referred to the National Referral Mechanism (NRM) and accommodated and supported by Unseen. Stephen kindly offered to speak with me for the purposes of this book.

Stephen was being supported by Unseen when I met him at one of the safe houses. We sat in the lounge and had a cup of tea together – he was excited about featuring in a book and made sure I knew he wanted a copy when I finally got it finished. He was jovial, positive, and a super-smiley guy. Stephen was determined to get his life back on track and could not speak highly enough of the support he was receiving from his support worker. He explained to me that he was due to move into independent accommodation soon, and even though the thought of no longer living at the house made him feel nervous, he was also excited about his new start and the next steps he was taking. He had plans to find work and move forward. Stephen had moved into Unseen's services when he was identified as a potential victim of trafficking; he was now far from home and knew that, as hard as it was to be away from his family, it was the best thing he could do to give himself some distance from those who had exploited him. He was starting to reconnect with his family and this was part of his journey he was proud of.

Stephen had been released from prison; I do not know what he was serving a sentence for and nor did I ask or need to know. When released, he moved into accommodation authorised by probation officers. What transpired was that they had not done their due diligence on who Stephen would be living with. It was here he met the people that began to exploit him, forcing him to transport drugs for them. Stephen had previously had issues with drugs before he had been in prison and it was this vulnerability that was exploited.

Those he lived with asked him if he had a driving licence and if he wanted to earn some money driving for them. That money never transpired, and before he knew it, he was driving the length and breadth of the country, transporting guns and drugs for them. He was at their beck and call, and described violent beatings if he took a wrong turn, went to the wrong place, or was late.

Stephen commented that even prison was better than what he experienced once he was 'free', referring to the beatings he experienced in prison being better than the broken bones he had since experienced.

For two years he described being enslaved; he was always watched and controlled via his phone. He described that he began missing appointments due to his exploitation, but his neighbours, family, and probation workers were all unaware of what he was going through.

Name: Mihaela

Age: 24

Nationality: Romanian. As an EU citizen, Mihaela was eligible to live and work in the UK with no restrictions, as long as she was able to support herself.

Type of modern slavery: Trafficked initially for the purpose of sexual exploitation, with the intention to exploit her criminally for the purpose of a sham marriage.

How I came to be involved: The male officer involved in the case had contacted me for my thoughts and advice in relation to this case.

This is the only experience of a sham marriage case in my time working in the sector, and it was part of a far wider case of an individual being held in multiple exploitative situations, being forced to sell sexual services on the street and in private residences. When she argued she did not want to do it any more, she was told she could earn her way to freedom by paying off the debt she had accrued either by carrying on selling sexual services or by using her European citizenship to marry a non-EU national. Mihaela was arrested at her 'wedding ceremony' and sent to prison.

Experiences of organ harvesting

I have only met one person who had their kidney taken against their will. He was presenting at a conference I was at, not in the UK, and shared his experiences with the participants. I am not going to reshare his account of what happened to him as I do not remember it accurately and was one of 50 people to hear it.

This does mean that I cannot introduce you to anyone who has been trafficked for the purpose of organ harvesting, which I guess is a good thing. There have been a couple of cases identified in the UK but the procedures had not occurred here.

There is an international market for organs due to the length of transplant waiting lists. This is well known, and people offer financial reward to those in tough financial situations in exchange for an organ, usually a kidney. Organ trafficking happens in two main ways: either an individual agrees to have an organ removed for financial benefit or an organ is extracted forcibly. It is a technical procedure and requires the input of medical professionals. Trafficking organs goes against all the principles of organ donation. The United Nations Office on Drugs and Crime (2015, pp.9–10) list these as: brokering is not allowed; organs required cannot be advertised; organs must be donated freely with no financial payment; those who donate must receive proper medical care after any removal and must be free of any undue influence and be able to give voluntary consent to the procedure. None of these principles will be adhered to in a case of organ harvesting as a form of trafficking and exploitation.

Experiences of domestic servitude

People who have been trafficked for the purpose of domestic servitude may:

- live with a family
- not eat with the rest of the family
- have no private space
- sleep in a shared or inappropriate space
- be reported missing by their employer even though they are still living in their employer's house
- never or rarely leave the house for social reasons
- never leave the house without their employer
- be given only leftovers to eat
- be subjected to insults, abuse, threats or violence.

(UNODC 2010)

Domestic servitude involves an individual working in a household where they experience ill treatment, humiliation, and long working hours, and have no private space. People in this situation will have limited control over their own decisions and movements. They are unable to come and go from their accommodation, needing the permission of their employer for the simplest of tasks. They are expected to serve the household and be on call for any task that may need doing, at any time of the day or night.

I have not met many people who have experienced domestic servitude; by its very nature it is less overt than other forms of trafficking. It is not on our high streets – it is hidden in plain sight within people's homes, behind closed doors.

Igor and Arfas experienced situations of domestic servitude, one in the UK and one abroad. For both men domestic servitude formed part of their accounts of exploitation rather than the entirety of their stories.

Name: Igor

Age: 40

Nationality: Polish. As an EU citizen, Igor was legally allowed to live and work in the UK.

Type of modern slavery: Trafficked, initially forced labour, and subsequently domestic servitude.

How I came to be involved: I was contacted by a nurse from the local hospital who was concerned about a patient. She asked me if I would be able to offer her advice and meet with Igor to help understand what was happening and to see if we could work out any alternative options.

When he fell ill and Igor could no longer work outdoors in harsh conditions on the car-wash forecourt, his employers made a different plan. Transporting him across the South-West of England so he could wash cars day in day out was no longer a viable option. He looked sick – he was sick – and people would start to ask questions. The solution was easy for Igor's employers: there was still a debt to be paid and this could be managed by Igor staying at the house; he would cook for the others and keep the place clean. Igor was not given any choice in this matter. One day when the van arrived to pick everyone up, he was told to stay home, that he would not be going out today. He did not go out to work again. He was being taken to receive the treatment he needed, but the nursing team were concerned about what was happening when he left the hospital.

Name: Arfas

Age: 36

Nationality: Burmese. Arfas required a visa to be granted in order for him to be allowed to live and work in the UK.

Type of modern slavery: Trafficking for the combined purpose of domestic servitude and forced labour.

How I came to be involved: I was contacted by Arfas's legal representative and asked to meet with him and offer my opinion as to whether his account contained indicators and elements of trafficking. From memory, he was facing potential removal from the UK and his legal team thought this may not be appropriate if indeed he was a victim of trafficking.

When Arfas and I met, he'd been through a lot: his experiences were complicated.

As a young boy, Arfas lived in a refugee camp in Bangladesh. He was an orphan; his parents had been killed as they fled from their village. As a teenager, having made the decision to leave the camp, he was abused and exploited by those who should have looked after him. He was made to live and work in a family home in Bangladesh, pretty much as their slave. On a daily basis, he would leave the camp to walk around the local area and ask tourists for money and cigarettes. It was one of these tourists who offered Arfas the chance to leave with him – to live in his home and to work for him. This man would become referred to by Arfas as his master. Arfas would be expected to do all sorts of chores, including walking the children to school, cleaning the home, and serving food for functions held at the house, while sleeping under the stairs, eating leftovers, and being physically abused by his master's wife. For three years Arfas served his master and his family. I am not clear on how Arfas got to the UK, but certainly the work he described to me in our meeting suggested that he had continued to be subject to exploitative practices in restaurants and takeaways across the UK.

Experiences of sexual exploitation

People who have been trafficked for the purpose of sexual exploitation may:

- be of any age, although the age may vary according to the location and the market
- move from one brothel to the next or work in various locations
- be escorted whenever they go to and return from work and other outside activities
- have tattoos or other marks indicating 'ownership' by their exploiters
- work long hours or have few if any days off
- sleep where they work
- live or travel in a group, sometimes with other women who do not speak the same language
- have very few items of clothing
- have clothes that are mostly the kind typically worn for doing sex work
- only know how to say sex-related words in the local language or in the language of the client group
- have no cash of their own
- be unable to show an identity document.

The following might also indicate that children have been trafficked:

- there is evidence that suspected victims have had unprotected and/or violent sex
- there is evidence that suspected victims cannot refuse unprotected and/or violent sex
- there is evidence that a person has been bought and sold
- there is evidence that groups of women are under the control of others

- advertisements are placed for brothels or similar places offering the services of women of a particular ethnicity or nationality
- it is reported that sex workers provide services to a clientele of a particular ethnicity or nationality
- it is reported by clients that sex workers do not smile.

(UNODC 2010)

Sexual exploitation is not only an issue that faces women and children; men are also subjected to this form of slavery. Sexual exploitation may involve violent, humiliating, and degrading sexual assaults, without the individual's consent. People can be tricked into believing they are in a loving, consensual relationship and then duped into providing sexual services under the guise of love, when in fact they have been groomed for this very purpose.

It is the manipulation or deception of a person into sexual activity against their will.

Depending on how you view it, sexual exploitation could be another form of work extracted, another form of forced labour. In the UK, it is a discrete form of trafficking.

As we saw in Chapter 1, some like Anatolyi's mum are abducted, forcibly taken from their normal lives, and forced to provide sexual services. Often they do not receive any financial benefit from this arrangement, are unable to refuse 'customers' and can be locked into the location they are working from. Some will be drugged to ensure compliance and continued reliance on those who are exploiting them. Some are offered the opportunity to travel, to see the world, offered a job that never transpires, and then made to work in the sex industry. Anna, Zara, Elbina, Olga, Ling, and Maria were all trafficked and sexually exploited.

Name: Anna

Age: 20

Nationality: Romanian.

Type of modern slavery: Trafficked for the purpose of sexual exploitation. As an EU citizen, Anna was able to legally seek employment anywhere in the EU.

How I came to be involved: I met Anna when I was working a shift in the women's safe house.

Anna was forced to sell sex and have her body used and abused against her will. She was held in servitude and deployed for her body at the beck and call of her trafficker. Anna believed, when leaving her home in Eastern Europe, that she would be heading for a better life. With limited access to education, the job market, or, in her mind, much of a future, she jumped at the chance to work abroad. Anna did not realise that the lady she befriended would not fulfil the promises that she had made to her.

I first encountered Anna when on shift at the women's safe house. I was there one evening, covering for a team member who had called in sick. This was not my usual place of work or a role I felt particularly comfortable in, and I was hoping for a quiet evening and not much to hand over to the night shift. It was one of my first lone working shifts at the house and I was having to put into practice all the policies and protocols I had written, trying to put the theory into practice.

I had been told to expect a new referral at some point that evening and had spent time making sure everything was ready and that I knew what I had to do. The room had been cleaned and checked, a welcome pack of basic toiletries and necessary items was awaiting the new arrival, and her key was ready for her. Forms had been printed off (yes, we were still using paper at this stage!) and the referral re-read. Then the waiting began. The safe house was quiet, with other residents having retired to their rooms after an evening of a communal meal and watching a film together. No doubt, they needed time and space to themselves, away from the other residents and the staff team.

Night-time always proved to be an interesting time for those we worked with. Night-time can feel more dangerous. It is the time when the house is quiet, when the noise and clamour of the day evaporates and the distractions subside. Some describe this as the time when they remember what they have been through, when night terrors hit, memories are relived, and panic attacks are most common. The coping strategies employed in the day are no longer present and managing emotions, feelings, and memories can be hard. Aside from feeling this way, body clocks can be out of sync. For some who have experienced sexual exploitation, night-time was time to work. As the rest of the world was winding down, they were being told to get ready and service customers and clients. Sleeping during the day and working during the night is a routine that many have found hard to change.

Anna arrived in a lurid, fluorescent pink, fluffy dressing gown. She had nothing else with her – no bag, no possessions, literally the clothes on her back. She had travelled dressed like this and no one had thought to see if they could offer her a different outfit. What I was meant to do – assess risk and do a health and safety briefing – went out of the window. The decision was made that this could all wait. She needed space, to see her room, to be given her key and told that this was hers. A shower and some fresh clothes later, we sat with a cup of tea. The tea had inordinate amounts of sugar in it and we spent time together while waiting for a pizza to cook. Anna was offended by the questions that needed to be asked – of course, she was not suicidal and she had no thoughts of harming herself; she had nothing on her to do herself or anyone else any harm; she was on no medication and did not have any immediate medical needs. She was hungry, tired, young, trusting, timid, smiley, vulnerable, and in desperate need of sleep. She was grateful for her room, the clothes, and the food, and to be away from those who had been exploiting her. Anna stayed at the safe house for some time and was supported to establish connections in the community and to access health care, education, and legal advice. Anna, like many other women, had been forced to sell sex; she received no benefit for the service she supplied and did so under the threat of force. Anna had been deceived, believing England would offer her better job opportunities. She was naïve and trusting, and this was taken advantage of. She had very little in her home country, nothing to lose, and the promise of better and more was alluring and attractive. The woman who offered her the job had selected Anna specifically, pretended to befriend her, and appeared to be a good friend by helping her to arrange her travel documents, her transportation, and organising the job that never transpired. This woman knew what she was doing; she knew Anna had little to lose and trusted her. Preying upon Anna and using the relationship she built with her, she brought her to the UK and forced her to sell sex.

People often freely agree to take up work, and only once they start working, discover that they have been deceived about the conditions or the nature of the work, and that they are not free to leave without repercussions. It has been established in international law that when deception or fraud is present, the initial consent of a person to do the work is rendered irrelevant.

The money Anna earned for her trafficker was set against the debt she had accrued. The debt was never discussed when the job was offered. But transport, travel documents, accommodation, food, and rent all cost money and culminated into a debt that Anna owed. Groomed into believing that she was complicit in the process, that it was somehow her fault, and unaware of support structures and her entitlements, she was dependent on the woman who was exploiting her.

Name: Zara

Age: 26

Nationality: Albanian. As an Albanian national, Zara did not have the automatic right to live and/or work in the UK.

Type of modern slavery: Trafficked for the purpose of sexual exploitation by her boyfriend.

How I came to be involved: I met Zara at her lawyer's office in London. I had been asked to write a report to challenge the decision that had been made in relation to her case: she had received a negative decision on her NRM. Zara had been sold into prostitution, forced to sell sex against her will by the person she thought loved her. Worried that her father was arranging her marriage, as was the custom in her culture and as had happened to her older sister, she believed she had a way out of this when she met her boyfriend. She was groomed by him. They had travelled to England together and then he had sold her. She had fallen pregnant during her exploitation. Zara had been entered into the NRM but her account of what had happened wasn't believed by the authorities; her credibility was challenged.

Name: Elbina

Age: 27

Nationality: Albanian. As an Albanian national, Elbina did not have the automatic right to live and/or work in the UK, and required a visa and permit to continue staying in the UK.

Type of modern slavery: Trafficked for the purpose of sexual exploitation.

How I came to be involved: I was contacted by Elbina's legal representative and asked to offer my opinion on her case. She was facing being removed from the UK and her legal team were concerned that she may be a victim of trafficking in need of support rather than immigration enforcement action. There was concern that she would be at risk if the UK government made the decision to return her to Albania.

I don't know how Elbina came to be in the UK, but she shared with me some of what had happened to her before she had managed to seek safety in England. Elbina was at the start of a promising career in her home country; she was educated, recently married. The beginning of her account did not sound like that of a trafficking narrative to me when I first met her. Her experience challenged what I thought I knew: she was educated and had a husband she loved and who loved her – to the outside world, an ideal set-up. Her first year of marriage did not turn out as she had imagined. Her husband became abusive towards her. She turned to the police for assistance, but even with a restraining order in place, she felt they were unable to offer her the protection she needed. Emotionally, the events she had been through took their toll and she decided to take a break and go and stay with a friend to rest and recover.

It was here, as she was walking to the shops, that she was held at gunpoint, thrown into the back of a car, and taken to a hotel room by three men. She believes this was all organised by her husband and that she was being punished for leaving him. Once at the hotel she was forced to provide sexual services for the various men who arrived at her room. This was not easy for Elbina to share with me, and she expressed frustration and embarrassment at being overpowered by those who had trapped her. She described being locked in with someone watching her 24/7. She tried to speak to clients to help her, but they were all scared of the people who were holding her captive. On the day she managed to escape, she called her sister for the first time in three months and planned to get herself to safety.

Name: Olga

Age: 26

Nationality: Ukrainian. As a Ukrainian national, Olga did not have the automatic right to live and/or work in the UK and would need a visa/permit to do so.

Type of modern slavery: Trafficked for the purpose of sexual exploitation.

How I came to be involved: I was in a London borough, invited to assist in an operation relating to potential sexual exploitation occurring across a group of establishments selling sexual services. A father-and-son business that ran numerous brothels around the area was suspected of being involved in the exploitation of those working within their premises. With a warrant, police had visited all the properties at the same time to gather evidence, to arrest the father and son, and to remove all those working from the properties. Olga had been removed from one of the establishments earlier that morning by the police and was now sitting in the hall, designated as the reception centre, along with numerous other women, being given a cup of tea and some food while she waited for the police to speak to her. She had appeared timid in the centre and had sat on her own. I had joined her for a cup of tea, shared a smile but not spoken. When the time to interview her came, I was asked to accompany Olga. She told the officers that she was being forced to do this work. As she spoke, she was visibly distressed as she described her experiences; she didn't know the work she'd be doing, she didn't want to do it, and yes, she wanted help. The police probed gently and carefully, and moved at her pace. Police explained that she could be taken to a safe place and people would help her there. Olga wanted to leave her situation and asked the police to assist her.

Name: Ling

Age: 32

Nationality: Chinese. Ling required a visa and work permit to live and work legally in the UK.

Type of modern slavery: Trafficked for the purpose of sexual exploitation.

How I came to be involved: I was part of a welfare visit with a local police force. I was part of the team and tasked with checking on the welfare of the staff and giving out information of support services if required.

Ling was another woman I met who was being forced to sell sexual services. This interaction was not at the safe house, but in a house on a normal street, in a normal city. She had no control over who her customers were, when they would arrive, or what services they would expect her to provide. Unlike Anna and Elbina, she was not out of her exploitative situation when we met, and leaving her behind that day was hard. At one point, I thought there was a glimmer of hope that she may accept our offer of assistance and take the opportunity to leave with us. This was before she realised that we were not able to pay off her debt to those who had brought her here; without that reassurance, she felt the lives of her parents and disabled son back in China were at too much risk. I was to learn that this was a common narrative and one that I was to come across several times over the next few years: people with issues at home – gambling debts, broken-down relationships, owing money to the wrong people – being offered the opportunity to earn money abroad, escape their situation at home, and pay off their debts. The work being offered was always ambiguous, but high wages were promised that would easily cover the debts once the accommodation and travel cost were paid off. For Ling, this debt was currently at £20,000; from what we could work out, this was for her travel, rent, and food bill. To pay this off, she was not given any wages and she did not know how long the debt would last, how much she had paid off, how many customers she would need to see, or how long she would be expected to work. Presumably, she also did not know that a flight to China costs in the region of £500, so somewhere something had gone very wrong. She would be moved regularly between new cities and locations; taxis would turn up at a pre-arranged time and take her and her one bag to the next location. She would stay there for a few weeks before being moved on again. At each location, there would be another person responsible for the bookings and for making sure Ling did what she was meant to. She was being completely controlled and could not see a way out. In some ways, I admire Ling: she knew that what she thought she would be coming to had not transpired, and she certainly felt stuck, but she made the choice to stay to protect her family and her son. She had first-hand experience of what those she was working for were doing to her, and I think had no doubt in her mind that her family would pay the price if she tried to leave. She put their needs before hers.

Name: Maria

Age: 36

Nationality: Romanian. As an EU national, Maria didn't require a work permit and was able to live and work in the UK.

Type of modern slavery: From my recollection, linked to forced labour and/or sexual exploitation.

How I came to be involved: Maria had been housed at Unseen's safe house. Staff sought my input with her case at the point when her support was coming to an end.

Maria had come from a lifetime of abuse and trauma, and had been positively identified as a victim of trafficking. As a Romanian national, Maria was able (pre-Brexit) to stay in the UK and to exercise her rights as a European citizen. This meant that if she could support herself, she could stay. She would have access to some benefits offered in the UK but would need to work and be self-sufficient. No one involved could see how this might be a viable option for Maria: she had never had an official job or agreed terms of employment, she had left school as a young child, her English wasn't good, her ability to retain information was poor (the result of traumatic experiences and her learning disability), she trusted everyone and anyone, and she had never had any money of her own. Her whole life she had done what someone else had told her to do.

A common theme for lots of those I have met is that they are genuinely unaware of their rights and entitlements in a UK setting. They have entrusted the employment, the journey, and all its planning to a third party. Sometimes this third party is known to them, sometimes not; in some instances, regardless, it is the only option they believe they have. In some cases, the person who offered them the job, the person who arranged their travel, and the person who eventually employs them are all different: people are passed off to different people at different parts of the journey. This means that they are easier to control and easier to isolate.

Marios, Dung, Ly, Arfas, Zara, Elbina, Olga, and Ling all came from countries where they needed to have visas to be in the UK. Although some of them may have originally entered using these, it is common that passports and documents are removed – preventing people from authenticating their identity and from physically being able to leave the situation of exploitation. The lack of documentation and the lack of a visa allowing them to work puts them in a precarious position – when they seek help and assistance, will those who are designated to give this support (a) identify them as victims and (b) believe their stories, or will they face deportation and criminal charges? It is these sorts of fears that traffickers prey on: they tell those under their control that they will not be believed, that they will not be helped, and that they will be returned home – home to the exact location the traffickers recruited them from. Unfortunately, on too many occasions I have seen this chain of events come to pass and those I would consider victims of trafficking treated as criminals and illegal immigrants. Not all the indicators listed in this chapter will be present in every case, not every person will neatly fit one definition or type of exploitation, trafficking, or modern slavery. It is fluid and it is complex. No two victims' experiences are the same, and nor should we expect them to be.

CHAPTER 5

Support for Victims of Modern Slavery

> The NRM is the UK's framework for identifying victims of modern slavery. It is also one means of ensuring that adult victims receive the necessary support and assistance in the period immediately after their identification as a potential victim.
>
> **(HOME OFFICE 2021, P.38)**

Anyone identified in the UK as a potential victim of modern slavery is entitled to support.

Identification of victims and their subsequent support is delivered via a system called the National Referral Mechanism (NRM). It is a mechanism that sits within the Home Office and is regularly reviewed and revised.

The NRM was introduced in 2009 to meet the UK's obligations under the Council of Europe Convention on Action against Trafficking in Human Beings (known as the Convention) (Council of Europe 2005). The NRM system specifically allows the UK to comply with the following convention articles:

- Article 10 – identification of potential victims
- Article 12 – assistance to victims
- Article 13 – recovery and reflection period
- Article 14 – residence permit
- Article 15 – compensation and legal redress
- Article 16 – repatriation and return of victims.

The content of the articles can be found in the Legal Appendix.

The Convention (Council of Europe 2005) requires that potential adult victims of trafficking are provided with a period of a minimum of 30 days' reflection and recovery, during which they will receive support, including accommodation, subsistence, access to relevant medical and legal services, and potential eligibility for discretionary leave to remain in the country if they are recognised as a victim.

The UK currently provides this initial support to potential victims, referred to as the NRM, for a minimum of 45 days, or until a conclusive grounds decision is made. This time is known as the recovery and reflection period and is in place to ensure that immediate needs are met and to support recovery from exploitative experiences.

The NRM provides potential victims of slavery access to a range of services, via a government-funded care and support contract.

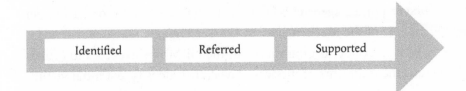

Figure 5.1: NRM process

Potential victims can be identified by a range of different agencies in their day-to-day work. These will include health care and NHS staff, law enforcement officials (as part of targeted activity or linked to other criminal activities), immigration teams and border officials, prison and detention centre staff, Job Centre staff, local authority teams (e.g. those working in housing, homelessness, adult safeguarding, children's services, and social work teams), school staff, legal representatives, non-governmental organisations, faith-based organisations. Not all of these agencies are deemed to be official first responders within the NRM system (for example, health services and those working within them are not currently NRM first responders); it is important that those working in these agencies understand the signs and indicators of slavery and what support can be offered.

Under Section 52 of the Modern Slavery Act, the government has designated specific agencies to have specific duties in relation to identifying victims of modern slavery. These include a statutory 'Duty to Notify' the Home Office when they believe they may have encountered a potential victim.

This 'Duty' can be discharged in one of two ways: by entering someone into the NRM (if the person is an adult, this requires their consent) or by completing a Duty to Notify (if no consent is given), and is outlined in Figure 5.2.

In addition to those agencies who have a statutory Duty to Notify there are also first responder agencies that also have a duty to identify potential victims. There is some overlap between agencies with a statutory duty and those who are first responders. First responder agencies are not all public authorities and it is recognised that some victims will not feel comfortable or able to disclose to law enforcement agencies. The list of first responder agencies is far wider than those who are obliged under Section 52 of the Modern Slavery Act (see Figure 5.3).

First responder organisations (in the NRM) are expected to (a) recognise the indicators of modern slavery, (b) identify potential victims of modern slavery, (c) try to understand what has happened to the individual, (d) refer into the NRM, and (e) provide a point of contact throughout the NRM.

As well as identifying potential victims, first responder agencies are also expected to explain what support is on offer to victims and make a referral into these systems if consent (for adults) is given and if support is wanted.

To enter someone into the NRM and into the support offered by the system requires the NRM to be completed, signed by the potential victim, and submitted by a first responder agency.

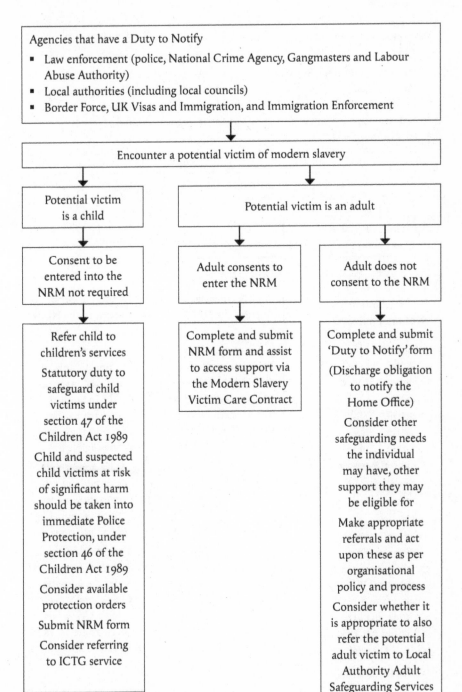

Figure 5.2: Overview of the Duty to Notify process

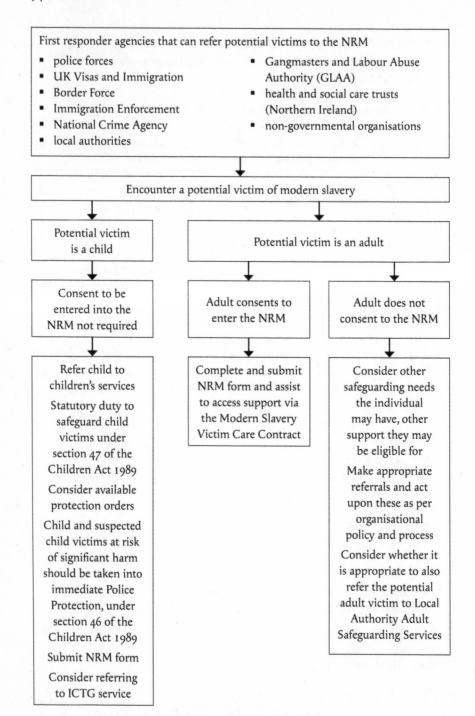

Figure 5.3: Overview of the first responder process

Once someone is identified and consents to accept support, their details are sent to a body known as the competent authority (a department within the Home Office) to decide about their status as a victim of modern slavery.

The NRM form captures basic data about the individual – their personal details and contact information and the type of slavery, trafficking, or exploitation that appears to have taken place. It includes an indicators list that the first responder has seen, heard, or believes to be present for the individual and any narrative that the referrer considers necessary to explain the situation further. Finally, it includes information about the person completing the form and their contact details. The information submitted on the NRM form will be used to make decisions about their case and whether they are considered to be a victim or not – where the person was encountered, what the first responder identified, and what the potential victim disclosed at the time of identification.

It is not the job of the person completing the referral to decide if someone is a victim or not. This is the role of the competent authority. As the body with responsibility for decision-making functions within the NRM, there are two decisions that the competent authority has to make: the reasonable grounds (RG) decision and the conclusive grounds (CG) decision. The whole process is a civil, not a legal, one.

The threshold for the first decision, an RG decision, is a low one and should not take a long time to be reached. The RG decision has a threshold that is lower than the criminal standard of proof, and lower than the CG decision. If the competent authority considers there are reasonable grounds, a positive decision will be given within the expected timescales and the victim will be offered support via the care contract.

If the potential victim is destitute and has no safe accommodation, they are immediately able to access the support system. If they are not destitute or do not need to be accommodated immediately, they will need to wait for an RG decision before being able to access support. This may mean that they require a further safeguarding intervention between the time they have been identified and the time it takes to receive an RG decision.

Table 5.1: Outcomes for the NRM reasonable grounds decision

	Positive RG	Negative RG
British national	Access to support offered by the NRM Offered support and accommodation as needed until a CG decision is made	No support offered via the NRM First responder agency to consider other safeguarding needs and how these can be met with the help of other support agencies
Non-British national	Access to support offered by the NRM Offered support and accommodation as needed until a CG decision is made	No support offered via the NRM First responder agency to consider other safeguarding needs and how these can be met with the help of other support agencies May be limited support available due to nationality

Towards the end of the reflection and recovery period, the competent authority must decide whether, 'on the balance of probabilities', there is sufficient information to grant a CG decision. The CG decision threshold is higher than the RG one, but still lower than the criminal standard of proof. This decision means that the person identified as a potential victim via the NRM process is believed to be a victim of human trafficking or modern slavery. There may not be enough information on the original NRM form to make this decision, and during the period of support, the competent authority can request further information from those involved in the case to assist them in making their CG decision.

Table 5.2: Outcomes for the NRM conclusive grounds decision

	Positive CG	Negative CG
British national	Move on and exit support available – provided as an extension of the Modern Slavery Victim Care Contract or by other agencies	Asked to exit support Other systems of support available and should be referred into these as part of exit from the support of the care contract

Non-British national	No legal right to remain in the UK	No legal right to remain in the UK
	Positive CG does not come with any automatic status in the UK	Asked to exit support and offered a short amount of time/support to do so
	A positive CG decision does not allow for access to public funds	Negative CG does not come with any automatic status in the UK
	A grant of discretionary leave will be automatically considered for those with a positive conclusive grounds decision (those granted DL have access to public services and benefits and no prohibition on work)	A negative CG decision does not allow for access to public funds
		No grant of discretionary leave will be considered
		Potentially to apply for other routes to remain in the UK
	Even with a positive CG, nationality will dictate what a person is eligible for and this will determine move-on support and pathway	No access to public funds and would need to be able to evidence self-sufficiency to remain in the UK unless granted a form of leave, such as refugee status or humanitarian protection
	What a person is eligible for will depend on nationality – legal advice to navigate this and to see if they are eligible for other immigration pathways (visas, discretionary leave, asylum)	What a person is eligible for will depend on nationality and their experience – legal advice to navigate this and to see if they are eligible for other immigration pathways (visas, asylum, CG reconsideration).
	Move-on pathway for ongoing support and accommodation will be hard: • asylum support and accommodation • homelessness shelter or other NGO provision • friends or family • return home (voluntary or via removal proceedings)	Potential accommodation options/pathways: • asylum support and accommodation • homelessness shelter or other NGO provision • friends or family • return home (voluntary or via removal proceedings)

An agreed pathway to exiting support is put into place between a survivor, their support worker and the competent authority, regardless of if a positive or negative decision has been made. The timeframes in relation to exiting support vary and someone with a positive CG decision will have longer to move on from support and will be supported in this transition for longer than an individual who has received a negative decision. What someone is entitled to upon exit from the NRM is dependent on the outcome of their NRM decision and their nationality, as outlined in Table 5.2.

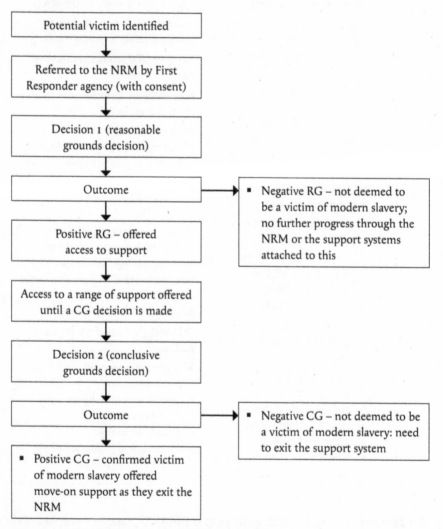

Figure 5.4: The NRM process and how it works

For an overview of the NRM Process refer to the Glossary of Terms.

Discretionary leave to remain

A positive CG decision does not result in an automatic right to remain in the UK. Whether an individual can stay in the UK or not is based upon their nationality and their immigration status. If an individual receives a positive CG decision, the competent authority will also consider granting a form of temporary leave as well – this is known as discretionary leave to remain. This policy and approach are outlined in government guidance (Home Office 2020). When the competent authority grants a positive CG decision, if the individual doesn't already have the right to remain in the UK, they also automatically consider if discretionary leave should be granted. However, this does not mean that all confirmed survivors automatically qualify to access rights to stay in the UK. To qualify for consideration of discretionary leave (DL), a confirmed victim of trafficking must either require leave to remain due to:

- personal circumstances
- pursuing compensation
- helping police with their enquiries.

(Home Office 2020, p.6)

As a result of helping with a police investigation, **Anna** had been granted DL. Discretionary leave to remain grants a confirmed victim's access to public funds and routes to employment. The amount of leave given differs depending on people's individual circumstance.

Help to return home

For individuals referred to the NRM, who are not British, there is the option at any point during the NRM and support process to opt for a voluntary return home. The government runs a funded service that is available to all potential victims during the NRM or upon receipt of a positive CG decision. The service can assist with:

- flights
- travel documents
- financial package for use on arrival home.

Adults and the NRM: Modern Slavery Victim Care Contract

Throughout the time a potential victim spends moving through the NRM process, the intention is that their needs are met via the Modern Slavery Victim Care Contract (MSVCC). This system of support doesn't and can't provide for all the needs in isolation and relies on being able to refer to other agencies throughout the NRM process, as needed by those being supported.

Riso, Andre, Stephen, Mihaela, Igor, Anna, and **Elbina** were all able to access support via the MSVCC.

The MSVCC is funded by the government, via the Home Office, and covers the support offered to potential victims in England and Wales. The model of support over the last eight years has been based on a hub-and-spoke set-up. A single primary contractor (hub) manages the administration, referrals, assessments, and data and coordinates a range of sub-contractors, based in different localities, to provide accommodation and direct on-the-ground support to those referred to them. The MSVCC commits to provide potential victims with the following:

- safe accommodation (where needed)
- outreach support (if already accommodated)
- practical help and advice
- interpretation and translation
- financial support
- health care (physical, emotional, and mental health needs)
- specialist legal advice
- education for children
- transport to important appointments

- assistance to return to home country (if not a UK national)
- and future planning support.

(Home Office 2021, p.62)

The system of support during someone's time in the NRM primarily provides access to safe accommodation and a support worker who can offer a coordinating function, advocating for access to the support a potential victim needs and is entitled to during their time in the NRM.

Some individuals referred to the NRM will be eligible for support from other agencies as well, and plans will be made as to if the care contract will offer them accommodation and support or support in an outreach capacity.

In practice, support may look like:

- assisting an individual to register with a GP, helping to arrange an appointment, and supporting attendance
- supporting an individual to find a lawyer so they can learn about and understand their options
- explaining what counselling is, how it may be able to assist, and discussing if this is something an individual may want to explore
- accompanying an individual to meetings with other agencies who are supporting their case
- providing for an individual's basic needs upon entry into support (e.g. clothing, food, items for children, and toiletries).

For lots of people, this may be the first time in a long time, or even the first time ever, they have had the opportunity to make choices and decisions for themselves. Support teams work hard to ensure the individuals they support understand the options available to them and support them to access these in the most appropriate way. Those in the NRM support system do not have to take up all the support offered and can access different elements at different times as and when they want and/ or need to.

The commitment to providing access to the support that victims and survivors often need requires engagement and advocacy with a range of other organisations to ensure that a victim can access what they need and what they are entitled to. Other agencies often involved in an individual's support are:

- medical practitioners including mental health teams, primary and secondary care practitioners and services, sexual health services, opticians, and dentists
- therapeutic practitioners and counselling services
- government departments including UK Visa and Immigration (asylum process), Department for Work and Pensions (access to welfare benefits and labour market, where applicable, via the Job Centre), and the Competent Authority (Home Office) (to get more information for the NRM process)
- local authority services including housing teams, adult care teams, safeguarding teams, and social care (in the case of children)
- law enforcement agencies including the police and National Crime Agency who may want to interview a potential victim as a witness in a modern slavery case
- lawyers and solicitors for advice on immigration pathways, criminal proceedings, and compensation claims
- educational services including schools, nurseries, children's centres, English language centres, and voluntary educational provisions
- other third-sector organisations who may be also providing support (depending on need) such as maternity support groups, drug and alcohol services, domestic abuse support, religious institutions, and migrant and refugee networks.

As part of support to access entitlements, support teams will also be looking at the wider needs people may have – social, spiritual, physical, psychological – and working out together how these may be able to be met, depending on the individual's current circumstances, what they would like to achieve, and what services are available locally.

The support system will also focus on risk and work with the individual to look at past, current, and future risks, and again work together to navigate these, putting in place mechanisms to support people to cope when risks arise.

The support given is required to be tailored to meet the needs of the individual being supported.

Children and the NRM: local authority children's services

The process described above is for adults only. Unlike adults, children, if identified as victims, don't need to be entered into the NRM in order to receive support. This doesn't mean that the NRM form shouldn't be completed as it may contain important information that can assist the care and support of a child or young person, ensuring they get what they need. But it does mean that all children who are thought to have been trafficked or exploited need to be referred to the local authority children's services, and the normal child protection and safeguarding measures need to be followed. Any child who is potentially a victim of modern slavery, regardless of their nationality or immigration status, must be appropriately safeguarded, supported, and placed in accommodation, in line with the relevant local authority's duties under various legislation in relation to the care of children. Children do not have to consent to being entered into the NRM.

Independent Child Trafficking Guardians (ICTGs)

Under Section 48 of the Modern Slavery Act (2015), children who are thought to be victims of modern slavery are entitled to access an Independent Child Trafficking Guardian (ICTG).

ICTGs provide advocacy and an independent source of advice for trafficked children. An ICTG will also ensure that all the professionals involved in a child's case are acting in the best interest of the child and focused on promoting recovery. An ICTG will be involved throughout the NRM decision-making process. Their role is to protect the child from further harm, prevent possible repeat victimisation, and reduce the risk of a child being re-trafficked or going missing.

To access the ICTG service, a first responder must complete an ICTG form (separate to the NRM form and process).

In **Marios**'s case, a referral was made to the social care out-of-hours service, the situation was explained, and accommodation was arranged for the night. We were told a social worker would be assigned in the morning and come out to do an assessment of Marios's needs. Along with the police officer, I accompanied Marios to the place he would be staying, logging his request for some new shoes as all he had were his work wellies. Some eight hours after we had first set foot on the car-wash forecourt, having identified a young person who was being exploited, we had safeguarded him, referred him to support with social services, and he was going to be safely accommodated overnight.

We had met **Dung and Ly** as part of a multi-agency welfare visit. When we had first started speaking to them, we realised we needed to get them away from their place of work and to a neutral, safe space to work out what was happening.

We had built up a rapport with the girls. We had been with them all day, and although the conversation was stilted, they wanted both the officer and me to be in the room with them when the social worker was asking them questions. As per normal process, social care had been called as Dung and Ly were both thought to be children. The wait for the social worker had been a long one, and we had all sat in a stuffy but sunny room in a council building for a good few hours. During this time, the girls had had food and water, they were worried about the woman who 'looked after them', and were insistent they stayed together, but mainly they slept. Arms folded on the table and their heads on top – they were exhausted. While they slept the officer and I spoke to children's organisations checking we had got the process right and trying to work out what agency would do what moving forwards; was there anything we were missing, anything we should consider? We decided it would be best to try and complete the NRM form with the information we had as this would assist the social worker to understand the situation, what they had been through and plan with them. We had to be professionally firm to stay in the room with the girls when the social worker arrived. Dung and Ly wanted us there and yet the social worker didn't. I am not sure why – it was a case that went on to need effective multi-agency working, and yet if we hadn't pushed for this at its outset and on the wishes of the girls, it may not have happened.

Getting people access to the NRM

The first responders, as outlined in Figure 5.3, all have a duty to identify and assist potential victims to access support. Where agencies and organisations who are not on the first responder list, such as health care professionals (in England and Wales), come across potential victims, they need to engage with an appropriate first responder agency. Some people will not want to speak to law enforcement officers and will prefer to disclose their experiences to a non-governmental organisation first responder, and this should be considered before contacting a first responder agency. The first responder agency will then be able to explain the process, complete the NRM form (if consent is given), and arrange for support. My main interaction in speaking to people about the NRM has either been through my expert witness work or as part of law enforcement and multi-agency activity.

With the focus of modern slavery as a crime, it makes sense that a lot of the identification and referrals into the NRM happen via police activity. **Stephen, Riso,** and **Mihaela** were all identified by police officers and entered into the NRM. Law enforcement agencies have the mandate to identify, disrupt, and prosecute modern slavery activity, are obliged to complete 'Duty to Notify' submissions, are a first responder agency within the NRM system, and generally have a safeguarding and welfare duty of care towards those they meet. During my time working in the sector, I have been part of both welfare and operational visits to protect and safeguard potential victims of slavery and this is, as you will have read, where I have met a lot of the people I have introduced in this book.

There are two main ways I have been involved in police activity over the years – operational activity and welfare visits.

Operational activity

Operational activity can be thought of as activity that is as a direct result of having received information about a crime or offence being committed and where further investigation of this is deemed to be needed.

When the police receive information about a potential crime or vulnerable people, they evaluate, assess, and analyse what they are going to do with it. There is the need to ensure a proportionate response to the information they receive. Information turns into intelligence via an analysis process. Police will consider the credibility of the report received, the source of the information, how it compares with other information and intelligence they already have – it is a process that allows evaluation of the information given and then the chance to work out what is next. Operational activity requires intelligence and evidence gathered from a range of sources to gain a warrant to allow police to go to a specific location to look for both potential victims and perpetrators of crime. It was operational activity, driven by intelligence that law enforcement had received, that was the catalyst for the set-up of the multi-agency reception centres where I met **Riso** and his friend and the men from Eastern Europe who had been living on the **caravan site**. Operational activity was also where I engaged with **Olga**, the Ukrainian woman removed from a brothel by the police.

The police conducted operational activity with a range of other agencies including UK Border Force, the local council, HM Revenue and Customs, the Environment Agency, and Unseen, following concerns about poor pay and living conditions of Romanian workers at car washes. After a briefing to ensure every agency was clear on its role and remit, we headed out to the car-wash sites to speak to those who were working. I was invited by one of them to visit their accommodation – attached to the car wash. Along with a plain-clothed police officer, I went to view how they were living. One couple lived in the lounge/kitchen area – the front door opened straight into this space. Their sleeping spaces were couches pushed back against two of the walls. The other two walls were taken up with a small kitchen area in which the oven door was open. They explain they had no heating or way of warming up after a day washing cars outside, so would turn the oven on as a heat source. We were shown up some less than safe stairs to the next floor. The stairs came up through the middle of the room and each side housed bunk beds and mattresses. A space that was not large and yet was housing up to ten people. The bedding was not clean, the space was not clean or big enough for the number of people it was housing – it looked like a travellers' hostel and not one anyone would want to stay in. There was a small bathroom at one end but it wasn't used – there was no hot water and the shower and the wash basin weren't plumbed in. The space was used for storage: the suitcases of those working were piled up in it. The workers told us they were paid no more than £5 per day for their work, had debts they needed to pay off (linked to their transportation to the UK and rent for their accommodation being provided), and didn't know who to go to for help.

Welfare visits

The other way I worked with the police was via welfare visits. Although technically still a form of operational activity, welfare visits don't require the police to have a warrant or any evidence or intelligence of crimes being committed. Entry to a premises or location is gained by asking and explaining the purpose of the visit. Unlike operations, there may not be specific information or intelligence that slavery or trafficking is occurring at the location being visited, but generally it may be considered that the sector being visited is 'known' for its links to slavery.

Over the years, I was invited to attend such visits at a variety of locations: brothels, car washes, takeaways, nail bars, restaurants, food processing factories, construction sites, farmers' fields – all places where nationally there is evidence that exploitative practices can occur. **Marios**, the **Slovakian car-wash workers**, **Dung**, **Ly**, and **Ling** were all encountered as part of multi-agency welfare visits.

The premises don't need to be searched under a warrant to look for evidence of a crime being committed, but there is a duty of care to check on the welfare of those inside – those who may not be free to leave their situation, may not understand their rights and entitlements, may not be free to come and go from their place of work as and when they choose or when their shift ends. Those who can no longer distinguish days or hours from each other, who sleep where they work, who are on call 24/7, who receive no time off and have been kept intentionally isolated from the local community – it is for these individuals that welfare visits are conducted. I first started attending welfare visits in around 2009 with the police. Officers attached to the policing team responsible for public order crimes such as prostitution, gambling, and drug-related activity had learned about the issue of trafficking and slavery, and were seeing trends in on-street prostitution that they weren't used to. They wanted to look further into this to see if they could understand what was happening. The idea was that we set up a problem profile group to understand what was happening locally – this was one of the very first tangible actions that came out of the Anti-Trafficking Partnership (ATP, as it was known in 2009). I had proposed the ATP, and with the assistance of the CEO of the City Council and a high-ranking police officer as co-chairs, we had managed to navigate the invite list and get all the people needed around the table. Agencies had come together to recognise trafficking as an issue, but it was early days in the life cycle of the trafficking sector and not much was known about the issue nationally or locally. In fact, most agencies that sat around the table had initially needed some fairly hefty persuasion that trafficking was even an issue in the city – the principle of if you don't lift the stone, you definitely won't find anything that was well embedded – and yet here we were preparing to lift that stone and deal with what we found. There was the recognition that to get buy-in from the powers that be, more information would be needed; action was unlikely without evidence and that was severely lacking – we needed to know what we were dealing with.

The overarching aim was to better understand the arenas in which trafficking and slavery may be occurring and, if possible, to disrupt the activity and assist those caught up in it. Working collaboratively with partners who were willing to support this activity, even if it technically sat outside the day-to-day obligations of their job role, there was a sense that this issue was bigger than job descriptions and that action was required to better understand what was going on. The plan was to visit premises locally to offer to support potential victims and to gain information about potential perpetrators.

We were to do a day of action visiting four establishments that were believed to be selling more than their advertised massages.

Different partners had different angles from which they were approaching this issue and different objectives they were hoping to achieve. The local authority wanted to understand what was happening, to try to pin some numbers, facts, and figures to the phenomenon of slavery in the city, suggesting that if the issue could be evidenced, they could secure political buy-in and then funding. Health practitioners wanted to ensure that those working had no immediate health needs and knew where drop-in facilities were, should they need them. The police wanted to gather information about what was happening both from a victim's perspective and also to try to gain an understanding of who was perpetrating these crimes (if there was any crime occurring) and how this was happening. Unseen was present to assist the agencies involved in identifying indicators of trafficking and slavery, and to provide support and advocacy if anyone wanted to leave the situation. On these first visits, immigration officers were also represented with agreement that they would be a silent partner at this juncture, understanding that the purpose of the visit was to understand the nature and scale of trafficking in the city, not to arrest people for immigration offences.

Ling was one of the people we met on this set of visits. As I sat on the floor with her, a police officer, and a translator, in a sparsely furnished room, a bed, bedside table complete with lotion and tissues, and a built-in wardrobe that contained a suitcase full of all her worldly possessions, we felt as if we might be making headway. The woman we were speaking to had confirmed she didn't want to do this work, that she didn't realise this is what she would be forced to do, and if there was a route out, she would consider it. She then asked about her family and her debt. Would her parents be safe? Would her disabled son, whom she had left in their care, be safe? Would her debt of £20,000 be paid off so she would be truly free from the people who had brought her here and forced her to do this work? The translator looked at us expectantly for an answer. Earlier in the conversation, it was the translator who looked embarrassed as the woman had disclosed the sexual services she had been forced to provide. The translator, obviously uncomfortable and struggling to find the right words in Mandarin and English, admitted they were unsure of what to call what was being described, and resorted to painful actions to try to translate for us what had been said. Now it was the police officer and I who looked uncomfortable. We knew the system of support in place couldn't offer safety for her family or her son; it sometimes couldn't even give this guarantee to potential victims within it, let alone wider family members in far-flung nations in which we have no jurisdiction and, bluntly, even less political will. We knew the accrued debt, however falsified, was not going to be paid by any agency in the room. The things she needed reassurance on before she would consider her own needs, we were unable to offer.

All the agencies involved debriefed and reflected on this visit and continued to do so over the years – checking motivations for going, checking what we could offer those encountered – and still the decision was always that it was better to try. Better for someone to know there were agencies out there that did care and could offer support. That there was a pathway, however insufficient, out of their current situation, should they need it one day. Better to have offered and walked away than not offered at all.

A welfare visit may offer, for some, a way out of their situation. An interaction may provide clarity on entitlements and how to access services and may begin to break down control that has been asserted. Visits can provide an opportunity to connect with someone outside of the normal day-to-day routine, to understand the services available, to gain knowledge and information on rights and entitlements in the UK, and to understand where help can be accessed as and when needed. Visits ultimately offer individuals the opportunity to leave the situation should they want or need to, either in the moment or at some point in the future. They can be a proactive way of checking in on potential victims, a way of agencies being able to gather information and decide on the best course of action, if any, to be taken. They can be a way to remind police and potential victims that the police don't only have a duty to detect, investigate, and prevent criminal activity, but also a duty to protect and safeguard those who may be at risk of crime and provide support to victims of crime. Police have a criminal justice function – we want them out there identifying and arresting the 'bad people', investigating the crimes, and assisting with prosecutions – but they also have a prevention and protection remit. Meshing these expectations together in relation to modern slavery can be incredibly complex and at times they appear to conflict with each other.

It is fair to say we learned a lot and continued to do so throughout the years we embarked on multi-agency visits, refining our approaches, techniques, the information we were able to provide, the locations we visited, the agencies that attended. Always the intention was to ensure the welfare of those we encountered.

All of those I have met over the years have shown indicators of modern slavery and trafficking. All of them should have been entered into the NRM when they interacted with first responder agencies. **Matt, Elbina, Arfas**, and **Pham** had all had interactions with members of the public or with agencies with safeguarding remits or first responder duties under the NRM, yet when I met them, not one of them had been considered to be a potential victim. Signs and indicators had been missed by the agencies who should have spotted them.

Anna, Stephen, Riso, and **Mihaela** were all in the NRM when I met them. Anna and Stephen had both been entered into the NRM by law enforcement and were in safe accommodation and receiving support, as they should be, under the NRM and Modern Slavery Victim Care Contract. Riso was entered into the NRM; accommodation had been secured for him locally and he was to be supported to find alternative employment. The police officers involved and I were able to complete the NRM form for **Dung, Ly**, and **Andre** with the information they had given us. Mihaela, when she had been released from prison (having been arrested at her 'wedding ceremony'), contacted the police officer who had first encountered her when she had been forced to work on the streets. He was able to enter her into the NRM and ensure that she moved from prison to safe accommodation rather than back to those who had been trafficking her. Like Mihaela, each of the other individuals already in the NRM when I met them had been identified and referred into the NRM by police officers.

Over the years I have acted as a first responder and entered people (who consented) into the NRM if I thought what they had told me might amount to modern slavery; part of my role when I met these individuals was to be considering the NRM and explaining this process to them, and what would potentially happen if they decided to enter it, or not.

Igor had been identified as a potential victim. The nurse who was caring for him was worried about him and what he was experiencing; other patients had also shared concerns with the nursing team who needed help to work out what to do next and how to approach this with Igor. Health professionals are not first responders in the NRM system, meaning they are unable to refer people into the support offered. It is unclear why they are not first responders, but there is a suggestion that this is due to confidentiality processes. The nurse didn't know what to do next and called Unseen and a local homeless shelter for advice. Between us, we managed to work together to explain the process to Igor and he consented to enter the NRM. It was important that all the information the nurse had was captured, and as a first responder, I took the decision that I didn't need to hear all of this again from Igor, unless he wanted to tell me. I needed to be mindful of re-traumatisation and the fact that he had already given his account of what had happened to him to someone he trusted, so although I didn't need to hear it all again, I did need to explain the system of support, what his choices and options were, and why there were concerns for him and his current situation.

When I met **Matt**, **Elbina**, and **Arfas**, I had been asked specifically by their legal representatives to see if what they told me about their experiences showed indicators and signs that could amount to them being victims of slavery. I was brought into these cases as an expert witness to look for signs and indicators, things that their lawyers thought other agencies had missed up until this point.

I met Matt, and once I had heard his account of what had happened to him and read the accompanying paperwork (health records, prison records, police interview transcripts, legal opinions), I assessed his case and, as an expert witness, put forward a report and recommendations, including that he should be entered into the NRM and receive support. Matt consented and we completed the NRM together.

I completed interviews and wrote reports for Elbina and Arfas, as well as Matt. In all of these cases, I recommended that a referral into the NRM would be appropriate. What I had heard from Elbina, Arfas, and Matt, in my opinion, had shown the elements of trafficking: the act, the means, and that this had happened for the purpose of exploitation – for sexual exploitation, for domestic servitude, and for criminal exploitation.

For all of those I have met, I have explained the NRM to them and what it does and doesn't offer. Some decided they didn't want to enter the NRM or seek assistance via this route – certainly, the **Slovakian car-wash workers**, the men who were brought to the reception centre and then left, did not consent to be entered into the NRM. **Ling** also didn't want to be entered into the NRM – she decided she couldn't leave her situation without putting her family at risk, and this was not something she was willing or able to do when we met her. I met **Pham** as part of research that I was doing; he was serving a sentence for the production of a controlled drug – in this case, cannabis cultivation.

For those adults who do not want to go into the NRM and seek support, there is the expectation that the suspicion that they may be experiencing trafficking is to be recorded by the professionals engaging with them via the Duty to Notify process. The purpose of this is to try to gather data and information about where people are being enslaved and exploited, to build a better picture and understanding of what is happening and why people didn't want help.

Although the numbers of people whose life paths have been diverted by slavery are uncertain, I've met countless individuals like **Marios, Riso, Andre, Dung, Ly, Pham, Stephen, Arfas, Anna, Elbina, Olga**, and

Ling. All of them believed they had limited choices, finding themselves in positions of vulnerability, carrying burdens that they should not be expected to. Some were children when their exploitation occurred – some still are children. Some, we may think, should have known better but...

There is a subtle difference between sympathy and empathy. Sympathy is when you feel pity and sorrow for someone's situation. I think this is a normal feeling to have when learning about slavery and trafficking, but it is not a good place to stay in. Empathy is the ability to understand and feel what others do. As humans, we are intrinsically programmed to separate ourselves from the things we fear and from people who have experienced the things we fear; we do not want to feel what those we have met in Chapter 4 and again in this chapter did. This is OK: they are tough stories. I feel pain, anger, confusion, frustration too when I think about those I have met.

In truth, let's not say 'I am sorry that happened to you' and then move on, as if we were nothing directly to do with that individual being exploited. Sympathy for those I've met and for those they represent who continue to be in their situation of exploitation is OK as a starting point, but it runs out quickly, especially if we cannot relate to them. Rather, let's try to foster empathy and understanding toward them and to those who are still enslaved today. Change will come from an appreciation and acceptance that the situations they faced were often impossible, that their freedoms were limited, and that if we were in the same situation, we may have made exactly the same choices. For us to truly start working out how to tackle slavery, we first need to break down the barriers and notions that it only happens to people who are not like us.

As Brené Brown says in one of her podcasts (2020), we have a need to believe things are not true, because if we believe they are true, it hurts too much, and we are too afraid because it requires us to reflect on our own experiences. She proposes we are increasingly depleted of compassion and are slowly losing our capacity to hold others. To think about slavery, trafficking, and exploitation requires empathy; it requires compassion. It is taking a step back, monitoring our own preconceived ideas, our judgements, our internal 'isms', and hearing about the experiences of another human. To be/sit alongside them in their moment of telling and to truly hear what it is they have to say.

Once identified, an individual is eligible for support if they want and need it – it is at this juncture that there are common recurrent issues that arise for victims of slavery and trafficking. Even though they are free from exploitation, the journey they are embarking on is neither easy nor straightforward.

CHAPTER 6

Disconnected Systems

> The moral test of Government is how that Government
> treats those who are in the dawn of life...those who are in
> the twilight of life...those who are in the shadows of life.
> **(HUMPHREY 1976, P.4)**

We say we want to tackle slavery, but we don't put the structures in place to do so effectively.

At a systems level, our approach to slavery is viewed via a criminal justice lens – government statements refer to heinous crimes and criminals who smuggle people across borders and the threat they pose. Government officials have been clear that they are 'acting at every level to tackle modern slavery, ensuring that victims are supported to rebuild their lives, and the criminals and perpetrators of slavery face justice for their crimes and activities' (Patel in HM Government 2020, p.2). It has been further acknowledged that modern slavery is an international issue that requires a collaborative and global response with Government stating 'we need a radically new, comprehensive approach to defeating this vile and systematic international business model at its source and in transit, and we need to flex the muscle of all parts of the UK government and collaborate with international partners' (May 2016). The language used is confusing and agendas of immigration, economic migration, asylum seeking, smuggling, and modern slavery are conflated and confused – often the victims and their experiences appear secondary in our approach to understanding and tackling the issue of modern slavery. The rhetoric suggests that if the criminals are tackled, the problem will disappear. This is far too simplistic: people have inherent reasons, sometimes necessities, for leaving one place and going to another – drivers, push and pull factors, things that we are just unaware of. We appear to forget that people need choice and alternatives, and yet the approach we currently take risks curtailing both things.

Managing to stop those facilitating movement, who are arguably responding to a demand and a need, is only part of the solution.

We are nervous about creating loopholes in immigration processes and opening the flood gates. We are nervous about people abusing the systems we put in place to help.

What we say we want to achieve and what we are able to do within the systems created are disconnected.

The UK states that we want to be the 'world leader' in tackling modern slavery, that we want to make sure we offer long-term, holistic, and needs-led support for those impacted, and that we want to tackle those who perpetrate this crime.

We are committed to doing the right thing, we say we want to do the right thing, but we haven't yet worked out how to join the dots. In some instances, we haven't even worked out where the dots are, how they link, or the order they come in. When the systems put in place to help are not connected to what the people being helped need, we fail those we are trying to assist.

The experiences of **Andre**, **Anna**, **Elbina**, **Olga**, and others I've met over the years reveal the brokenness and disconnections in the systems that are meant to support them. The current set-up of systems involved in the identification, recovery, and support of victims and survivors is failing.

No one system, organisation, or sector is at fault in isolation. No one policy or system is individually to blame. What is to blame are the punitive immigration policies, the increasingly hostile ways in which we deem those less fortunate as 'other', and a reduction in workers' rights and protections.

For those identified who are not UK nationals or eligible to be resident in the UK after an initial period of support (available to everyone, regardless of their status in the UK), an individual's options and access to meaningful, long-term support is currently determined by their immigration status, rather than by what they need. Even for those identified as British nationals, access to appropriate support is not always easily available.

The backdrop of a hostile environment, the differences in what each individual agency can and can't do and in what timeframe, when combined with a wide range of different needs individuals have, make journeys and access to support systems fraught with difficulties – even once identified, the path ahead for any potential victim of modern slavery is rarely clear or straightforward to navigate.

The support system and the general systems that offer support, protection, redress, compensation, and restitution *must* do better for all identified victims and survivors. They can't and shouldn't be a lottery, based on nationality.

However, it is not only the systems at play that are disconnected.

We are all detached, remote, and disconnected from the issue and from the people it impacts. We want to help our fellow human, but this ability, understanding, and willingness often only goes so far. Fear of the 'other' comes into play. We see this in our politics and in our media, and then it filters down into our opinions and our critiques of people that we don't understand and of people who we think aren't like us. We tell ourselves that there were underlying vulnerabilities and burdens, mental health issues, problems with addiction, a lack of education, poverty, a poor family environment, and although this can often be the case, it isn't always.

We find it hard to believe at times that it is only by degrees that we differ.

It is easier sometimes to compartmentalise and pigeonhole people, but the world isn't black and white; it is glorious shades of grey, and in this greyness we discover, when we look, that we can find connection. Some connections will be harder to uncover, harder to maintain, harder to articulate, but they will be there if we take the time to look hard enough. By sheer misfortune or unfortunate circumstance, through difficult choices, or no fault of our own, we could find ourselves in similar or the same situations, but we don't like to think about this. It is easier to assume and highlight the differences rather than see the potential for the similarities.

Sometimes we associate underlying vulnerabilities with previous actions and choices people have made or even brought on themselves. We make blanket statements that show our often subconscious fears of anyone who isn't like us, anyone whose experience we don't understand, anyone who we think has made a mistake, one that we wouldn't have made.

It is an innate human reaction – we judge, we criticise, and we critique. These reactions are how we protect ourselves from our underlying, subconscious fears – we propose we would do something different if faced with the same set of circumstances, but deep down there is a niggle, a fear that we would do the same as those we are viewing as different, as having made duff decisions. A fear and a recognition that if we would do the same, then maybe we really aren't that different after all.

We forget that there may be really good reasons why someone made the choice or choices that they did, and that if we were faced with the exact same set of circumstances, we may well do exactly the same. We forget that although there may always be choice, sometimes there are no *good* choices for us to make.

CHAPTER 7

Problems in the Identification Process

Effective prevention, enforcement of laws, and protection
and assistance envisioned for victims of human trafficking
are not a reality in many countries. As a result many
traffickers go unpunished and many victims of human
trafficking are not identified and assisted.
(SIGMON 2008, P.245)

I dentifying people at risk of harm and who need support is hard. Explaining
the system of support and what it can offer is hard. Sometimes what we can
offer isn't what people need. Sometimes people don't see themselves as victims.

The knock-on effects of 'helping' and of accepting help are far-reaching. Sometimes we end up putting people at more risk in our attempts
to help. Sometimes we don't see the things that are right in front of us.
Sometimes we don't understand the consequences and see the choices
people are having to make. Sometimes we see it and can do nothing about
it. Sometimes we have no choice but to walk away.

When we go to work, we put on a uniform (real or metaphorical),
we represent the agency we work for, we take on board their policies,
procedures, and approaches, we adapt them to fit our styles and approach,
while still following the rules. Although we may be able to leave some

of us behind as we take on our professional roles, we still hold on to our own personal biases and opinions, and I have seen this directly impact the way professionals have interacted with, believed, and responded to potential victims.

What responding properly to a victim should look like is tough to define, and different agencies have different roles and remits that sometimes appear to take precedent over and above the duty to protect and safeguard someone in an exploitative situation. Not that this responsibility should fall solely upon the professional – the person being exploited has a voice and should be presented with options and choices so they understand what is available to them. Identifying that someone may be in an exploitative situation, understanding why they may not see it that way, explaining what can be done to help, the systems in place and how they can access them should be standard practice for any professional who may come across a potential victim of slavery. Members of the public need to know when they report a concern about people, that this will get dealt with sensitively and well.

We must be up to date on this stuff, and if we are not, using Google to work it out in the moment is absolutely fine. Not spotting the signs, not explaining rights and entitlements, not believing someone and having preconceived ideas about how a 'victim' should present are not OK.

We have to listen, we have to try to understand, and when we don't, we need to ask questions, sensitively, as part of a normal conversation. We also need to know when to stop asking questions, when it is no longer appropriate and is putting people at risk.

We must avoid asking questions in a way that makes people think we doubt them and what they are telling us. We must remember that people often think that they are in trouble, that they feel guilt, shame, and embarrassment about their situation and think that what has happened to them is their fault.

Those we identify need to be treated well. We must treat people as we would want to be treated ourselves. We must try to connect with them, we must try to build trust and rapport, and do what we say we will.

Indicators such as those in the boxes in Chapter 4 are a useful tool, but the absence of them doesn't mean exploitation isn't occurring. They shouldn't be used as a tick-box exercise.

A professional approach

I remember sitting with a police officer at a table in a restaurant as he tried to engage with a potential victim – I am not exaggerating when I say the officer spent the whole time looking at his piece of paper, reading off the indicators as a list: have you experienced this, that, and the other? It was clear to me he didn't want to be there. Even though the living conditions, the work environment, and the intelligence suggested people were being forced to work long hours in poor conditions for little or no pay, he was not interested.

He made no effort to connect, no effort to care, no effort to believe. If we are presenting this activity as potential lifelines for people to leave their situation, or understand their rights for the future, we must at least try to work out how to connect with them on a person-to-person level.

I have been invited into police stations to speak with people they have thought may be victims of modern slavery but were not comfortable with engaging with officers. Realising the individuals may fear police or that officers were not confident to explain the systems of support that they could access, I would be asked to meet with them and outline their potential support options.

In one case, I was asked to speak to a woman who had been arrested at a cannabis farm. Police were concerned about her presentation and suspected there was more to her experience than she was saying. They thought she might speak to a non-law-enforcement professional and asked for my assistance. I got the same response from the woman as the police did. Her solicitor had advised her to give a 'no comment' interview, and even though I explained to her that I was not a police officer and was there to explain the support system she might be able to access, she didn't want to engage. I was able to pass information on to her, but she didn't want to accept any help at this point. As I left the interview room, the translator walked out with me and in an animated way expressed how horrified he was that this woman didn't want to accept any help. He continued, sharing his opinion that it was all her own fault, that she had put herself in this situation, that she had been stupid to believe such an opportunity would ever exist. This was the person who had been translating for me, whom I had trusted to communicate that we were concerned about this person, that there were options we could consider, that we would try to help. To this day, I am not convinced that this message was communicated in the way in which it was intended.

I have also seen the polar opposite response from officers who exude care and compassion. Sitting for hours trying to work out plans to help the individuals who have asked for assistance. Visibly shaken and upset by what they have seen and frustrated by the lack of power they have to help someone. I remember one officer's frustration at a situation we were facing as part of a welfare visit. **Zhang Li**'s experience was reminiscent of **Ling**'s. Zhang Li expressed to us that she didn't want to be doing this job, that she was moved around the country on a weekly basis, that she was in debt, and that she was being forced to sell sex. She never knew where she would be going, but a taxi would arrive for her and take her to another residential home in another town or city, another house, with another housekeeper who would be responsible for ensuring the woman did what was expected of her and didn't leave.

Always on the move, always isolated.

She was nervous about leaving but was considering it. She had asked a lot of questions and was trying to understand what accepting help and support would look like. In the end, she decided she couldn't leave – the risks, whatever they were, were too big or too many. The unknown was too much. She made the choice, in that moment, to stay.

Unfortunately for Zhang Li, it was at this point things took a turn for the worse. A message came through on one of the officer's radios requesting an arrest be made for immigration-based offences. It tran-spired that Zhang Li had been encountered previously by authorities and identified not as a potential victim of trafficking but as someone who had overstayed their visa. As a result of this, she had been required to attend a police station regularly and sign on. She had failed to do so, but this was completely out of her control. She hadn't understood what she had been asked to do or the consequences of not doing it – in any case, she was being moved around the country on a weekly basis. Zhang Li didn't know where she was, she wasn't allowed out of the houses she was in, and her missing appointments resulted in a warrant for her arrest being served.

The officer who had identified her, spent hours with her explaining the situation, what support would look like and how she could assist, was visibly broken – someone we both felt sure was a victim of modern slavery was now going to be arrested for immigration reasons. Had Zhang Li agreed to the support being offered, all immigration proceedings would have been put on hold while she accessed support and got assistance to work out what was next. But now, in this situation, even with our professional judgement indicating slavery was occurring, without her consent we could do very little. The officer and I left the room we had occupied for the last few hours, and another officer arrested Zhang Li.

The officer tried again to get her to accept help that night, and the following morning, after she had spent a night in the cells, we both tried again. The signs and indicators of slavery were clear; other professionals had already interacted with her and missed the signs. But still her answer was no, she could not accept the support on offer.

Tough choices

Even when we get it right, the outcome isn't always what we would want to see; different systems come into play and take precedent, and we are unsighted on the pressures and the choices people are considering in that moment.

People make the hard choice to not say anything and to not take up the offer of support. For some, this will be because the support is not what they need; for some, it will be because traffickers have told them they will be deported or that the authorities are corrupt. Some may have experience of corruption in their own countries; for some, the last person they trusted got them into this situation. For some, the threats to themselves, the threats to their family, the fear of what may happen if they leave, and the debt they owe all mean it is their best option to stay in their situation and not accept help. **Ling** made this choice when she realised her debt couldn't be paid off; she decided it was better for her to stay than put her family at risk.

Olga had been taken out of a brothel, along with lots of other women, and taken to a reception centre. During her interview with the police, she expressed wanting to leave the situation she was in. Towards the end of the discussion, she asked the officers when everyone would be going; they had been waiting all day at the reception centre and she was tired. When she realised that she was the only one out of 20 or so women to tell the police what she had experienced, a shutter went up. It was immediate: the realisation that she was the one who had let the cat out of the bag – no one else had complained, no one else had shared that they were being forced, that there was no payment, no days off, and no way to say no, just her. As soon as she realised this, she wanted out – she refused to say any more. The change was almost immediate and she somehow managed to get all her emotions back in order and walk out of that interview room with the same swagger she had had coming in, hoping to indicate to all those in the room that she hadn't said anything. Identified as a victim, she needed and wanted help, by her own admission, but when she realised she was the only one, the choice between leaving and staying became too much for her.

I was frustrated and angry as I walked to the tube station. Angry that even with the police seemingly doing all they could, the hold of those exploiting some or all of these women was stronger than what they could offer. That support and the opportunity to leave the situation they were in were not at that moment a choice they wanted to or could make. That even when someone had asked for help, once they realised no one else was leaving, they decided not to either. As I walked and contemplated all I had seen and been part of, I saw women I recognised from the centre being picked up – car after car along the local high street pulling over to collect those who worked for them.

The grapevine was working. Word had got out, and although where the women had been for the last few hours was probably at this stage unknown, a call had been placed and the collections began to happen. The network the police were trying to disrupt was in play; they were taking back what they considered to be theirs. The women needed to get back to work, and those picking them up needed to check what had and hadn't been said to the authorities.

Traffickers, as I learned, always seem to manage to be at least one step ahead of the authorities in one way or another. They offer those working for them accommodation, some form of payment, and sometimes, in the eyes of those like Olga, the only viable option. Whether they are one step ahead or not, what can we realistically offer as an alternative? The promise of a safe place wasn't enough for Olga – yes, if she left her situation she would need somewhere to live, but she also needed alternative ways to earn money. The system in that moment couldn't offer what she needed and the risk of leaving with so many unknowns was a risk she couldn't take.

One of the men from the car-wash site decided he wanted to leave with us on the day of the police activity, and along with colleagues we facilitated his entry into the National Referral Mechanism (NRM). The other nine or ten people we had met weren't sure and had decided to stay on site. It was an odd moment, when all of those involved in the multi-agency visits began to leave the site; there was no one asking for help – everyone was legally allowed to be in the UK, we had explained people's rights and entitlements to them, answered their questions about the minimum wage, about workers' rights, about the support they could access if they needed to. The officer I was working with made the decision to leave a contact number, just in case. Knowing that we had viewed indicators of exploitation, he didn't feel right leaving those he had met with nothing.

I heard from the officer a few days later – he wanted to update me that he had received a phone call and that he had been able to facilitate a further four people leaving the car-wash site. He had arranged to pick them up after work and a little way down the road; they didn't want it to be too obvious to their boss that they were leaving. He said it was quite a sight to see this group of people shuffling down the road with all their belongings in bin bags and starting to run when they saw he had come, as he said he would.

When **Mihaela** initially interacted with the police, she was selling sex on the streets. She was noticed by an officer because her behaviour seemed out of place: she was standing away from the roadside, hiding in the shadows and not actively engaging with customers. Officers learned that she did not want to be doing this but was being made to. She didn't want help or assistance right now. Mihaela then disappeared off the radar. What transpired later was that she had been taken off the streets after the interest the police had taken in her, made to work from a residential house, and then, when she challenged her exploiter, presented with the choice of selling sex or getting married. Upon her release from prison, she saw her chance to not have to go back to those who had been exploiting her and remembered the officer who offered support if she ever needed it and asked for him to be called.

I don't know why the **Slovakian staff from the car wash** decided not to leave the car wash with us that day, but I can hazard guesses. What other options did they have? Better to stay together. Better to stay with what you know. A sense of loyalty to the man who had offered them the chance to leave the streets in Slovakia. A debt? I don't know for sure. I think if one of them had decided to come, they would have all come, but even though there were clear indicators of slavery and trafficking, they were not wanting to leave at that time. It was uncomfortable that evening thinking of them locking up the car wash, being transported to their cleaning shift, and then preparing to sleep in the loft space I had seen.

The men from the reception centre, recovered from the **caravan site**, left one by one. I am sure they had their reasons for not wanting to stay, one of which may have been that they were reluctant to take the risk of leaving what they knew, however appalling the conditions.

I didn't see the conditions they lived in on the day of the operation as I was at the reception centre, but I did get to attend a follow-up visit with the police and local authority. We visited one of the men from the site who had been identified as a vulnerable adult as it was thought he may need safeguarding. He lived with his mother, who struggled with an alcohol addiction. The house was full of rubbish and not clean, the floor was covered in dog faeces, and finding somewhere to sit was tricky. The man's mother said she liked who he worked for; it transpired they visited her often to deliver a bottle of her favourite tipple. They would pick him up for work, he would stay with them, do some odd jobs, and then they would bring him home. It wasn't clear if he got paid, but what was clear was his mother's opinion that no one else would employ him and that they should be grateful for what was being done for them. It felt like a desperate situation in which there were limited solutions to be found. He and his mother were adamant they didn't want help or assistance. But I was left wondering about the balancing act of providing options and choices for people versus stepping in and taking control.

Zhang Li had been identified as a victim but she didn't want to enter the NRM or support at the time we met her. When an individual doesn't accept support, the system views them as not needing support and the protections afforded to someone deemed to be a potential victim of modern slavery are no longer applied. The system presented Zhang Li with the choice of entering the NRM or of being arrested for an immigration offence. The system no longer saw Zhang Li as a victim; she was now considered an illegal immigrant.

Ling did not have a valid visa either, but as this was her first inter-action with the authorities, there was no information about her on law enforcement systems and she was not arrested on the occasion we met her. Like Zhang Li, she declined assistance, and although we walked away leaving her in a less than ideal situation, she was not arrested. As a non-UK national with an expired visa, arrest could have resulted in her removal from the UK, or at least the start of this process.

Those at the **car wash** and **caravan site** all declined assistance. As UK and EU nationals, their ability to reside and work in the UK legally was not in question; unlike Ling and Zhang Li, they faced no threat of deportation. But declining help doesn't mean they didn't want or need help.

Leaving people behind, knowing full well that they need help, is not pleasant. I also know full well that if I or others involved in their cases were in a position to offer viable alternatives, people may make the choice to leave.

By viable alternatives, I mean offering people things that they need and want. This means engaging with them on a human-to-human level and finding out what they want. It isn't just the lack of help offered by the system that is frustrating, but the stark reality that you are often unable to offer an alternative, present different choices, or propose potential solutions. It is at this juncture you realise how rigged the system is to maintain the status quo. It also means gauging when it is right to let people make their own choices and whether, as professionals, there is the need to step in and take control of a situation. When does the risk become too high, when does walking away truly put someone at more risk, and what, in this scenario, can we do, if anything?

Rescue, recovery, extraction

Rescue, recovery, and extraction are all words I have heard in relation to proactively identifying potential victims. We know slavery is a crime and we want to give people the chance to leave their situations, but I am not sure we do this in the right way. Welfare visits and operational activity disrupt business and this has been seen as a frustration tactic by some forces, but disrupting business (a) for those who are found to be running legitimate enterprises and (b) in which no one discloses they are being exploited or forced into the work they are doing is not a great tactic for community cohesion and has the potential to breed institutional racism towards certain sectors and people. The visits may identify people that have been under the radar and unknown to the authorities, but what starts as a visit to check on welfare can become by proxy an immigration raid unless managed well.

Although I have been part, over the years, of a lot of welfare and operational visits via my involvement in the Anti-Slavery Partnership, including assisting to create a problem profile model to help us better understand the issue of modern slavery and how it impacts people and communities, I feel conflicted about these visits now and the approach taken and the impact they have. I have been part of some that have worked well, with officers determined to go the extra mile, and I have been on others where the approach and the attitude has been less than ideal – focused not on welfare, protection, and support but on getting information from potential victims in relation to potential perpetrators and not engaging well with those who have been found. I found the visits, especially the first ones, challenging – all the partners wanted to understand the issue more fully, we genuinely wanted to help, but I think we were initially shocked that people didn't want the support when it was offered – we have to rightly adjust our expectations and put ourselves in their shoes. They are at work when we interrupt their day, checking to see if they are OK. Our visits were unannounced (although often if we were visiting more than one location in a day, people were expecting us and arguably any trafficked person would have been removed or told not to say anything before we arrived), we walked in, we offered support, we walked away again, we left people behind. Yes, they may now know more about their rights and their entitlements, but we often ended up leaving them there in a potentially exploitative situation. Not all police forces have dedicated modern slavery teams. Outside of days of multi-agency visits, there aren't always the available resources for follow-up visits. The welfare action becomes a one-time only thing and provides a limited offer to those who are being exploited.

Whenever we interact with people who may be being exploited, we must start from a position of belief and from a position of having an adult-to-adult conversation. Of course, some people will be incredibly traumatised when they are identified, and in that moment we may need to decide a plan of action on their behalf, to ensure their protection. But we must not do things to people; we must not remove agency and be yet another person who has told them what to do. We have to work on the principle of doing no further harm and presenting the choices, however limited, available to them.

Welfare visits and operational activity, when done well, can some-times provide the opportunity people need to leave. Done poorly, they drive a wedge between victims and authorities and confirm everything traffickers said would happen to them.

People come forward when enough is enough – and when an opportunity and an alternative presents. It is not always professionals that interact with potential victims; members of the public may do so and victims also self-identify, as **Andre** did – he saw his opportunity to leave and he took it.

Mihaela and the **guys from the car wash** didn't leave their situations straight away, they wanted time to consider the options, to think about their choices, to process, to understand, and then decide what they want to do – what is the best choice they can make with the information they have and considering the situation they are in? For those at the car wash, this took a matter of days; for Mihaela, it came after a prison sentence.

Unfortunately, for some, like **Zhang Li**, there are repercussions of not accepting help and support, and for others like **Matt** and **Pham**, they will be in prison or facing sentencing when someone spots tell-tale signs in their account, indications that they may have been forced, controlled, deceived, or manipulated into what they were doing.

Igor attended hospital for treatment regularly, and the nurse who cared for him had raised concerns about exploitation with the safeguarding team at the hospital but they had dismissed her concerns and decided not to take this any further. She was not happy with this response and knew something was wrong. She took a risk and went against her superiors, contacting me and the homeless shelter for further support – in Igor's case, this was the right thing to do, but she put herself at risk to do this. She knew something was wrong and that he needed help. It transpired Igor had been trafficked for forced labour. We explained the support on offer to Igor and tried to understand what he wanted and what he needed. It became clear he wanted to leave his situation but was terrified to do this. He went away to think about it and we arranged that I would be at his next appointment to answer any further questions. He wanted out. We had to make a plan that (a) would allow him to leave safely and (b) not compromise his health. We needed to arrange accommodation and support via the NRM, but also once this had all been confirmed, all his health care needs had to be transferred to the local hospital. Everything needed to be set up before Igor could leave. This meant that he had to go back to his exploiters – we were nervous that something would go wrong, that his exploiters would think something had happened, or Igor would change his mind or miss medical appointments. But over the next ten days he attended appointments, and each time he brought a shopping bag full of his belongings. He was determined not to leave anything he had behind, but realised walking out with everything at once would alert his traffickers. This period gave the medical team time to hand over to the new hospital and explain Igor's medical needs to the support provider. The day he was due to be transferred into NRM support, I was not at the hospital – the plan was in place and I learned how it had gone a few days later. Igor had attended his appointment as usual, and after his treatment he was assisted to leave the ward by an alternative route, accompanied by security guards, and with all his belongings gathered and packed, he was picked up by his new support provider and taken out of the city. The nursing team and security guards had to navigate the exploiters who were insistent they had dropped Igor off and that he hadn't returned to them. Igor's nurse went the extra mile; she was isolated and ignored by the organisation she worked for and yet knew her patient needed her to go above and beyond for him.

Missing the signs and making assumptions

Multiple organisations and people missed the indicators and signs that the **men and woman from Slovakia** were potentially being exploited. The van was dropping them to and from their cleaning jobs each morning and evening. They made weekly visits to the Job Centre to claim benefits, all arriving at the same time, all presumably recording the same address, but no one putting two and two together. The customers using the car wash and the neighbours living next door – no one spotted what was going on.

Matt and **Pham** weren't identified as potential victims of slavery. The agencies that initially interacted with them had their blinkers on. Both were criminals from their first interaction with the police. The police didn't look for any reasons why Matt, a young British man, may have been over 100 miles away from home; they didn't ask him questions about how he got from London to sleepy villages in the countryside, or who provided the drugs, or what would happen if he didn't deliver them. They didn't ask him if he got paid or if he was free to come and go. They focused on seeing a young black man who fit the profile they had of someone who dealt drugs. Matt had got a positive decision from the NRM, identified as a victim of slavery for the purpose of criminal exploitation.

Pham was serving a sentence for drug cultivation when I met him. The others who were arrested at the same time as him he told me had already been deported. It appeared as if immigration officials and police involved in the case were focused on the cultivation of the drugs and looked no further. They didn't question how five Vietnamese men came to be locked in a container, had food delivered, and weren't allowed to leave – they didn't ask the right questions, they didn't spot the potential signs and indicators. In Pham's case, it isn't just the arresting police officers who missed asking the right questions and spotting the indicators, but his legal team and the judge. We came across him in prison as part of some research looking at perpetrators of offences that could be related to modern slavery. As a result, one is now serving a sentence and four have been deported. As Pham is a British citizen, he wasn't deported but charged with a criminal offence.

Not identifying someone, missing the signs, will not always be simply the fault of the professional or the person interacting with a potential victim. It is a systems issue compounded by an individual's own blind spots and lack of understanding of slavery and the hard choices people are having to make and further compounded by the person being spoken to not identifying as a victim.

I was introduced to **Sam** by his lawyer and asked to speak to him about his experiences. Sam genuinely believed he would be killed if he 'snitched' – he thought that by telling the authorities about his situation he would be in trouble with the gang that were making him sell their drugs. They had moved into his flat, and what had started as needing to stay a couple of nights had turned into his flat being used as a storage unit for drugs and him being made to run them across the city whenever he was told to. He told me he wanted to tell the officer what was happening to him and that he wasn't safe at home, but he didn't trust the police and he was scared of the death threats that had been made towards him. It was easier for him to keep his head down and not say anything that might put him at more risk. This did mean that the police were investigating him as a potential person involved in the criminal activity rather than a potential victim.

I met both **Esther** and **Ruth** when they were living in a safe house. Both had been trafficked for the purpose of sexual exploitation. Both were from African countries, and both felt their families were at risk as a result of their decisions to accept support to leave their situations.

Esther was identified; she left her exploitative situation and entered the support systems on offer, only to call home and learn that someone linked to her trafficker had visited and threatened her mother – he would be taking Esther's sisters if she didn't return.

Ruth's experiences were similar. She was identified and out of her situation of exploitation, but her traffickers had threatened her family at home, broken her brother's legs, and burned down the family shop.

These are things we are unable to counteract or to provide a solution for. They help us to begin to see why saying yes and leaving a situation may not be a 'choice' someone is able to make in the moment we encounter them.

The accounts I have heard over the years have at times felt as if they are from a movie script. They can be hard to hear, hard to rationalise, hard to understand, and at times hard to believe. But we have to try. We have to try to remove our unconscious biases that mean we may fail to identify someone for all that they are.

Viewing a potential victim as less than us – just a prostitute, a foreigner playing the system, a liar, a criminal, or someone who should have known better – is not OK. We must not jump to conclusions. This is not our job and we must press pause on our own assumptions.

Assumptions put barriers in place.

We must not assume because someone is working in a particular sector or is from a particular country that they are or aren't a potential victim of slavery. Yes, the evidence and data may suggest this is a possibility, but we have to ask the questions on an individual basis. Does this person want or need our assistance in this moment and what is the assistance they require? Is it even possible for us to do? We have to care and we have to connect.

Over the years, I have told myself that if we give people knowledge and information about their rights and entitlements, offer the pathways and the exit routes, we then have to trust they can find a way to use these in the future – at the right time, when they can, they will use them. It doesn't make leaving people behind any easier and it isn't always the case that this will provide the lifeline to people that I hoped it would – in some cases, in fact, being found and identified puts them directly at more risk.

Identifying at ports of entry

I always found it interesting that Border Guards were expected to identify the signs of trafficking in people at point of entry to the UK and act as first responders. I never really understood how this would be practically possible. Profiling potential victims of trafficking and slavery and increasing screening and vetting accordingly feels like an incredibly hard task at the border, with automated passport control and the pressures to process people efficiently via the manned posts. Often people will be entering on legal visas that wouldn't flag an issue in any systems. At the point of entering the UK people genuinely believed they were coming to study, travel, or work; they didn't necessarily know what was going to happen. As such, they do not necessarily raise concerns for border officials.

Before developing and delivering training for staff at a provincial airport to spot the signs of trafficking and to have effective responses, an officer showed me around behind the scenes and took the time to explain the processes and policies that were currently in use and what it was that officers and staff were seeing. She shared how it was the same van picking people up on a weekly basis from the provincial airport that gave her team cause for concern. None of the passengers seemed to have any issues and everyone appeared to be travelling freely and under their own volition – between disembarking from the plane, through border control, and picking up luggage there were no obvious or overt signs to be picked up on, no indication that people were going to be exploited. But what would people be looking for in this situation as indicators anyway?

It is hard to identify people who may be victims, especially at ports of entry. The fleeting moment a border guard has to look at a passport or an identity document, confirming the picture in it looks like the person who is standing in front of their desk, is hardly an obvious opportunity to ask someone whether they are being exploited or not. The reality is that at this point someone may not know.

The jurisdictions of agencies at points of entry to the country also cause identification issues – if someone is identified air-side (at border control) as not having the right documentation to enter the country, they may be returned to where they came from without their lack of documents being considered a potential indicator of trafficking. This may result in people being deported before ever being identified as a potential victim – their immigration status, or lack of it, taking precedence. There is a fine line to be walked here. Do we expect immigration officials to ask everyone from a particular country if they are aware of trafficking and exploitative work practices as they enter the UK? We would run the risk of breeding institutional racism towards certain nationalities if this was to be the case, but it does mean we are potentially returning vulnerable people to unknown situations – although this process may mean they avoid exploitation in the UK, we don't know what they are returning to and what other routes they may use to try to enter. Once land-side (after border control and customs), they are in police jurisdiction, but looking for indicators here can also be tough. An officer once told me about a case he was working on – he was investigating a group that seemed to be bringing women in and out of the UK on a regular basis. As the flight boarded in Romania, police had identified passengers that fit the usual profile of the women they were concerned about. They forwarded this information to English counterparts, who decided to speak with the women upon arrival in the UK. The officer I knew ended up speaking with a young woman of 19 or 20 about her reasons for coming to the UK. He explained that sometimes people were offered work that didn't transpire and that they were running checks on various flights to make sure everyone was OK. The young woman confirmed she was fine, that she was expecting to have a live-in cleaning job and was being met from the airport. He gave her a contact card should she need it, explained that there were services that could assist if needed, and wished her the best of luck with her new job.

Two weeks later, he got a phone call from a hospital – the young woman he had spoken with needed his help. The job hadn't transpired as a cleaning job; rather, she had been forced to sell sex and, seeing no way out, she had run through a second-storey window in an attempt to escape, breaking both her legs in the process. A passer-by had called an ambulance for her and she had asked the nurse to call the officer and ask for help.

A disconnected process

The responsibility put on agencies to identify people is not always practicably possible – people may not know what is coming, people may not want to admit what has happened, some may feel guilt, shame, and embarrassment about the situation they are in, some may fear for themselves and their families if they say anything, some may not want help at the moment it is offered, for some what they are experiencing is better than they would have at home – and although this doesn't excuse exploitative practices, it means that identifying them by relying on potential victims to come forward and explain the situation they are in is incredibly tricky and puts a massive burden on the people we are aiming to assist and support.

When I have sat with people I believe to be in a situation of exploita-tion and tried to explain their options to them, I have realised time and time again how disjointed the system is and how powerless I am to offer help at that juncture.

The conversation to explain what I think may be happening, exploring options, rights, and entitlements, discussing the NRM and the system of support they may be able to access, is complicated enough, and yet I know that I can't even suggest with any certainty that this is what will happen.

I can't promise they will be believed or that they will get the support they need and want. The identification process is disconnected.

It is unclear if the agencies assigned as first responders are the right ones. The whole process of identification is heavily biased towards statutory and law enforcement agencies, and this may not be what potential victims need – it may not always provide them with a trusted connection.

The obligation and status as a first responder can, in some cases, contradict the mandate given to first responder agencies in their day-to-day role. Is it realistic to think that each first responder agency can manage the dual remit this role presents?

Sometimes people aren't identified; the agencies they interact with have blinkers on and don't see or attempt to see the whole picture.

Matt was arrested for committing drug offences; he wasn't seen as a potential victim.

Pham was convicted for drug offences and serving a sentence. Those he was arrested with were deported. None of them were identified as potential victims.

Sometimes people can't share their experience in a way that we understand. Sometimes people aren't identified because they don't know what is going to happen to them. Sometimes people aren't identified because they are unable to ask for help. Sometimes people don't realise what is happening to them is wrong, and sometimes even when they do, the thought of leaving their situation puts their families and them at a level of risk they are just unable to take.

Sometimes, even when a first responder does everything right, everything that they can do, things don't always go smoothly or how you expect them to.

Igor was identified by a health practitioner who couldn't refer him into the NRM.

Zhang Li was arrested for an immigration offence when she declined assistance and faced deportation.

Ling stayed in her situation, being forced to sell sex.

Olga returned to her situation of exploitation when she realised no one else was leaving with her.

Those from the **car wash** and the **caravan site** all decided to stay in the situations they were identified in.

Sometimes, you get to see the glimmer of hope that the system may work, as in the cases of **Andre, Mihaela,** and **Riso**.

CHAPTER 8

Problems in the Support Process

> The support currently provided to survivors of human
> trafficking and modern slavery is not meeting recovery
> needs. Government funded support ends abruptly and
> too early and there is little information or data as to what
> happens to survivors in the longer term. The current
> situation leaves survivors with little realistic opportunity
> to rebuild their lives, with some ending up destitute,
> vulnerable to further harm or even being re-exploited.
> **(INDEPENDENT ANTI-SLAVERY COMMISSIONER 2017, P.1)**

S upporting survivors is hard.

Explaining the system of support, what it can offer, and how it works is complicated.

Sometimes what's on offer just isn't enough. Sometimes the systems don't join up, leaving people in a perpetual state of limbo. Sometimes the support does more harm than good. In the moment, agreeing to accept support may be the only option someone has – this doesn't mean it is the right one. Sometimes people don't realise what they have agreed to.

There is limited recognition that we have in our minds what an 'ideal survivor' should look like, how a 'deserving victim' behaves, and a notion of who is worthy of support.

The services people need around them to form an effective support package all work on different timeframes and have different thresholds. There are different criteria, different priorities, different budgets, different focuses, and different quotas to be met.

The UK's support system could be described as a crisis intervention, an 'accident and emergency' response to those found and identified as victims of slavery. A patch-them-up, ship-them-out mentality.

It doesn't really matter what support systems look like if the overarching immigration policies and pervading attitudes of hostility towards migrants don't change.

Sometimes being free from a situation of exploitation isn't really free at all.

There is a clear disconnect between the intention behind a rest and recovery period and what happens.

Allowing and enabling survivors to begin to develop trust and feel safe to engage should be the primary focus of all support providers. According to the *Human Trafficking Care Standards* (2015), in addition to ensuring accessibility, confidentiality, maintaining of professional boundaries, and effective multi-agency working, the following professional approaches should also be adopted and incorporated into practice when supporting survivors.

Support should be:

- culturally sensitive
- empowering
- gender-sensitive
- holistic and victim-centred
- human rights-based
- trauma-informed.

(Human Trafficking Foundation 2015, pp.32–34)[1]

---

1   For a full explanation of what is meant by each of these professional approaches, please refer to the Glossary of Terms.

The current approach to supporting potential victims during their reflection and recovery period is based upon their nationality and the options available to them. If housing can be provided in some way other than via the Modern Slavery Victim Care Contract (MSVCC), then the stance is that this should be considered. In essence, this is spreading the load across a range of services. What this means is that it is preferred that British nationals who are eligible for local authority housing should go down this route, those claiming asylum should be in asylum support accommodation, and those who have neither of these options will be provided with accommodation under the MSVCC.

Although this may seem like a sensible approach that sees every identified victim accommodated and given support, practically it means different survivors are getting access to different levels of support and different standards of accommodation, not dependent on their need but potentially based on their status in the UK. This means that not every victim identified gets to access accommodation under the support system specifically established and contracted for trafficked persons. Some will be placed in unstaffed asylum accommodation, rooms in houses of multiple occupancy, or a local authority hostel or support living provider. What this means is that from the moment of identification potential victims are seen as a burden, and I am sure that they must feel this.

Over my time working in the sector, support teams have reported on numerous occasions the inappropriateness of some of the accommodation survivors are in. Simple things that the system doesn't consider, that may compound the trauma experienced:

- One woman was so scared to visit the bathroom down the corridor from her room at night in her hostel that she used plastic bags.
- One woman would have men knocking on her door, taunting her, and asking her to do things for them.
- One woman was housed in a single room with her toddler and baby – with a shared kitchen and bathroom facilities and no space to move.

- One woman was housed with men – this triggered for her memories and traumas from her exploitation.

Men reported issues about their accommodation far less. Reports of people bringing 'friends' and associates back to accommodation, and that this on occasion was linked to illegal activities, were not uncommon. This resonates with **Stephen**'s experience. He was, after his release from prison, housed in inappropriate accommodation – accommodation from which he ended up being coerced and controlled, forced into illegal activities, trafficked for the purpose of criminal exploitation. Inappropriate accommodation impacts people.

When people don't feel settled, are unable to rest effectively, when they can't shut their doors and feel safe, it's so much harder for them to engage with any support they are offered.

This does not mean that safe houses are always the right option for people. They are not always peaceful places where everyone feels safe the whole time but they should be fundamentally established on the principles and professional approaches outlined. There are, of course, sometimes clashes of personalities, trauma triggers, or mental illness that mean behaviours can be unintentionally disruptive. Living with other people is not always easy, for anyone; living with other people who you haven't chosen to live with, in a place that has been designated for you by someone you have never met, with people who may not speak the same language as you, in an area you don't know, on top of everything else you have experienced, can compound frustrations, traumatic experiences, and an individual's ability to engage with support.

Not everyone identified needs, wants, or is given the opportunity to enter a safe-house environment. Some are offered outreach support only. For some, this will be exactly what they need – they may have left their situation of exploitation some time ago and not need a period of concentrated support, they may have sorted out their own safe accommodation, they may be settled where they are living and not want to move – but it may also be that the system has decided for them that they don't need accommodation.

Getting support

Step one complete, a potential victim has been identified and wants assistance. The first of many hurdles has been navigated. On paper, the process appears straightforward – identify a potential victim, gain their consent to enter the NRM, and ascertain if they want support, complete the NRM form, and then speak to the agency able to offer support, as set out in the MSVCC.

What won't be clear at this point is the time it will take to get someone into accommodation and support, the different forms in play, the different questions that will be asked, and the apparent repetition that will occur, all of which, while understandable, will delay someone getting to a place of safety and settling, decompressing from the day, beginning to process what has happened, having a shower, putting on clean clothes, having some food, and sleeping. The identification system and the support system are not effectively joined.

By the time people arrive to safe houses, it can be hours and hours after they were first encountered, first offered support. This does not mean they should remain at their site of exploitation during this time, and professionals need to consider where they can go to complete these processes safely and who needs to be involved. This is not a process to start near the end of a shift; it takes time and it relies on the trust and the relationship that has been built with the person who has asked for help.

We waited all day with **Andre**. He'd been taken away from the car wash by a member of the public and then we had met with him and taken him back to the police station to discuss his options. The officer and I completed the NRM form with him, and he signed to say he was happy to be referred to support and agreed with what we had put on the form – we had entered the information he had given us already rather than ask him more questions about his experiences, aware that he was still shaken and somewhat overwhelmed by all that was happening. Once the NRM form was submitted, we started the process of getting Andre support.

Support for potential victims is arranged centrally via a referral line. An assessment will be made via phone as to the potential victim's needs, and then they will be assigned and transported to accommodation and support accordingly.

We called the referral line and explained the situation – yes, we had completed an NRM form, yes, the person did want and need accommodation and support, yes, we were with the potential victim, yes, he was safe, yes, he would need a translator, and yes, we would wait for a call back.

What followed was a frustrating and convoluted process that involved a multitude of calls and long wait times. The information on the NRM form had to be repeated, not only by myself and the officer, but by Andre as well. The same information had already been given on a different form, but it couldn't be transferred across – everything needed to be said again. Then there were more questions. It is, of course, understandable for an agency to want to understand the risks to the person, the risks they may present to support teams, and the needs that have to be met.

But there is a time and a place for such detail and, arguably, that is not on immediate exit from an exploitative situation. The reality of the situation is that most of the time, at this stage, we just don't know the detail.

Andre's case was particularly memorable because we felt the tone taken with him was not appropriate. It was obvious he was becoming distressed by the questions being asked and expressed to us his confusion at their relevance.

With his permission, the officer and I ended up putting the referral call on speaker phone to try to assist him to navigate this – the main sticking point appeared to be that the person on the other end of the call would not believe Andre when he said he didn't drink. The questions were endless and started from a position of doubting what Andre was saying. The same question was asked time and time again in slightly different ways.

The officer and I confirmed we had been with him for the last five hours – there were no obvious signs of him withdrawing or being reliant on alcohol, he was coherent and engaged. There was no reason to doubt what he was saying and yet this is what was happening.

What transpired was a grown man in tears, apologising for the couple of beers he had drunk for a friend's birthday a few weeks ago and worrying that it would impact the decision made about his support.

There is a way to approach the questions that need to be asked and a way to work with and trust the other professionals and their opinions – those who are actually in the room and with the person.

This was a clumsy and inappropriate approach.

It also is one I know not to work. On numerous occasions, survivors have arrived at accommodation projects, their referral form stating they have no 'issues' with alcohol – this has not always been the case. It may have been that this wasn't disclosed at the time of the referral. The anti-slavery sector has asked for more accurate detail in referrals to ensure they are able to effectively support someone's needs. Support teams are aware that unmanaged withdrawal from alcohol can be fatal and most safe houses are not set up to be able to manage this process.

There are issues with making referrals into support services over the phone, things being misunderstood and misinterpreted by both the potential victim and the person assessing the referral. The referral process is long, drawn out, and, in some cases, re-traumatising for the potential victim. The work the officer and I did in Andre's case was nearly undone by the approach taken to him over the phone – he was upset he wasn't being believed, the questions confused him, and he didn't understand what was happening. All of this can lead to people who need assistance and support walking away. This puts them at risk of re-exploitation, of returning to the situation they came from. Faced with the choice of returning to the known or continuing into the unknown, it takes guts and strength either way, and we are too quick to forget this.

The support system is at odds with itself. We want to support someone, but we want to manage all the risks we can in relation to this, and these can be opposing aims. We are not willing to accept that sometimes we just don't know and the impact of grilling someone may in fact not be appropriate or needed at this juncture. If we want to 'help', we need to accept that this offer comes with some unknown territory, territory that will look different for every person.

There is also the risk of the potential victim being unable to offer enough information or the right information as part of the referral process, and this can sometimes result in their referral for support not being accepted. The other stumbling block at this juncture is that support doesn't technically kick in until they have received an initial decision (reasonable grounds) about their status as a potential victim of trafficking. Unless there is evidence that they will be destitute in the interim period, there is no requirement for support and accommodation to begin immediately. Destitution means someone has nowhere to live safely while this decision is being made. Andre had accommodation, but it was accommodation sourced by his boss, the man who owed him money, who had made him work excessive hours, and who had that morning held his throat so tightly he left bruises. He knew where Andre lived, so for Andre to remain there, in our minds, was not a safe or viable option for him. He was not technically destitute but he would be at risk if he was asked to return to his accommodation until an initial decision about his status as a victim was made.

On paper, this decision should take a matter of days; the reality on the ground can be different. If a referral is not accepted or is waiting on an initial decision, professionals can find themselves in the ridiculous situation that the central support system established for victims of modern slavery is not able to assist.

It is here that any trust built can be damaged. The systems offered and explained not coming to fruition.

In such instances, police and other first responder agencies are literally left with someone they deem to be a victim, someone who wants and needs support and yet is unable to access it. Faced with limited options, agencies need to make decisions about how they discharge their safeguarding duties towards the person they are sitting with, the person they believe to be vulnerable and a victim of modern slavery. This is when conversations begin about using budgets for hotel accommodation, accompanying people to homeless shelters, questioning if there is anyone the individual can stay with. It is uncomfortable and not the system that has been described; it's not what was offered. The system puts first responder agencies in an impossible situation – here is what I think is happening to you, here is what you may be entitled to and able to access, would you like to access this, yes, great, we now need to call someone else to make this decision…so I can't promise anything. It is understandable why people choose to stay in the situations we encounter them in – we aren't able to offer anything concrete.

Not everyone who receives a reasonable grounds decision will then access support. Some will disengage from the process, some will decide it isn't for them, some will make other plans, some will not have understood the system, some will return to their place of exploitation thinking this is their only option.

When we offer a system of support and then can't fulfil what we have offered, we leave people, yet again, with impossible choices.

After some eight hours of waiting and speaking to professionals, Andre was accompanied to his accommodation by police. He wanted to pick up his belongings before he moved into his new accommodation. The system, convoluted and tricky to navigate, had worked for him.

Being moved out of area

Sarah's experience highlights the geographical challenges that affect access to support. Accommodation and appropriate support services may just not be available locally. For some individuals, the situation they were identified in may necessitate a move out of area.

Sarah quickly realised that she was leaving the city she knew as she was transported to a women's safe house after agreeing to enter the NRM. She panicked and tried to get out of the car while it was moving. The drivers were able to convince her to continue on her journey to safety. It was a traumatic experience for all three of them and meant that Sarah was understandably suspicious of the help she was going to get when she arrived at her support provider's location.

Sarah may not have been told she would be moved out of area, the person referring her into support may not have known, Sarah may have been told and not understood or remembered. Whatever did or didn't happen, something had broken down in the communication between the professionals and the person needing assistance.

Although the volunteer knew the city Sarah was being taken to, we must remember that even if they are told, people may have no concept of where a place is. Depending on their experience, moving to a safe house in a different area may not mean anything to someone who hasn't had the freedom to move as and when they wish to – they may not realise where they are going, how far away this is, or how long it will take to travel there. People may be unaware of what they have agreed to.

The other elements of Sarah's life, those that may not have been necessarily linked to her exploitation, hadn't been considered as part of her referral and entry into support. We find it hard to get our heads around the fact that people can be exploited and in horrific conditions but sometimes still have connections and ways they have developed to deal with the environment they find themselves in. Not everyone fits the media portrayal of being chained to a radiator and physically restrained. Control mechanisms are far more subtle than that – it's how slavery can continue hidden in plain sight. People can appear to commute under their own free will, coming and going between their place of work and their accommodation (the overcrowded accommodation with extortionate rent that means they are in debt), and to the untrained eye, and even the trained eye, people are making these choices freely, but these may be the only choices they have, there may be no other options.

Sarah had a life outside of her exploitation. She had children in the care system in another city and moving away meant the little contact she did occasionally have would not be possible. The professionals had focused on Sarah as a potential victim, as someone who needed help, needed saving, and in the moment this may well have been understandable and justified, but sometimes getting support has those knock-on effects we just don't appreciate at the time – **Esther** and the threat to her sisters, **Ruth** and the family shop being destroyed, Sarah being moved halfway across the country for her protection without anyone considering she may have commitments and a life outside of her exploitation.

It is now standard practice upon referral to ask about children and relatives, but if there is no locally available accommodation, an individual in a situation like Sarah's will still be asked to move out of area. Once again, this means people are facing tough choices.

The principle behind moving someone out of the area they have been found in is a sound one. Putting distance between the exploiter and the exploited sounds sensible. If you are being trafficked and exploited by an organised criminal gang with networks in and around the area, there is the risk they will (a) locate you, (b) locate others in the same location as you, and (c) put support staff and survivors at risk. As I said, it sounds sensible and will be necessary in some cases, but it is also sometimes naïve and not what people need.

It is naïve because not all traffickers and exploiters are criminal masterminds; some are the people that the day before were in the same position as Sarah, **Anna**, and **Pham** – they have been 'promoted'. Now, instead of watering the plants, selling sexual services, or washing the cars, they are responsible for making sure the others do. Respite for them and yet they become involved in the control of others – unintentionally. They complete the cycle of abuse and exploitation and move from exploited to exploiter – not that those involved would necessarily view themselves like this.

Moving people to new locations and away from where they've been living may also impact their ability to support any criminal investigation (should they choose to) – as they may then come under a different force area. Although this shouldn't impact the investigation, in practical terms it makes it harder for officers to maintain contact and keep in touch about a case and may mean the force area the person is now residing in also needs to get involved.

Moving to a new location may also mean losing access to local authority services. If I entered the NRM, I may move to a new area as part of my decision to accept support, but I may not have the right to access housing or other local authority services. Once I'm ready to move on from support, my access to support services may be limited because I'm unable to evidence an existing connection to the local area. I may be housed in asylum accommodation and I may face multiple moves. As a potentially trafficked asylum seeker, the asylum and trafficking systems may be running in parallel. I may be housed in 'initial accommodation' to begin with and then moved again to longer-term housing while a decision is made about my asylum claim. At the same time, I'd be eligible for support under the MSVCC, but support would likely be provided purely in an outreach capacity. There is no guarantee that my longer-term accommodation would be located close to where I'd initially been housed. It's likely that my support worker would change – and this would feel incredibly disruptive. Multiple moves would be traumatic for me in their own right, with the need to adapt to a new area, where its shops are, what bus I need to take, where the services I need to get to are. Connecting and learning to trust another professional all over again, retelling them my experience, having them reassess my needs and risks, putting in place yet another plan may all become just a step too far.

When we consider that this process happens to an individual *in addition to* any trauma they may have already experienced as a result of their exploitation, it's clear to see just how little focus the current process places on the needs of the survivor, on basic human comfort and needs.

When we move people out of the area in which they were identified, is it for their own protection or because it is what we have available at the time their referral comes in? Both are considerations that come into play, but the narrative shared as to why we do what we do has to be more transparent, especially to the people it involves. Moving people out of the area they were found in is not always serving the best interest of the person being moved. We must, wherever possible, involve survivors in the decisions we are making about them and for them. They need to understand and consent to what is being offered – they need to be presented with choices.

Rest, recovery, and reflection

I do not want to confuse the issues with the system with issues with those providing the support.

As one survivor reflected:

> '[We were] all women who had been through something, some spoke about
> it, some didn't, which is fine, fair enough, but we were all in the same boat.
>   We weren't judged.
>   Not made to feel little.
>   We were encouraged.'

Survivor (2020)

The system of support is a short-term fix, it is a chance to meet someone's
basic needs, needs they may well have been denied during their situation of exploitation. It can provide the basics in Maslow's hierarchy of
needs (1943) – it can ensure access to food, water, warmth, rest, a space
that belongs to you, and safety. It may even allow for the beginnings of
connection with self and with others.

The support systems in place are a short-term thing, a brief respite,
a chance for the situation to de-escalate.

For **Stephen, Anna, Elbina, Esther, Ruth**, and the thousands of
other individuals offered this support, it is needed and welcomed.

> 'The support from you [Unseen] and others…financial, emotional, phys-
> ical…has kept me going. The support for me and my child has been the
> driving force to move forward and survive this situation.'

Survivor (2020)

> 'Need help to get out of old ways, scary to go into a safe house and meet
> other people…it's what you need…you think everyone is against you…you
> think you will never get anywhere, you never going to get somewhere to live,
> you never going to get another job, nobody's going to believe you, you not
> entitled to benefits or this and that, but they help you.'

Survivor (2020)

Despite support staff's best efforts, it is often not quite the rest, recovery,
and reflection it is intended to be.

Some referred to the NRM will not be accommodated by the support system but will receive support in a community setting – if eligible, they may be housed via the local authority or in asylum accommodation, while some may stay with friends or be able to rent somewhere privately.

Technically, those who are not accommodated or are considered to not need accommodation may receive less support. They may be assessed to need less support at the point of referral, they may have other accommodation options available to them, or there may not be accommodation (in the NRM) available for them. It does mean, though, that identified trafficked persons are not given access to the same level, intensity, or amount of support. Staff will be onsite at accommodation projects; sometimes this is during office hours, for other organisations it will be 24/7 cover – so regardless of whether someone is in a support session and directly working with a support worker on things related to needs and support required, there is someone there should they need them – someone to grab a cup of tea with, to chat to, to connect with. This will be different for someone who lives elsewhere, and although frontline teams need to maintain the boundaries of being a friendly professional rather than a professional friend, being in the same space as someone on a regular basis can build trust and cement an understanding of each other more quickly than meeting people in the community for one-off support sessions. Arguably, this connection may also improve the support that an individual receives.

The teams I have worked with have shown me that the support can work against the systems in place – yes, this can often only go so far, but it can offer people the space they need.

The other support systems people need in place are where the frustrations often come into play and mean the support that can practically be offered is stifled. Over the years, frontline teams have reported frustrations in the coordination of support with other agencies and advocating for access to support for survivors they were supporting. An example of the issues that would come up time and time again over the years are as follows.

Long waiting lists for counselling – so long that even if a survivor needed counselling, they might not be able to access this while in the NRM. Even though it is listed as a core part of support, waiting lists, the availability of the right type of therapeutic intervention (at the right time), access to translators, all put barriers in place to actually accessing this form of support, even when it is needed and wanted.

> '*It's not just the interview and travel, it's also the 4–5-hour wait they put people through. [They] advise [you] to be there at 9am and don't start the interview until afternoon! And yell at people non-stop in the waiting room for using phones to play games on to pass the time.*'

> **Frontline Practitioner (2021)**

The invitation to an immigration interview is not arranged at a time and place that is suitable for a survivor; it is on the Home Office's schedule. Asylum interviews are usually held in Croydon, and depending on where a survivor is based, this can take all day to travel to. The impact not only of having the asylum interview, the way survivors are spoken to and approached, but also the emotional turmoil involved in recalling events and having to provide evidence of what did and didn't happen, on top of a physically long day of travel and meetings, is less than ideal. Such interviews also mean that a support worker will spend all their allocated time with a survivor on this one activity, when there may also be other support needs that need addressing. For those with children, making this journey is even more complicated.

Priya asked to speak to me when she knew I was writing the book. She was being supported and in the NRM and wanted to voice her opinion. Priya was a 40-year-old woman from Pakistan. She had been forced into marriage, abused, and exploited by her husband. As Priya told me when we spoke:

> '*The Home Office always want evidence, they ask me why I didn't take a movie, why I didn't take a picture [to show the abuse I experienced]. What sort of proof do they need? Why didn't I get to the police or the hospital? This is impossible in my country...*'

Encouraging local authorities to collaborate with survivors' support networks to ensure a seamless transition into move-on accommodation (where individuals are eligible), minimising disruption, and ultimately avoiding inappropriate accommodation placements or homelessness, would be an ideal way to partner effectively and support survivors. Sadly, in my experience, it seems that local authority policy only allows for a response at the very last possible moment once all other options have been exhausted. Structured, planned move-on rarely seems to be the norm and disruption is rarely minimised.

Maria had come to the end of her support. Her support team had tried to plan a pathway and an exit for her but were worried about her. Lots of agencies had been involved in her case, but no one, it appeared, was able to take responsibility for her ongoing support needs. An extension of support had been applied for, and the team had worked tirelessly to try to secure move-on accommodation. Maria had a learning disability; it was picked up by her support team and, three assessments later, social services also were of the same opinion. Maria had left some of her belongings at the safe house, partly for safety, but also we hoped that the local authority would accept her as a priority need and offer her supported housing – we had hoped this would happen before her scheduled move-on date. It had already been agreed that if the local authority managed to find accommodation in the next few days, Unseen would continue to accommodate Maria until she could move across, but there was no news from them. Maria was street homeless for a time and this fundamentally impacted her well-being and her engagement with support services. It was unnecessary and could have been, should have been, avoided, but sometimes the systems are unable to work together.

Some survivors may use substances to cope with what has been happening to them; some may also have addiction issues. Addiction may have been a precursor to their trafficking experience – a vulnerability that was used by their exploiter. Some professionals report that issues with alcohol and drugs start as a direct result of the waiting times associated with being in the NRM, the sense of hopelessness survivors feel at not knowing when decisions about their status as a survivor of slavery will be made. One professional told me that a young Polish man, waiting for a year and a half for his NRM decision, had no purpose, no distractions, and was traumatised from his experience. He started drinking heavily to cope with the situation he found himself in. Drinking led to his behaviour changing: he became violent and ended up being evicted from his accommodation. To access support for drug and alcohol issues, survivors have to be ready to accept there is a reliance on substances – understandably, not every survivor will be in this position. This isn't the case just for drug and alcohol services: to access mental health support, it is often a prerequisite that no substances are being used.

A young British woman of 19 had been in the care system since she was a child and struggled with self-harm and suicidal ideation as a result of her exploitation. It was a complex case.

> 'Because she could do all the basic functions and life skills, she wasn't considered a priority. The fact that she was chaotic, couldn't manage her finances, was using drugs and putting herself in dangerous positions with some interesting people, agencies didn't seem to care about.'
>
> **Frontline Practitioner (2021)**

Her behaviours linked to mental illness resulted in her continuously being evicted from accommodation – it wasn't necessarily her fault, but no one agency was willing to take her or her extreme behaviours on. However:

> 'She was not considered to be in crisis [multiple suicide attempts] because for her this was normal behaviour. It also hadn't been happening for long enough for her to access immediate crisis support... She was put on the list for counselling... I was worried she would be dead by the time her turn came up.'
>
> **Frontline Practitioner (2021)**

For some, poor mental health will have been one of the vulnerability factors that were taken advantage of and used to exploit them. Survivors may have diagnosed mental illnesses, undiagnosed mental illness, or be struggling with trauma symptoms because of what they have experienced.

All elements of support offered are objectively good and needed – but practically, on the ground, hard to achieve. For many survivors, the agencies that sit outside the specific support systems are unsure of their role in relation to slavery. The irony of this is that the support system relies on them and the services they provide. Survivors can have a range of complex needs that require a range of agencies to work together on their behalf to ensure support is accessible and appropriate. Unfortunately, many support agencies tend to be stretched and no one organisation is willing to take the lead, to coordinate ongoing support.

What then happens is that frontline practitioners and charities step in to fill the gaps, to provide for the needs those they are supporting have. Although for the individual survivors benefiting this is incredible, it is firefighting mode and not a long-term solution. It gives the appearance of a system that is working. It means the support given and accessible is reliant on the support worker/charity an individual is assigned to. It means the system isn't challenged to be any better or to change, because it is 'coping'. If we continuously fill the cracks, we can avoid looking at the overarching system and working out how to make this better.

The system of support offers general support delivered by generalist support workers, who over the years will build up expertise in modern slavery and trafficking and do an amazing job, but the support needs they are expected to deal with and navigate are unreasonable.

Survivors can arrive with mental illness, diagnosed or otherwise, with prescribed medication that they may or may not have been taking, or had access to; with dependencies or addictions to drugs and alcohol, used by exploiters as a control mechanism or by survivors to cope with their experiences. Some survivors will experience moments of disassociation, flashbacks, nightmares, trauma triggered by their experiences. Some will self-harm, some will have suicidal ideation. Some will arrive with physical and sexual injuries that have been left untreated. Some will arrive pregnant. I remember one woman who arrived at the safe house and genuinely didn't understand the mechanics of becoming pregnant or how this had happened to her, and another who arrived pregnant and wanted an abortion.

Survivors don't come with a predetermined or predefined set of needs.

Every survivor is different and will need different things, access to different services, and this is where the system of support falls down.

The fact that every agency that needs to be involved in supporting a trafficked person is working on different referral pathways, different referral criteria, different thresholds, and different timeframes makes the wider system of support almost inaccessible.

Assumptions are made by the system about what people can and can't do on their own, what will be paid for in support-worker time, and what isn't covered – based on the opinions of those who I imagine have never been practitioners.

The system forgets the practicalities and the realities of those it is intended to support. It forgets that when people live on a minimal income, they are having to constantly make decisions about what they can and can't do.

People are reliant on appointments being walkable, on their children being entertained or looked after, on having enough data left on their phone to call and arrange meetings or let people know if they are still able to attend as planned. People are dependent on being able to read and understand the letters from their solicitors, from police, from support agencies, or on being able to decipher the processes to access support – to understand the bus timetable, the ways schools, doctors, hospitals, and counselling all work. To understand the expectations those who are meant to be offering support have of them. It is a minefield to navigate.

The systems don't consider that people may not have been used to working 9–5, that night-time may have been the time they were up and working, or the time when memories or traumas are triggered. For lots of people it is not a restful time, not a time when sleep comes easily, and we fail to see that making a 9am appointment, which requires an hour-long bus ride to attend, may not be possible. The system doesn't consider that people may not always understand what is expected of them and what documentation they need to take with them to various meetings – for lots of the things people are having to do, it will be the first time for them – the system expects them to be able to navigate it, often without providing access to the support they need to do so. There is little understanding that sometimes people don't have the ability to retain information or understand the systems they are part of – this can be as a direct result of the trauma they have experienced, the lack of such systems in their own country, their lack of experience of having to navigate them, language barriers, or learning difficulties. Sometimes people, understandably, need things to be repeated multiple times, explained to them in a way they can process and decipher, in a language they can understand – sometimes services and agencies don't have the time, money, or resources to do this.

Zara, the young Albanian woman who had been trafficked for sexual exploitation by her boyfriend, arrived with her two children, one a baby that she needed to breastfeed during our interview and the other a little boy of not quite school age. Both Zara and I were aware that what she was going to tell me would be hard for her and hard for her eldest child to hear. She was very clear that she didn't want to show emotion in front of him. We managed to distract him with a phone and he was soon engrossed with Peppa Pig. Zara had no one to rely on, no one she trusted to leave her children with. She was understandably distracted at various points during the interview and had to attend to her children throughout.

When I met her, Zara was living in a double room she had found and was paying for this using asylum support money. She explained she got a small amount of financial support every two weeks, relied on the Red Cross for things the children needed and for clothes. To have enough to eat, she depended on the local food bank. She was technically receiving support but nevertheless was struggling.

The best pieces of 'support' I have seen are often those that the system doesn't 'require' – getting someone a health check, registered with a GP, setting up a legal appointment, making a referral to counselling and education services, sorting out subsistence payments. These are all the boxes that need to be ticked but it is the other things outside of this that I think have had the bigger impact on people.

The relaxation and yoga session run by a support worker before bed, the communal meals, trying different food from different countries, movie nights, exercise classes, accompanying people to groups they want to attend, being present in the middle of the night when someone has night terrors or can't sleep – the simple things that bring human connection.

'Art therapy, I am not doing it, I don't need therapy – I have still got those drawings, I am glad I made the decision to try it, I loved it.'

Survivor (2020)

We must be:

- honest about what we can and can't do
- honest about the short-term nature of support and what can be achieved
- honest about the options, potential outcomes, and choices people do and don't have.

We must remember what people have experienced, that their hopes, dreams, and ambitions of a better life have been dashed, their trust has been broken – sometimes they have been broken, too. Sometimes people make poor choices, sometimes people make the best choice, the best of a bad bunch, sometimes people have been duped, tricked, and forced into all manner of things – we need to remember this in our interactions with them, we need to believe them, we need to hear what they want, we need to treat them as we would want to be treated ourselves and help them to find their voice to fight for themselves.

On paper, the support system offers people access to services to meet their basic needs. The support teams across the country fight hard to ensure the survivors in their services are supported and cared for.

But the odds are stacked against them, and the support system people are offered is a temporary fix, a sticking plaster, that quickly begins to peel off.

We want to focus on individual needs, on individual journeys and pathways through support, and provide what each person needs, but the reality is we haven't worked out how to do this yet. The number of agencies involved in an individual's case – police, health care professionals, support workers (in the NRM and out of the NRM), local community groups, immigration officials, Home Office officials (decision making on NRM and on immigration), education providers, and counsellors, to name a few – all working on different timeframes, under different policies, and with different expectations.

A person's entitlement to access anything (outside of the NRM) being based on their immigration status means we can never truly have equitable access to all the support services an individual will need. The NRM offers a short-term stop-gap, a period of 'rest and recovery', but that is all – for some this will be enough but for many it is far from sufficient. Wider than equitable access to support is equitable access to options, viable alternatives, clear pathways to move on, to rebuild, to make decisions, and to have choice. What an individual can do, what they are entitled to, and the pathways available to them are based on their immigration status within the UK. The lack of choice once again means individuals could be facing yet another series of equally poor options. Without being given the options to learn, to work, to seek further support, we exacerbate the situations people face.

Support for children who have experienced trafficking or modern slavery

My interactions with children over the years have not been as extensive as the adults I have worked with, but this section is based upon my observations of **Marios, Dung,** and **Ly** as well as my experience of developing and designing the first Ofsted Registered children's home for children who have experienced trafficking, a pilot project Unseen ran in 2018. This does not mean that there are not numerous disconnects in the identification and support offered to children who have experienced trafficking and exploitation, but that I am not necessarily the right person to expose and speak to these in detail as my experience of them is limited.

My colleague, Andrew, was the first person to bring child trafficking in the UK to my attention through his work in a young offenders' institution (YOI). He told me about a group of young Vietnamese boys who had been arrested, investigated, and all given custodial sentences after being found in cannabis grow houses. One of their case files noted that one of the officers in the case suspected they may have been trafficked, but this wasn't taken forward by any professional agency – the police, legal representative, social worker/advocate, or sentencing judge. Andrew, with the assistance of staff at the YOI, identified indicators of trafficking and, together, referred them into the NRM.

We decided to develop the children's home in direct response to the increasingly reported trend of children who had been trafficked going missing from care. The home was a pilot to see if we were able to offer an alternative support model for trafficked children, with a specific focus on trying to reduce the number that went missing. Although the numbers of children supported during the pilot were low, we did achieve our aim of having no episodes of any child going missing while in our care.

Certainly, in relation to children, some of the central issues we found through running the children's home were similar to those that presented for adults. In the evaluation report written by Unseen (2020), the following issues were identified as needing to be addressed if we were going to be able to provide effective, collaborative, appropriate support for children.

There was a lack of:

- effective collaborative working between involved agencies
- appropriate accommodation options for trafficked children
- understanding among frontline professionals in relation to identifying the signs and putting in place appropriate safeguarding measures
- specialised training
- clear pathways into and out of appropriate support.

We had taken **Marios** from the car wash to the police station and then on to local authority supported accommodation for the night. When the social worker went to meet him the next morning, Marios wasn't at the accommodation. I found out about this the following day when a police officer called me – he had left shortly after we had dropped him off. It was believed he had returned to the car wash.

Dung and Ly were exhausted, and after hours of waiting, questions, and assessments, they were placed in foster care. They were housed separately; they wanted to be together but there were no suitable placements available. Within a matter of days, they were both missing from their placements. This was a pattern that was to continue for some time: every time they were found (usually in a new city staying with another family connected to the nail bar), they would be placed in care and then go missing.

Independent Child Trafficking Guardians (ICTGs) act as an independent source of advice for all trafficked children. No ICTGs were assigned or available for Marios, Dung, or Ly. The service is not yet available across the whole of the UK. It is hard to know whether having access to an independent advocate would have assisted Marios, Dung, or Ly, whether they would have managed to meet and speak with them before the children left their placements. It is not fair to place the responsibility on ICTGs to prevent children going missing, but it is believed that having access to an independent advocate has some influence over reducing the number of children who go missing (Kohli *et al.* 2019, p.36).

In addition to ICTGs not yet being available across the country, they are also currently no specialised modern slavery accommodation services for children. This has historically been due to local authorities' duties to safeguard and promote the welfare of children in need in their area under section 17 of the Children Act 1989 – a trafficked child fits this category. (In Wales, different provisions apply, with councils having a duty to meet the needs of children where these meet eligibility criteria or where it is necessary to protect them from abuse, neglect, other harm, or the risk of harm.) It has been recognised, however, that trafficked children may require specialised support that sits outside what local authorities can offer as their standard provision.

The system of support offered to adults and children is disconnected.

It can't fully meet what people want and need. Every survivor is different and has different needs, but our system has a cookie-cutter approach – a minimum you will be offered and then an over-reliance on support workers and other services to sort the rest out.

The disjointed nature of an arbitrary process with no shared timelines, thresholds, or access criteria directly impacts survivors. From the start of the support process, how a person is able to interact with the support offered (accommodation and support or just support) is impacted by their immigration status.

Pham was in prison and the Vietnamese children in a YOI were unable to access the support they were entitled to.

Zara was surviving on donations; she had no one she trusted to leave her children with as she sought to seek support for herself.

Priya was asked whether she had evidence of her exploitation.

The system couldn't provide safety for **Marios**, **Dung**, and **Ly**, all of whom went missing.

Maria was made street homeless because of statutory systems and working practices that didn't line up.

Andre had to wait for hours to access support and was questioned inappropriately about his situation.

Sarah was moved halfway across the country so she could access the support that was on offer.

Whatever the support that is to be offered via the centralised system, we must:

> recognise the impact of traumatic experiences upon survivors' lives and behaviours and always strive to do no further harm by ensuring that support is provided in a way that is respectful of their need for safety, respect, and acceptance. (Human Trafficking Foundation 2015, p.34)

Once again, it comes down to choice, or rather a lack of choice. What people can access is dependent not only on their initial identification as a potential victim and their consent to be supported but also (a) what is available at the time of referral and (b) what other services they are eligible for.

Our system of support doesn't always manage to 'do no further harm'.

CHAPTER 9

The Problem of What Comes Next

> In order to emphathise with someone's experience you
> must be willing to believe them as they see it and not how
> you imagine their experience to be.
> **(BRENÉ BROWN 2020)**

S ometimes people leave support and are still in limbo, thrown into more
systems and more waiting. People's lives are on hold.

In some cases, being conclusively identified and given the label of 'victim of
modern slavery' means very little.

Ongoing access to support is based on your immigration status. As
standard, survivors do not get the right to remain in the UK. This means
they do not get the right to work, the chance to rebuild themselves. They
are churned out of the system that is meant to assist them to fend for
themselves. They have limited options.

Limited, too, is the willingness to offer people the opportunity to stay,
to work, to rebuild, to contribute. Limited is acceptance that the system
of support has, in some instances, added to their distress and not offered
support or access to the services needed.

From the moment of identification, we like to think that a victim
moves to being a survivor. Although this notion of having survived may

be accurate, often people remain in survival mode. So although the current system maintains survival as a status once out of exploitation, the sense of isolation, powerlessness, and loss of control often do not subside.

While the support offered via the NRM has been extended over recent years, there is in many cases still a cliff edge, a moment when centralised support ends and there is no clear pathway on what comes next.

The impact of an NRM decision

The impact of an NRM decision on an individual is minimal, as outlined in Chapter 5. As shown in Table 5.2, what happens next is based largely on an individual's immigration status within the UK.

There are two outcomes in relation to an NRM decision – you are either believed to be a victim of trafficking and receive a positive conclusive grounds decision – this was the case for **Anna** and **Stephen**. Or you are not believed to be a victim of trafficking and receive a negative conclusive grounds decision, as was the outcome for **Roze** (see below) and **Zara**.

The experiences of those I've introduced reflect a higher number of positive conclusive grounds decisions, but this does not reflect what happens in reality. As well as those who receive negative decisions, there are those whose NRM decisions I will never know – they received their initial NRM (reasonable grounds (RG) decision) when we interacted, but this doesn't mean they will have necessarily received a positive final decision.

Some survivors will be asked to attend an NRM-specific inteview but this is not standard practice for all – decisions will be made on the information available at the point of identification and on any further information submitted throughout the NRM process. This means that the basis of information on which decisions are made will vary.

A negative decision doesn't mean someone hasn't experienced some form of exploitation or an abusive situation; what it means is that the threshold for identification as a victim of modern slavery hasn't been met – this could be for a range of reasons. It may be that:

- there wasn't enough evidence either way
- the police couldn't take a case forward
- the potential victim didn't know details that could be used to build a case against potential perpetrators
- the NRM form was poorly completed
- there was no time or resources for follow-up interviews
- the individual's asylum claim becomes conflated with their trafficking claim
- they were seen as a criminal, like **Matt** and **Pham**
- they weren't a victim.

There is rarely, in my experience, conclusive and objective evidence in any direction as far as an NRM decision is concerned.

The current system of support offered in the UK is retrospective – an individual is identified and receives support while a decision (NRM) on their trafficking status is being made. Regardless of the outcome of this decision, positive or negative, they will have had access to support. A positive NRM decision will give some survivors access to routes that may offer them the opportunity for some form of leave to remain, as it did for **Anna**, but this is not the case for all people.

The NRM final decision does not grant an individual the right to remain in the UK automatically.

If an individual doesn't have status in the UK (after the NRM), they can't stay here legally, regardless of a positive or a negative decision.

The NRM decision doesn't give automatic access to anything that someone wouldn't have already as a direct result of their immigration status and nationality. Government and policy purists will point out that a positive conclusive grounds (CG) decision may give access to discretionary leave (DL), but 'may give access' is not good enough and the anti-slavery sector has long argued for everyone with a positive CG decision to be given an automatic right to remain in the UK.

Discretionary leave (DL)

Anna had been made to believe she was complicit in her own trafficking, that it was somehow her fault. Being unaware of support structures and her entitlements, she was dependent on the woman who was exploiting her.

During her time in support, Anna made the decision to assist the police to bring a case against the woman who'd instigated her exploitation. She never got her day in court. As she and her support worker sat outside the court room ready to go and give her statement, her trafficker pleaded guilty to a lesser offence and the case was dropped.

For many, this may not sound like a big deal, but for Anna it was her moment, her time to look her trafficker in the eye and tell her she wasn't scared of her anymore and that she wouldn't be able to control her. It was a chance for her to tell the judge what had happened to her, to show she was no longer afraid and was ready to move on. She wanted people to see she was strong and that what she had been through would no longer define her. She was gutted not to have this opportunity and felt robbed by the criminal justice system. It had not been an easy decision to be a witness in the case; with the support of the police and her support worker, she had decided she could do it. To be denied her day in court was soul destroying. This wasn't about the perpetrator getting a longer sentence or a bigger fine; it was about Anna having her voice heard and for people to understand what she had experienced.

The charge against her trafficker provided evidence to support a compensation claim and showed that she had been physically and mentally injured because of what she had been forced to do. She was awarded compensation and, in hindsight, this put her into a position of vulnerability again; for the first time in her life, she had access to large amounts of money.

The positive trafficking decision and the temporary leave allowed Anna's support to continue and for her to get access, initially, to supported accommodation and to apply for benefits while she worked out her next steps. With support, Anna had moved out of the safe house and into independent living locally. Not everything that had happened to her had been worked through, and elements of her life and behaviours were still, at times, chaotic, but the support Anna was able to access had reached its end.

Anna was granted DL because she had assisted the police and was eligible to claim compensation – two of the three criteria outlined in guidance that support an individual to make an application for this form of leave.

Grants of discretionary leave, in comparison with the number of victims identified, are low, and DL doesn't provide a route to secure indefinite leave to remain (ILTR). This is a policy concession that shows that the intention to offer an option to remain continues to exist. In practice, it is rarely utilised as such.

Not everyone gets access to temporary leave as Anna did. The granting of a decision about status as a trafficked person, a victim of modern slavery, comes with no automatic right to remain in the UK. With no leave to remain, survivors are unable to access legal and safe employment, accommodation options are limited, and access to health care and wider support, if needed, will not be available.

Believing what we are told

The decision mechanism is over-reliant on a professional's limited and brief initial interaction as they entered someone into the NRM and on an individual's recollection and narrative of what has happened to them. There is rarely someone who can corroborate their version of events. These recollections of what has happened to them may be incomplete, appear implausible or unlikely, and lack detail. Shared accounts may be tentative and they may develop and morph as someone becomes more stable; details may change slightly depending on the agency being spoken to or the way in which the questions are being asked. The NRM is a civil process and relies on working out if the victim is considered objectively reliable – if they can remember facts, evidence, and information, depending on their experience, this may be information they may not have access to.

People don't always know the answers to the questions we are asking. Not knowing, not having access to information, not having the ability to manage your own movement, the work you do and when, are all mechanisms of control that are used.

In one case, a survivor I met knew he had started in Russia and ended up in the UK – he was able to tell that he was in different places based on the change in the road signs. He described in detail his journey – the houses he stayed in, the places he was locked in, the roads he walked, the cars he was put in, the vessel he had to inflate, the travelling by dark to avoid detection, the different people who joined him along the way, the different people he was handed to, the paperwork he was sometimes handed so that an official could check it. He could tell me what had happened, but he had no idea of the names of those he travelled with, location names, or how long this had all taken. The information provided and his account of the exploitation he had experienced had been enough for him to receive a positive NRM decision but not for him to receive the right to remain in the UK.

For many victims and survivors, there is a period of reconstruction as they process what has happened to them. They tend to 're-interpret events and try to come to terms with their experience, to find an explanation for what has happened, or to evaluate the event' (UNODC 2009, p. 10).

As with all potential trafficking and modern slavery cases and narratives, the accounts we have available to rely on are often one-sided. We do not get to hear or understand the full story from all involved as we are often not aware of who these individuals are. We are overly reliant on victim testimony. Victim testimony and accounts often don't have the key pieces of information to satisfy the authorities that exploitation has occurred. Sometimes there will be no usable evidence; survivors will have been unknown to services and authorities until identified and until they consented to be supported. This doesn't mean that what they recall as having happened to them didn't happen. It just means our system, because of the embedded hostile environment, is unable to function from a position of believed until evidenced otherwise.

It can appear as if the system judges experiences and accounts based on status rather than experience. If **Roze** and **Zara** were legally allowed to stay in the UK, if they already had residency through some other means, would the outcome of their NRM decision have been different?

We struggle to believe that someone would take a job offer without knowing the details, without seeing the contract, without negotiating, and without asking where the job would be, if a visa would be needed, or what the hours of work would be. We attach our lens and our understanding of the world to their accounts and to the decisions they have made – we doubt what they are telling us. We forget the limited choices they may have been facing.

Believing people becomes even more important in cases like those of **Matt** and **Sam**, both young British men exploited for criminal activity. They were both facing custodial sentences because of the crimes they had committed. If the crimes had been committed under duress or because they were being exploited, there are protections outlined within the Modern Slavery Act (2015) to assist their defence and overturn any criminal convictions gained as a result of being trafficked. Overturning of any convictions, especially for foreign national victims, is incredibly important as any criminal conviction can prevent a grant of leave being given. The issue with the statutory defence (Modern Slavery Act 2015, s.45) is that it has to be invoked by the individual. They must instruct their legal team to use it.

Roze had been thrown out of one system, the NRM, and into another, the asylum process – she was exhausted and struggling to muster the little fight she had left.

Roze had asked to speak with me – her support worker had told her that I was writing a book and she wanted to tell me about her experience. When I spoke with Roze, I was brutally aware that although we were in the same city, probably no more than three miles separating us, our lives couldn't be more different at this point in time.

Roze had requested a translator for our call. She was learning English but wanted to speak in her native language, as she would find it easier to express herself. As we spoke, it became apparent that her toddler was becoming unsettled. I offered to call again another day, but she wanted to carry on – Roze was always juggling her various roles and assigned labels: mother, victim, woman, asylum seeker, foreigner.

Roze told me about the impact the waiting had on her, on her mental health, on her ability to feel settled and stable, and on her ability to concentrate. At the time Roze and I spoke, she had been in the system for four years. Roze had initially been supported by Unseen in safe-house accommodation – she would have had her needs assessed and the team would have worked with her to meet these needs.

During her time at the safe house, Roze had received a negative decision. The authorities did not believe she was a victim of trafficking. With a negative NRM decision, Roze would not be in receipt of discretionary leave to remain in the UK. Roze and her legal team challenged this decision, during which time she remained at the safe house. Roze's legal team asked for the NRM decision to be reconsidered. For Roze, **Elbina**, **Zara**, **Priya**, and others like them, who are reliant on a positive CG decision as a mechanism to apply for discretionary leave to remain, being believed is really important. In all these cases the granting, or not, of a CG decision has far-reaching ramifications. As Priya reflected to me: *'I didn't come here to be a princess... I want to work, I want my dignity... The NRM accepts you are a victim, it gives hope and then it gets taken away.'*

NRM reconsiderations

There are no set timeframes for reconsiderations. There is no formal right of appeal in the NRM process and decisions can be challenged via judicial review or a reconsideration can be requested if (a) more information about the case has come to light or (b) there are concerns that the original decision was not in line with Home Office guidance. Because **Roze** had received a negative decision, she was expected to exit support. Technically, during reconsideration of decisions, unless an extension of support is also requested (and approved), people need to exit support. The decision was made to continue to support Roze, outside of the MSVCC, until her reconsideration was made and until an appropriate move-on pathway was available. Roze's negative decision was overturned and she was given recognised status as a survivor of trafficking. Unlike **Anna**, this decision did not come with leave to remain.

Asking for a reconsideration of a negative NRM decision, while enabled via policy guidance, has parameters.

Until recently, a reconsideration had to be completed by the same first responder who had entered the individual into the NRM – a process that made the reconsideration policy all but useless. It would be nigh on impossible for a first responder – whose involvement in a case may have been as limited and brief as completing and submitting the NRM, several months or even years previously – to be expected to offer any effective or relevant commentary.

It is now the case that:

> an individual, or someone acting on their behalf, may request reconsideration of a negative RG or CG decision…if additional evidence becomes available that would be material to the outcome of a case, or there are specific concerns that a decision has not been made in line with statutory guidance. (Home Office 2021, p.141)

There is no formal right of appeal within the NRM process. If legal representatives believe an incorrect decision has been made, a judicial review is the only option available. This can be an expensive, convoluted process in which survivors may not be supported. The lack of legal pathways available to survivors compounds how they are disempowered by the processes in place to support them.

Lack of status

As a potential victim, my account of what has happened to me is believed – like **Anna**, **Stephen**, **Matt**, and **Maria** – and I have a legal right to remain in the UK, or it is not – like **Zara**, **Elbina**, and **Roze**.

If my experiences were determined to have met the definition of slavery or trafficking, but I have no status in the UK, I am not able to stay here legally.

Although there are ways I can apply for status and regularise my stay, these are not guaranteed to give me the right to remain and can be lengthy and complex processes.

Without status and the right to remain in the UK, I can't access services, benefits, housing, or employment.

Roze's legal team advised her to apply for asylum at the same time as asking the competent authority to reconsider her NRM decision, and this provided Roze with a pathway to move on from her initial NRM accommodation into accommodation provided by the asylum process to wait for her asylum decision – her lawyers believed she was unable to return to Albania for fear of persecution and via the asylum process should be offered either refugee status or humanitarian protection. At the end of the NRM process, people face yet more tough choices, some of which are completely out of their control: remain or return.

Remain or return?

To remain legally, an individual needs to have status.

If people can remain, they then must navigate more complicated and complex systems.

Some then make the decision to stay but go under the radar – deciding that this is the best option available to them at the time.

Some individuals will be returned to their home countries when they don't want to be.

If people choose to return to their home countries, there are programmes available to assist and support this.

The pathways ahead for people after the NRM are (a) not always clear, (b) not always flexible, (c) not always accessible, (d) not always well travelled, and (e) based on an individual's immigration status.

Before Brexit, all EU nationals had the right to continue residing in the UK and exercising their European Economic Area treaty rights. This meant that if they were able to work and support themselves, they were able to stay.

Non-British nationals must apply via normal immigration processes for leave to remain. For many, this will be via the asylum process or via an application for discretionary leave that is available upon receipt of a positive conclusive grounds decision.

It is not so much the NRM decision given but the individual's status in the UK that enables or curtails what can happen next.

There are limited options available to trafficked persons after the initial support offered. If someone does not have status or the right to remain in the UK, the pathways available when they come to move on are inadequate: homelessness, staying with friends and family, voluntary return to their home nation, living in asylum accommodation (if able to apply for asylum) are the options available. For those who do have status, the same options are on the table, with the addition of being able to access local authority accommodation and private rented accommodation options.

Maria was clear that, upon leaving the safe house, returning to Romania was not an option for her. She was of the opinion that it would be far better to stay in England, even if that meant being homeless here – for her, this was safer than going 'home'. This was something that came up in a couple of survivors' cases during my time at Unseen – people actively not wanting to return home. Some believed there was nothing there for them, some were afraid of ramifications from exploiters or their own communities and families if they were to return, and some had been gone for so long that they had no family unit left to return to. Others wanted to stay simply because that's what they wanted to do.

With no family, friends, or connections in Romania and her support coming to an end, options were limited for Maria. She had felt safe at the women's safe house; it was where she was beginning to work out who she was and what she needed. She had people there with her 24/7, people who cared and were helping her find her voice. Her final NRM decision confirmed that she was a victim of trafficking. This decision triggered an arbitrary move-on process that she was not ready for and was unable to navigate alone. That once again put her at risk.

I am not advocating for people to stay in safe houses and supported environments for ever. Although made as homely as possible, the reality is that people become institutionalised and over-dependent on the con-nections they have built. These connections are professional ones and come with boundaries, caveats, and parameters – they provide the first stepping stone to reconnect with life and to discover what life out of exploitation can be like, but they are only part of the picture.

Maria had to move on – but to what? The team felt that they could not in good faith support her to sign a rental agreement with a private landlord. Even if we covered the first few months' rent, she was not in a position to get work and then manage these payments herself – we would be setting her up to fail. She had no connections locally, no friends or family she could stay with. She agreed she would be happy to move out of area if she needed to, and a referral was made to another charity that was able to offer longer-term support and a slower reintegration into the community. The charity declined the referral: Maria's case was too complicated and she still required too much support that they didn't feel they could offer.

On the day Maria's support ended, there was no accommodation lined up for her. I drove Maria to the homeless shelter – we had managed to get her a bed in the women-only section for that night. The shelter team had offered to look out for Maria and support her during her time with them. I tried to explain to her that tomorrow she would need to come and queue up again to get a bed. It was painful to leave Maria at the shelter – it was a chaotic environment. Yes, it was a roof over her head, but Maria was back into survival mode.

Maria came back to the safe house the following night – staff didn't let her in and she ended up seeking shelter in the porch. It was my call not to let her in.

It wasn't possible for us to let people come back. What would that show to all the other people that were due to move on soon? What would it say to the staff about the boundaries of care and support we put in place – to protect the survivors and the team? How would we stop it happening again and again and again?

Maria was housed, eventually, by the local authority in supported housing – it would have been great if this move could have happened straight from the safe house, if the systems of support had aligned and focused on her needs – in Maria's case it would have avoided a period of homelessness, a time when she would have been at risk and vulnerable. Maria's case is not a one-off; it is an example of how the centralised government-run support system and the localised support systems don't always work together.

The system fundamentally let Maria down and then I compounded it – I was worried about agreeing to let her back to stay at the safe house, worried about the impact of this on the team, on other survivors, and on Maria. Her arriving at the safe house each night and asking to come back in was not a viable option for her or for us. But on that one occasion, could I, *should* I, have done something different? Could I have connected with her in that moment as another human, a person who needed assistance and had come to the only place she knew that might help? Rather than look at the knock-on effects, the bigger picture, should we have allowed her in for that one night? Would it have helped?

It was one of the trickiest cases I have ever been involved in, and to this day it serves as a reminder to me that the system failed, we failed, I failed.

The system is failing people, and while support workers, charities, and other organisations in the sector can jump in and save it, prop it up, choose to help out the individuals we come into contact with, we also need to be looking at how we avoid this happening in the first place, how we develop systems of support that are effective, that allow people access to what they want and need, that create clear and accessible pathways that aren't hidden behind layers of bureaucracy, reliant on already stretched local services, or based on immigration status.

For Maria, receiving the decision that she was believed to be a victim of trafficking triggered the beginning of the end of her support in the NRM.

Anna's outcome after moving on was initially smoother than Maria's. Again, like Maria, Anna was a European national (pre-Brexit) and able to exercise her treaty rights and remain in the UK. Because she had assisted the police with their enquiries, she was also eligible for a form of temporary discretionary leave that granted her access to welfare benefits for a set amount of time.

Roze did not get refugee status or humanitarian protection – her claim was refused, with the authorities stating that they believed she could safely return to Albania and be accommodated in a safe house and receive the support she needed there. The Home Office publishes guidance on every country, noting their ability to support people who return; on paper, it looks as if Roze may be able to access support, but she is currently challenging this decision. She does not think she will be safe in Albania; she does not think her child will be safe there.

Roze has been waiting for an outcome on her challenge for the last four years. That's four years of not having secure status, four years without being able to open a bank account, to seek employment, to access benefits or support services; four years of not having stability, of living in inappropriate accommodation, of living hand to mouth and being reliant on the generosity of organisations to provide what her and her son need.

She has been in limbo for four years.

In her words, she has waiting fatigue. She has been waiting and it is tiring. Roze struggles with the knowledge that her future is in someone else's hands and that those hands have already refused to believe her. She says that when people don't believe you, it is damaging.

She felt tired when we ended the conversation. She had spoken at a rate of knots throughout our time together – at times the translator struggled to keep up. Roze was astute in her reflections on the damage waiting does to someone. She wants to work, to contribute. She wants her son to grow up in a safe environment, and she wants to put what she has experienced behind her. She is in survival mode; she is not yet free.

Her positive status as a survivor of slavery hasn't helped her move on with her life.

What comes next for survivors?

The system of support does not currently provide standardised long-term support for trafficked people to rebuild their lives. Data is not currently collected on longer-term outcomes for those identified via the government-funded identification and support systems. Understanding what happens in someone's life after they have experienced trafficking is certainly a significant current gap in understanding in the UK. Many in the sector call for the support systems currently in place to offer more and for longer.

Many want to see identified victims being given access to a resident's permit, access to the labour market, and continued psychosocial and general support according to each individual's needs. Such ideas have to date been sidelined, the subtext being that the support systems shouldn't offer too much and that they offer some a loophole through which to access the immigration system and leave to remain in the UK. No system wants to be providing an incentive to pose as a victim. Although this may be a known risk, many find it an affront to those they have worked with and supported to suggest that they are being penalised and prevented from accessing necessary and needed support just in case someone 'plays the system'.

Elbina was in the NRM when I met her; she was still receiving support and living in a safe house. Her lawyer was concerned that she might receive a negative NRM decision and as a result would not be afforded the opportunity to remain in the UK. Her legal team were worried about the risks to Elbina should she be returned to Albania and wanted an expert report to further evidence the indicators of slavery in her case. They were aware of a worrying trend in the approach being taken to Albanian women and didn't want this to happen to Elbina.

Increasingly, there were reports of Albanian females arriving at police stations and asking for help, claiming they were victims of slavery. Some were pregnant and some already had legal advisers in place. It soon became anecdote, with professionals warning each other to watch out for Albanian females presenting in this way. As a direct result, the way in which Albanian women were seen and their stories believed had started to change. Rather than professionals viewing them as potential victims, they were seen as potential criminals, playing the system to access support.

This rhetoric was hugely damaging to the way every Albanian woman was viewed, and the system showed its inability to treat people as individuals. Elbina's lawyer was aware of this bias and wanted to give her client the best chance of being fairly heard.

We need to understand what the systems do to people, we must understand what they are going through, the perpetual limbo and the lack of pathways and options available to them.

Roze wanted to share what had happened to her, how she felt the system needs to change, from her first-hand experience of it all. It is tiring to continuously be in survival mode. She was and she is exhausted.

Stephen shared with me some of the practical issues that meant he was finding it hard to move on from Unseen's accommodation and support. As a British national, he faced no immigration issues but this didn't appear to make the pathways available to him any clearer or easier to navigate.

His last supported accommodation placement was the place he had been exploited from, and he was understandably nervous about something similar happening again. He was really pragmatic and knew it was a step forward, but also expressed concern and worry that it would be like the old place. He told me that the local authority had offered him a place to move on to, and he had been to visit it with his support worker. He didn't get the right feeling from the place, but this was his only option. He explained if he said no to this, there was no guarantee of him being offered another place – he didn't like it, but what choice did he have?

What he really wanted was to move into private rented accommodation and to get a job. But without a guarantor for a rental agreement, without a deposit, and without explaining the gaps in his employment history when he had been in prison and then exploited, he wasn't sure either of these would be an option. He still had work to do on himself and wanted to rebuild his confidence. He was glad that Unseen would continue supporting him in the community as he didn't feel ready to leave the safe house, even though he knew this was what he had to do. Stephen was still scared; he described being triggered by shouting and loud noises. He was finding it hard to move on from his exploitative experiences. Support from the safe-house team and living with others, while hard at times, gave Stephen purpose and distraction from his thoughts. He could help those who didn't understand the systems, whose first language wasn't English; he was involved in photography classes, gym sessions, and leading house meetings. He was also trying to rebuild relationships with his family.

Even for those with the right to remain, with access to housing, benefits, and ongoing services (non-slavery specific), navigating the move-on pathways available is tricky, stressful, and fraught with practical barriers that people find really hard to overcome. The lack of choice about where you get to live or who you get to live with, the area you are housed in, explaining your work history, the constant change, the feelings of isolation, the lack of community, of not feeling confident that you are able to manage all the things that come up in life generally when you are living alone – these are but a few of the issues survivors face at the end of their time in support.

Stephen's feeling was that the systems people are expected to move on to were not fit for survivors of modern slavery – in fact, they had a negative effect on his experience of support.

The risk of re-trafficking

It was some years later that I next encountered **Anna**.

We had ad-hoc reports from other agencies about Anna and the potential of her being in an abusive relationship but were unable to provide her with any support or ongoing contact.

I was part of a panel providing my opinion on NRM decisions along with a range of other professionals. On one occasion, as I was reading through paperwork, I began to feel my stomach churn and bile rising at the back of my throat. I couldn't believe what I was reading and hoped it wasn't true, but the wind was knocked out of me. Maybe 'Anna' was a popular name, maybe it wasn't the person I knew three years previously who I was reading about all over again. I dearly wished it would not be the girl who'd successfully moved on from her experiences and been strong enough to give evidence in a criminal case. But it was. For the first time in my career, I was reading about someone I knew being re-trafficked, re-exploited. Up until this point, all the information about re-trafficking had been anecdotal, based on the assumption that if people didn't get access to longer-term support and the right to work and support themselves, they may be, yet again, faced with tough choices about how they would support themselves and be vulnerable to exploitative practices.

According to the reports, Anna had moved in with her boyfriend, leaving the city she had been relocated to and supported in – leaving any support structures that had been established. Her boyfriend had access to the compensation she had received and took advantage of this. When the money ran out, she was expected to sell sexual services to provide money. She didn't do this consensually and was forced by her partner. She was a victim of circumstance and her own vulnerability, twice. I don't know what happened to Anna in the end. The group of professionals reviewing her case agreed she had been trafficked and fit the criteria under the NRM, and she had previously been given the right to stay in the UK, so I can only hope she was able to access the support she needed.

There are currently no assurances that victims, once out of their situation of exploitation, will not find themselves in another similar situation in the future.

Matt's legal team and I were informed that he had been recognised as a survivor of slavery. Around the same time, I was told that the case against him had also been dropped – his involvement was believed to be as a direct result of him having been exploited and forced into county lines activity. This was all looking positive for Matt. In a follow-up email, I was told that support services had tried to get in touch with Matt, but as he hadn't been contactable on several occasions, they were closing his case.

In our previous interaction, Matt had told me that those he had worked for were a thing of the past, that he was out of it, and that he was safe.

It transpired that the reason Matt was not able to answer a call about the support he needed was because he was in prison.

After his NRM referral and the case being dropped, Matt had subsequently been arrested, for county lines activity, this time by a different police force. Matt's original legal team asked me to speak to him, and from prison Matt and I had a video conference call. Matt wasn't sure if he wanted to speak to me because, as he described it, he was weighing up the cost–benefit of speaking – he thought that speaking up again would put him in more trouble with the gang; he had already risked it once speaking to me and going into the NRM – and he wasn't sure it was worth it. He had ended up back in prison anyway.

A 20-year-old deciding his options based on fearing what might happen if he said the wrong thing, to the wrong person, about those who he had worked for – this fear was so real he was considering staying quiet and facing four years in prison on drug charges.

The system of support in place can do very little to protect those like Matt against the threats that they face from those they have been exploited by.

CHAPTER 10

The Problem of Viable Alternatives

Extending support, allowing access to employment, and creating pathways for survivors to access decent work, appears to make sense morally and financially; however, these increasing calls for creating safe, durable solutions for survivors of modern slavery are yet to be taken on board by government.
(RIGHTS LAB AND OFFICE OF THE INDEPENDENT ANTI-SLAVERY COMMISSIONER 2021)

*T*he hostile environment is pervasive; it snakes itself through the modern slavery agenda, and the mechanisms in place are unavoidably linked to the immigration agenda and rules.

Choices individuals have post-support will be based upon their immigration status and not their individual needs. The system set up to care, to support, and to tackle modern slavery only goes so far before remembering someone is not legally allowed to be here. Some people won't even realise they are not 'allowed' to be in the UK and to work; for others, the recognition of their lack of status is used against them as a threat and a control mechanism, traffickers and exploiters aware that there are limited protections for those deemed 'illegal workers'. Opportunities to regularise an individual's stay are limited, and people are denied the right to work and to access welfare benefits and support. During an individual's time in the NRM, they are viewed as a potential victim, as someone who needs and is entitled to support; once an NRM decision is made, regardless of whether this is positive or negative, individuals are no longer viewed based on their need but based on their immigration status. In the space of 24 hours, the system's approach to people alters.

Access is determined by status. Access to ongoing support. Access to employment. Access to stay. All determined by where you were born.

Even for those who are British nationals, legally allowed to reside in the UK, access to the labour market and to ongoing support can be hard to navigate. The impacts of trauma and having a criminal conviction or no work history to speak of mean that moving forward from experiences of exploitation can be problematic.

Navigation of the systems in place to identify and support victims and survivors of slavery is complex. There are, of course, success stories – people who have made it through, who have managed. I would suggest that it is against the odds to have navigated the systems of support and get access to what they have needed.

People make the choice to leave their home for the promise of a job – a job that they very much need to support themselves and their families. The individual circumstances they faced at the time will have dictated what they needed to do. Some won't have realised they were leaving their home country. For some, the journeys they took to get here were traumatic, and once underway, they saw no way of reversing the choices they had made. Some never left their home country. Even when the work that transpired wasn't what was offered, they were forced to do things they didn't want to do, the terms and conditions of the job offered changed, working hours were longer than expected, they faced abusive treatment, threats were made towards them and their families, and they were not paid for the work they did, they stayed – what choice did they have?

They accepted what they were told about the authorities not believing them, about being deported, about being charged as a criminal, about their families being a risk. For some, these threats turned out to be their reality. They were hurt. Their families were hurt. The authorities didn't believe them. They were arrested for crimes they were forced to commit. They were detained for immigration offences.

They came forward, sought help, and realised that some of the things they might need (work, housing, to stay in the UK) may not be available.

People want and need to work. People will always find ways to do this and there will always be other people willing to take advantage and exploit their situations.

For those who want to work, we need to find ways to make this happen.

The intention behind the time afforded to potential victims in the NRM to allow them to rest, recover, and reflect is well meaning, but it is not always possible, achieved, or needed. Until we listen to what those impacted by modern slavery want and need, we will not be able to develop systems, pathways, and support mechanisms that they want and need.

We must accept that while there may be some trends in experiences of exploitation and some generic needs that come from this, everyone is different; everyone's experience is different, and any approach must work out how to account for this.

At each stage – identification, immediate support, and ongoing support – there must be clear options, pathways, and viable alternatives – there must be the space for people to make choices.

Curtailing individual freedoms is a significant factor in the disconnect that survivors experience. Held in limbo, within systems of control reminiscent of those they've previously experienced, what they want and need is not offered to them. It's this that results in people choosing to remain in or to return to or being unable to escape exploitative situations.

Thinking about solving these issues will necessitate us thinking about it all in different ways. Starting from viewing the individuals affected as equals and delivering access to support that avoids triggering processes and inflicting further trauma, we'll begin to move away from a focus on corroboration, evidence, and bureaucracy, and towards a default belief in survivors' accounts of their experiences.

It's possible to develop support systems that look at individuals first and foremost as people, before any need to categorise them under 'sex worker', 'migrant', 'offender', 'illegal immigrant' labels. Effective and supportive processes will need the flexibility to hold in tension that people can be one, all, or none of these.

Systems of support will need to involve gaining an understanding of an individual's needs, and of the experiences that have led them to their current circumstance.

Slavery is linked to big, scary, and apparently insurmountable global issues: poverty, violence against women and girls, war, climate change, natural disasters, unstable economies, and lack of employment and educational opportunities. What isn't insurmountable is our freedom and fundamental ability to work out what it is we can do for the individuals who are affected, the people who reach a dead end on their journey and are left trying to make a choice from an array of – often unsafe – options.

CHAPTER 11

Can We Fix What Is Broken?

Capitalising on others' hardship and misery... We (an individual, the system, politics at play, organised criminal gangs, the law) take advantage of someone's suffering, vulnerability or burden to make it beneficial to ourselves.
(CONCEPT FROM SANDEL 2009)

To fix what's broken, we need to understand it.

It's impossible to propose effective solutions if we don't understand the issue, what it looks like and how it presents.

We need to connect with the issue of modern slavery, to the individual people impacted. We need to understand the part we play in keeping the wheels of supply and demand turning.

We need to consider what we can do about it. Sometimes we miss what is right in front of us, blinkers on. Sometimes our attempts to help only add to the problem.

There are no simple answers to tackling slavery, no magic wand, and no end currently in sight. We need to sit with this discomfort, the same tension I felt when leaving people I knew needed help behind in deportation centres, prisons, brothels, car washes, and restaurants. The same tension that still makes my stomach churn when I think about **Anna** or **Maria**.

Modern slavery cannot be solved by an organisation in isolation. It is a phenomenon that interacts with a range of systems, policies, and legislative instruments, and requires effective interplay between domestic and foreign policy makers, government departments, judiciary, law enforcement; it also requires action from civil society, survivor support agencies and the third sector, business, both big and small, media outlets, and, most importantly, survivors themselves.

Whatever action is considered should not be without the input and lived experiences of survivors. They offer a unique and pivotal perspective in relation to what actions professionals could have taken, what support systems could have offered, and an opportunity to be able to better understand the issue.

We must work together if we are to instigate successful change. Attempts to solve modern slavery country by country are also likely to be unsuccessful. The supply and demand of people, services, and goods is an issue that requires a collaborative and global response. Everything we change in one place has an inevitable knock-on effect elsewhere and just hides people from our sight, just as vulnerable, just as exploited, just not in our own back yards.

We can work out a way to deconstruct what we have created, understanding that at its very heart exploitation is the result of the systems instigated, the intended and unintended consequences of a capitalist society.

We can focus on the notions of justice, equality, fairness, choice, welfare, and freedom. These are all philosophical debates that can be approached from so many different perspectives but all elements that need to be considered if we choose to address an issue that we have allowed to weave itself into our social and economic fabric.

Slavery is not going away. As individuals, we are a part of the problem, so we can play a part in the solution. Governments are part of the problem, so they can play a part in the solution. Business is a part of the problem, so it can play a part in the solution. Media portrayals are a part of the problem, so they can play a part in the solution.

Considering and addressing how the systems we've put in place in good faith may be perpetuating slavery is one of many uncomfortable thoughts I've begun to consider after years on the frontline. Do we, as members of a capitalist society, accept slavery and exploitation of others as an inevitable byproduct? As with other far-reaching ethical and moral issues, this is something we as individuals, as communities, as a global society have a responsibility to wrestle to a conclusion.

For example, our behaviours impact the climate. As our climate changes and people's homes and livelihoods are threatened, do we offer them safe passage to settle and alternative employment options elsewhere or leave them to fend for themselves? Without options, as their homes disappear, they may be left with limited choices, put at risk at the hands of those willing to exploit, to offer seemingly viable alternatives, who then fail to deliver on their promises.

As we progress with electric cars and as cities across the UK decide to ban anything but electric transportation, do we consider the supply chain involved? The benefit to the environment is clearly evidenced, but are we considering the children expected to mine the lithium required to allow us to reduce our carbon footprints?

Similarly, with Brexit and the end of free movement between the UK and Europe, there are concerns that workers' rights, predominantly based in EU law, will be eroded. This may lead to an increase in exploitation of migrant workers. Restrictive immigration policies limit the number of pathways and protections to access work legally and safely in the UK. This becomes problematic when there is a clear demand for labour but not the routes available to meet the need.

Everything we do impacts someone somewhere. Deciding what it is that we have the capacity to fight for, or against, what we want to see change starts from an awareness of our impact, with informing ourselves and connecting with the domino effect.

Modern slavery by its very nature could be considered a 'wicked' problem. Wicked in the literal sense of the word as evil and morally wrong, but also in the way described by Rittel and Webber (1973). A 'wicked problem' is described as a complex social challenge that is dynamic and impossible to solve. A wicked problem is characterised by an incomplete or contradictory knowledge base, indeterminate in scope and scale, which has economic burden on the state and by its very nature is interconnected with other problems. They are problems that exist in an ever-changing environment.

The numbers of those enslaved and exploited are not clear, the definitions of trafficking, slavery, and forced labour, while defined in internal and domestic legislation, are interpreted differently, often depending on a country's approach to employment rights, sex work, issues that impact women and girls, and migration policies (to name a few of the interconnecting issues). Modern slavery is not a globally recognised concept. There is a range of exploitation that shows itself in a range of different ways; it is our interpretation of this that allows or denies access to support and choice. It determines how we view people.

Evidence thresholds required to pursue a modern slavery offence are different to those required under the National Referral Mechanism (NRM). Outcomes of an investigation impact the NRM decision and vice versa. However, just because law enforcement may be unable to gather enough evidence to show the criteria of a modern slavery offence have been met doesn't mean that it hasn't happened. It doesn't mean that a person isn't a victim of exploitation. It doesn't mean that someone isn't in need of assistance.

Poverty, violence against women and girls, gender discrimination, economic inequality, access to education, labour market access, war, natural disasters – these are all structural issues, root causes that link to slavery and create perfect environments that allow it to happen.

Modern slavery is ambiguous, ill-defined, messy. It is not a static phenomenon; it is dynamic, versatile, agile, flexible, and ready to take advantage of situations as they arise. It is the polar opposite of the systems we have in place to identify and disrupt it and protect those impacted by it, which are so often rigid and fixed.

It is a multifaceted issue that, if framed as a wicked problem, appears almost impossible to solve. This is not a justification to rest on our laurels and ignore it or assume the responsibility to solve it will fall to someone else.

If modern slavery is an impossible problem to solve, does considering how we control it or at least mitigate its impact become our imperative? This requires interdisciplinary collaboration and perseverance, and an acceptance that while current systems are incapable of preventing slavery, this doesn't mean we admit defeat.

We must unpack this issue, connect with it, understand its impact on individuals, families, and societies, and I hope this book has started you on your journey to doing so. Looking for innovative approaches is a starting point to understanding how this issue is a symptom of a broken world and broken systems – a world and systems of which we are a part. It's possible to choose how we contribute.

My aim was to:

- *reveal* the impact of slavery
- *expose* the systems involved
- *suggest* some ways we need to approach this issue in the future.

The experiences of every person whose story is told in this book – **Olga, Pham, Matt, Andre, Riso, Igor, Zara, Zhang Li, Dung, Ly, Marios, Maria, Ling, Stephen, Elbina, Anna, Arfas, Mihaela, Sam, Sarah, Esther, Ruth, Roze, Priya, Nadia, Anatolyi's mum,** those from the **car wash** and the **caravan site** – all meet the definition of human trafficking and modern slavery. All their experiences share common themes. What they've endured meets the criteria under act, means, and purpose.

They were all exploited, all forced to do something against their will for the benefit of someone else. But each experience was different. Different motivations, vulnerabilities, and burdens were at play for each of them. Each was faced with choices that meant they were in a position that enabled another person to take advantage of them. Some of them may appear to have had more or better options available to them than others; for others, all options available to them were equally unattractive. For some, I don't know the full story and never will; I merely glimpsed a part of their journey and experience.

To attempt to address the problem of modern slavery, understanding individual experiences and the issues faced is key. We've examined definitions of slavery and the wide range of people it impacts. We've looked at the systems in place to support survivors and the disconnects between what individuals who've been trafficked need and what the systems of support are able to offer them.

Some of these disconnects need to be addressed by governments, by policy and legislation, by systems change, professional approaches, and the inputting of resources. But some of the disconnects lie within us and our underlying, unspoken biases toward an 'other'.

There is little point in proposing changes to a political system or a system of support if these changes are not accompanied by changes in the public perception of the issue and those impacted. Any system change remains a sticking plaster until we are able to truly accept the human condition for what it is, accepting that if we were in a similar situation, we may do the very same thing.

We have a culturally embedded bias that allows the hostile environment to continue, that allows people to be held indeterminately in a state of limbo, that sees people deported instead of supported. We make assumptions about people's motivations for wanting to work in the UK; we see them as people who will take what is rightfully ours. We have established systems that require people to evidence their experiences, evidence that isn't available or may be so traumatic that more damage is done during this process. Our bias sees us viewing young British men as perpetrators of crime instead of potential victims. We tell ourselves that providing an immediate crisis response to those in need is enough. We have given them a foundation from which we expect 'them' to start again. We have done our bit, played our part – now it is up to them. But have we truly done enough? Have we truly connected? Have we walked in their shoes?

Have we treated 'them' as we would want to be treated?

I don't think we are there yet.

But I do believe it can be different.

Individuals

When we look beyond issues, headlines, and labels, we can connect to lives like ours.

As individuals, we have a powerful part to play. It is not enough to place any blame solely at the feet of government and the laws of the land. We are all parts of a society that wants cheap, disposable consumables because we are predominantly cash-rich and time-poor.

Change on a global scale is overwhelming and can feel completely out of our control. There are no simple answers. The politicians in power represent us; the things we make a noise about are the things that find their ways into debates, policies, and legislation. We are not helpless; we put people in power and it is our job to keep them accountable. We can use this power to facilitate change, to raise the issues that are important to us, and to use our voices for those who are unable to.

We can start small, influence what we can, change what we can about our lives, and influence the lives of those around us.

Signs to spot

Physical appearance
- Show signs of physical or psychological abuse, look malnourished or unkempt, anxious/agitated, or appear withdrawn and neglected. They may have untreated injuries.

Isolation
- Rarely be allowed to travel on their own, seem under the control, influence of others, rarely interact or appear unfamiliar with their neighbourhood or where they work.
- Relationships which don't seem right – for example, a young teenager appearing to be the boyfriend/girlfriend of a much older adult.

Poor living conditions
- Be living in dirty, cramped or overcrowded accommodation, and/or living and working at the same address.

Restricted freedom of movement
- Have no identification documents, have few personal possessions and always wear the same clothes day in and day out. What clothes they do wear may not be suitable for their work.
- Have little opportunity to move freely and may have had their travel documents retained (e.g. passports).

Unusual travel times
- Be dropped off/collected for work on a regular basis either very early or late at night.
- Unusual travel arrangements – children being dropped off/ picked up in private cars/taxis at unusual times and in places where it isn't clear why they'd be there.

Reluctant to seek help
- Avoid eye contact, appear frightened or hesitant to talk to strangers and fear law enforcers for many reasons, such as not knowing who to trust or where to get help, fear of deportation, fear of violence to them or their family.

(Unseen 2021)

We can work out where our inner biases lie, challenge ourselves, work out what we think about people that are different to us, connect with them and their life stories, search for the similarities instead of the differences.

Ultimately, we need to accept that we benefit from the exploitation of others. This means that if we want to be part of the solution, we need to be willing to change. It is not as simple as donating some money to charity and letting someone else do the work on our behalf. We have to choose change.

Slavery is an issue we knowingly or otherwise are perpetuating with our day-to-day actions.

We are accountable for contributing to its success.

In Chapter 1, I outlined how we interact and intersect with slavery, on a day-to-day basis, on a global scale, and the fact that the items in our kitchen cupboards, the clothes in our wardrobes, and our technological devices are all likely to be inextricably linked to labour exploitation and/ or abuse in some shape or form. Someone, somewhere in the supply chain will not be being paid properly for what they are producing, for the work they are doing.

It is common sense when we look at the price we pay for things. We are often disconnected from the source of what we are purchasing and people that made it or harvested it for us.

Sometimes the children mining, the women making clothes, and the men picking fruit and vegetables seem far from our frames of reference – they are. But **Anna, Maria, Andre, Matthew, Stephen, Marios, Igor, Dung, Ly,** and the others bring this issue closer to home. They were washing cars, painting nails, moving drugs, and selling sex in towns and cities in the UK, not in a far-flung, distant country, right here. Some were British, some European, some legally allowed to live in the UK, some legally allowed to work and entitled to decent work conditions, minimum wages, and time off. None of them deserved what happened to them.

Modern slavery is happening in our cities, our towns, our villages – sometimes at the end of our road, right on our doorstep.

When I last checked, I had 37 slaves working for me. This, of course, is an approximation and comes from an online tool, 'The Slavery Footprint' (Fair Trade Fund 2011). Try it for yourself: https://slaveryfootprint.org. It is a resource that helps us check out where our lives may intersect with slavery based on what we purchase and consume. It takes you through each part of your family and your home and asks questions about the technology you use, the food you eat, the toiletries you buy, the products you use. It allows us to see the products that may have slavery in their supply chain. It is pretty safe to assume that most things we purchase will be linked to some form of exploitation; it is endemic in a global, capitalist system with our far-reaching, hard-to-regulate supply chains.

We need to take time to consider the consequences and the impact of our consumer, capitalist lifestyles. I don't think we actively wish to harm people with the things we choose to buy, but just as we increasingly think about the impact on the environment and reducing our carbon footprint, we also need to look at ways of understanding and actively reducing our slavery footprint.

When we learn about modern slavery, realise our own individual connections to it, when we allow ourselves to connect with it on a human-to-human level, the opportunity to change is possible, and change is compelling.

I was compelled to do something when I met **Anatolyi**. Sitting under that tree in Ukraine, I connected with trafficking and slavery. I don't have all the answers, I still have 37 slaves I am connected to in the things I buy. Even with all I know and all I have tried to practically change in the way I live my life, I am still inextricably linked to the exploitation of other human beings.

Professionals

As professionals and first responders working for organisations more likely to encounter people who are enslaved, the approach we take to potential victims and survivors can bring about change in its own right. As professionals, we too need to educate ourselves and others and connect with modern slavery as an issue in order to connect with the people it impacts.

Looking for and identifying survivors may present challenges with the other remits we have in our roles and functions, but the most impact we can sometimes have is to step back, to try and understand others, to understand their situations, to look between the lines of what they explicitly tell us and what they don't. When we take our blinkers off, we'll see beyond 'The Sex Worker', 'The Addict', 'The Migrant', 'The Illegal Worker', 'The Drug Runner', 'The Criminal', 'The Runaway' – and beyond how things seem at first glance. When we arm ourselves with awareness and knowledge, we'll know how we can better become part of the solution.

For professionals involved in multi-agency visits, we need to check our motivations for our involvement in such practices. As I outlined in Chapter 5, these visits do not always have the outcomes we seek. The ethical considerations of the ways we choose to intervene and the potential that this has to do more harm than good for those we are aiming to identify and support should be considered, making sure that we are aware of the intended and unintended consequences – the direct impact such activity may have, the impact it did have on **Olga, the Slovakian car-wash workers, those from the caravan site, Riso, Marios, Dung, Ly, Zhang Li,** and **Ling.**

We can become informed about the systems of support that are in place, what our roles within these are, what we can and can't do, what helps and what won't. We can ask for training when we need it and refresh our knowledge on our organisations' policies and protocols. We can become aware of our own (and our organisations') biases toward certain people in certain situations. We can ask ourselves some of those uncomfortable questions that start to make the unseen visible: are we part of the solution, or are we perpetuating disconnection and difference in our professional approaches?

Remembering to explain things to others as equals, engaging with them, being a person they can trust, that first point of contact that offers them a chink of light at the end of the tunnel, that allows them to believe that life could be different, is being a living, breathing part of the solution. Explaining options to others, however limited they are at present, sharing our knowledge and understanding of individual rights and entitlements, the support that may be on offer, and how to navigate the systems to get it makes us part of the solution.

The systems we work in tend to be flawed and hard to navigate, but we can still treat others as we'd wish to be treated. The approach we take when we interact with a potential victim or survivor will always present us with an opportunity to reconnect, rather than disconnect. We always have a choice in how we behave.

Governments and policy

There is no denying that the UK has made progress since the advent of the Modern Slavery Act, including attempts to ensure supply chain transparency and the appointment of the independent anti-slavery commissioner. Survivor care standards, policy reforms, the focus on consulting with survivor voices, commitments to longer-term support, increased funding for research and training have all improved. Yet we still have a complex web of interconnected systems to dismantle in order to, at a minimum, 'control' the issue of slavery. We can dismantle these systems, reviewing our policies and legislation, reflecting and learning about what has and hasn't worked, reconnecting with the things that drive, sustain, and enable exploitative practices and considering collaborative actions that may prevent them.

We drew a line in the sand in 2015 with the Modern Slavery Act; a wide-reaching commitment was made to tackle this heinous crime.

Yet are those who profit from trafficking in fact just taking advantage of the principles of the free market systems of supply and demand – entrepreneurial in their approach to providing a labour force to those who need it and offering the opportunity to those who 'want' it or have such limited options that they can't do anything except take it – rather than so-called heinous criminals? Do our systems, our approach to the issue, our laws provide the perfect environment for the continuation of slavery rather than facilitate its demise?

Slavery being a present reality raises other questions. Do our laws and policies allow for those for whom there are limited choices? Do we welcome them or view them with suspicion? How much of this is determined by those in power and the rhetoric they share via the policies they implement? How much is determined by media influence? How many of our opinions are formed from political bias?

Modern slavery discourse frequently references 'coercion' – but if exchanges are not voluntary, if those involved have no other viable choices or options, could it also be viewed as extortion? Arguably, those coercing will be in receipt of financial benefits including but not limited to 'debts' 'incurred' by individuals towards their travel, accommodation, and visa (usually with a considerable amount added on to the figure), the payment for their services and labour once working that bypasses them, and then the ongoing debt (often unclear how accrued or calculated) that the individual is forced to pay back.

Modern slavery is a blatant, brash, global expression of injustice and inequality. It reveals (or hides in plain sight) and disconnects the haves and the have-nots, those with power and those with none.

Governments must ensure that systems improve in terms of holding businesses to account, ensuring supply chains are effectively tracked, offering safety and worker protections, allowing safe and legal routes for decent work, identifying survivors, understanding what individuals need, and providing appropriate pathways to appropriate support.

The support mechanisms and policies in place to support **Stephen**, **Anna**, **Nadia**, **Priya**, **Roze**, and **Arfas** may seem fit for purpose on paper, but it is clear that they don't always work in practice as intended.

Governments and policy makers can ensure that they understand the obstacles that prevent individuals from accessing the systems they need in order to gain support. Systems can be reflective and can be built on learned experience which places supporting survivors at the centre of delivery. Wider-reaching prevention strategies, foreign policy, migration policy, trade deals, expectations and standards for business, and workers' rights are all policy areas with the potential to connect and reconnect with features of slavery and those affected by it. It would be a mistake to continue to view modern slavery in isolation from these.

The anti-slavery sector has called for a range of changes to policy and law in the UK, with domestic laws expanded and elements of European law and directives more fully included in our response to modern slavery and those impacted. The main calls for change include survivors (upon being granted a conclusive grounds decision) being given access to longer-term support, regardless of nationality or whether or not they can/will assist with police enquiries.

With longer-term support would come access to welfare benefits and the right to work. Longer-term support and access to the labour market give survivors viable alternatives, provide choice, and offer clear pathways away from their experiences of exploitation.

Working out how survivors access the labour force, housing, and community support will also empower individuals affected and enable them to connect in ways that they choose.

We also need to be cognisant of the current unknown impact that Brexit may have on the modern slavery agenda and directly on survivors. There may be gaps in the workforce that need filling, restrictions on entry into the UK, fewer routes to access employment visas, less freedom of movement, and fewer protections on offer once identified as a potential victim. This may feed the inequality gap, increasing the potential for exploitative practices and modern slavery, as well as reducing the remedies and support available to those impacted.

It is within the government's power to address the disconnects in the system, to be part of the solution. Changes in policy and legislation would prevent survivors being held in limbo, provide meaningful support with clear pathways into future opportunities and access to the labour market, and offer routes, options, and choice for people as they journey towards being self-sustaining.

Government can be a primary driver behind helping the UK to change the rhetoric of the hostile environment, to view people as equal and as valuable.

To change the systems that mean that, once free from a situation of modern slavery, they are truly free.

Support systems

The systems of support we have in place try to quantify how much time and how much support an individual will need to reach independence, to be back to a position of thriving. What if the individual never started from a place of thriving?

What the system doesn't do is give all those identified as trafficked the prerequisite access to the routes in order to do this – we want people to thrive, but only the people we choose and allow to.

Where our responsibility towards those who have been exploited, entrapped, enslaved begins and ends is a contentious topic. Are we willing to accept that for some, no matter how much support, finance, and care we put in, their experiences may have broken them to beyond anything we can 'do', any help or support we can offer? But that, for others, when given the choices, opportunities, and the right support to access these, they will start to see all that is available. What this doesn't mean is that we don't offer the choices to all, but that we accept that for some they may not be viable options at the time we are able to offer them.

How can we get to a place that means we are able to view each other as individuals, with unique and different life paths? That, like **Andre**, wanting to get up and get back into employment may be what some people need and want to do, but for others working out how to process what has happened and get out of bed each morning may be all they can manage. Some don't want or need support, like those working at the **car wash** and those who were found at the **caravan site**, but they do want a job and they want to have rights and be protected within their workplace. Some will want different things at different times.

What everybody needs is viable alternatives, better choices.

The reality is that they are no different to us – people, people who have experienced things we hope we never have to, who have had to make impossible choices when facing impossible situations, but people who have the same hopes, dreams, ambitions, pains, fears, and feelings as we all do.

To truly tackle slavery, we need to challenge the deeply embedded cultural and systems bias that allows for a hostile environment, a culture of disbelief, and the notion that it is 'better than what they would have had at home'. Although it may be easier to think of those exploited and enslaved as faceless and far away, they are anything but. **Matthew, Roze, Olga, Stephen** (to name a few) are real people, with real dreams, hopes, and ambitions; they are resilient and determined people we can relate to.

The culturally prevalent hostile environment in the UK means it's easy to forget about the individual experience, the person. It also means that to support someone properly, we are already fighting against toxic but common narratives of 'You are not welcome', 'It's your own fault', 'You are just playing the system' – narratives that it appears have become increasingly acceptable to voice publicly over the last few years, since the EU Referendum. I am not arguing that every person you have met in this book hasn't had choice. I am proposing that we need to understand the choices they made from the position they were in. For most of those I have worked with, their choices were made from a range of unappealing, sometimes unsafe, choices. At the time, the choice they made appeared the least bad. Until we challenge tendencies to scapegoat, we won't be able to support those who have experienced exploitation in the way they need us to.

To effectively support someone, we need to first find them, then believe them, then offer them safety, security, and stability. We need to be prepared for system change across a range of policies, legislation, and approaches: a from-the-bottom-up and from-the-top-down approach which intersects wherever slavery is found.

What choices can we make when none are good?

The choices people face can be impossible. The choice to trust someone you have just met, the choice to believe the job exists and that everything will be OK, the choice to snitch on those who made you carry those drugs and risk the repercussions to you and your family, the choice not to snitch and potentially serve a prison sentence, the choice to leave the situation knowing the debt you owe may be recalled from a family member, the choice to leave knowing you may be deported, returned home, re-trafficked.

I am not sure these really are choices that any of us would ever want to have to make. Nor are they choices that have the possibility of a good outcome. They are all equally poor, and in the same position, I think we would all consider doing the same.

If we walked in others' shoes, our options limited, our support networks non-existent, if the systems designed to support and help us move away from our exploitation didn't fully comprehend what it was we were facing, we would be likely to go it alone and to make the same choices.

The decisions I've witnessed people making, while desperately sad, are completely understandable.

Reconnecting with what people need as individuals will improve outcomes for survivors of modern slavery across the board. We must learn from survivors and those with lived experiences, to understand the factors and events that led them to needing support and what it is they'll need to go forward and thrive.

Modern slavery raises hard questions of ethics, justice, equality, and law. Is it morally and legally acceptable that people offer opportunities to work, even if these opportunities are poor, to those with no other options? Is it acceptable when these 'opportunities' don't quite match what was advertised? Is it right that if someone seeks support and wants to leave their situation, they may be subject to immigration policies or seen as a criminal? What, if anything, should the law do about this? What, if anything, can citizens do about this?

We cerebrally appreciate that what has happened to **Anna, Matthew, Igor, Arfas, Riso,** and the others is appalling. We may change our buying habits, think more carefully about where we shop, engage with people in a more meaningful way, but this is where we stop. We pass responsibility (rightly so) to the powers that be to make the necessary decisions about an individual's life and we listen to the anti-migrant rhetoric and believe that someone has come to the UK to take advantage of what we can offer. I am not sure I see that in the stories shared here.

The issues are bigger than modern slavery. They are woven into the fabric of our society, intertwined with the way we view people and what we deem them to be worth.

We have to accept that we are unable to do anything practically to change the situations of exploitation people have experienced. We can't change the past but we can learn from the experiences people have faced and provide a system that, wherever possible, provides people with more options, better choices, and a range of alternatives.

CHAPTER 12

Hearing from Those Who Know

Every country wants responsible citizens. We need to know where our place is.

(PRIYA 2020)

Roze, **Stephen**, **Nadia**, *and* **Priya** *all have clear ideas about what needed to change. With lived experience of the systems of support, of living in safe houses, and navigating the processes, they were impacted when policies and people got it right or got it wrong.*

Stephen wants to see more agencies being able to refer to the NRM. In his experience, the fact the agency that became aware of his situation couldn't refer him into support immediately meant he was stuck in his situation for longer than he needed to be.

It is his suggestion that more checks might be carried out on supported accommodation and assessments to make sure the people living there don't pose a threat or risk to those moving in. From his perspective, the checks were insufficient. Following release from prison, instead of being able to restart and rebuild his life, he was exposed to being exploited.

In relation to moving on from support, Stephen proposed that more options needed to be specifically available for people that had been trafficked. He reflects that even though there is a housing crisis, more thought is needed as to how people move on:

'*Even if it's just sheltered accommodation, even it's just supported living, [a place they can go] after if they are not going home. It's just hard for everyone, it's like unbelievable.*'

He proposed that regulations in relation to renting and private landlords needed to be looked at, suggesting that '*putting more rent down instead of needing a guarantor*' could be considered and would support people to transition out of support.

His feeling was that governments need to do more for people and need to consider the timeframes that individuals are allowed to remain in support for in practical terms, as well as how they are enabled and helped to move on from support.

'*More care [is] needed over people who have been through this… You can have too much help and do nothing for yourself, too little help and do everything for yourself, but at the moment everything is going through my head – if I can't stay here I have a limited time to find somewhere and move out to.*'

Nadia is a British woman in her early 30s. She had experienced exploitation at the hands of her partner for criminal activities relating to drugs and sexual exploitation. Nadia's thoughts mirror Stephen's in that she feels her time in the NRM wasn't long enough. She proposes that six months in support would be good and that she felt the council needed to step in at the end of the support period.

'*Being put in temporary accommodation is hard. You need something that is permanent, something that is yours.*'

When I met Nadia, she had moved out of the safe house two and a half years previously. Her support had continued, via Unseen's outreach service, but this support had also recently ended. She had received compensation for what had happened to her, was back in touch with family and her children, in a new relationship, working, and participating in ongoing counselling.

She was complimentary about the support she had received via the NRM and the safe house, and about the approach the police took in her case. She knew that previous officers had viewed her as someone involved in drug supply and that they viewed her and her offences rather than seeing what was actually happening, but Nadia described meeting one officer who saw what was happening and got her out of her situation.

> 'I felt safe…not a policewoman, a woman, she was empathic…I am grateful and thankful. In some ways she saved my life. I know it sounds crazy, but she did. Because I would have either been dead or in prison but I got a second chance.'

Nadia articulated that she had already started again at the refuge (safe house), and the move-on stage, if not managed well, felt like yet another move, another upheaval at a time when people might risk going back to what they know. In her words:

> 'We need permanency.
>   [A place that] is mine; no one can take it away.
>   Permanent
>   You have something,
>   It may only be a bed sit, but it is yours.
>   Your palace
>   Your [place to] feel safe.'

Nadia and Stephen were not alone in voicing concerns about the lack of clarity for those experiencing the system, of not knowing how long decisions would take to come through and what the next steps would be, and what options they might have at each stage.

Priya and **Roze** talked about what it was like waiting for the outcome of NRM and asylum decisions. Both shared the need for clarity on timeframes and processes. Throughout all my experiences and interactions with potential victims and survivors and those that support them, time and time again the notion of clarity, of needing to know what is happening and when, comes up.

As Priya puts it:

'[It would be] better if they tell you at the start this will take two years, three years, or ten or eleven years. Mentally you will be prepared at the start – come with a lot of trauma, a lot of depression, a small thing is a big thing for us. Waiting, waiting, waiting... I entered with 45 days in my head. It is OK, I can wait and prepare. But 9–10 months and no decision, they have not replied. This is very frustrating.'

Priya has proposed a solution. She thinks the system would be better if there was no specific timeframe put on the NRM, if the authorities stated 'time duration is dependent on your case'. She feels this will mean people are able to prepare better, manage their expectations, and prepare for the emotional toll. She asks for transparency about how the process will work and for the systems and those working within them to avoid setting up false hope that in a set time period a decision will be made.

A common theme from those I spoke to about the system of support was the notion of being believed. **Nadia** expressed how important it was for her to be believed and to have been noticed by the officer who offered her a way out of her situation, as well as the impact of a positive outcome from the NRM process: '*Journey of support that helped discover self... Acknowledged me – the system believed me.*' This had not always been the case for Nadia, who described multiple arrests and interactions with the police when she had not been believed or considered to be a victim.

It is clear how hard it is to evidence what has happened to you, and how the emphasis is placed on a requirement for this. Evidence may not actually be available. For Nadia, the person who exploited her didn't face charges and she knows he is still out there, '*doing what he did to me [to others]*'. She knows the police and other agencies tried to take the case forward but that the evidence to do so wasn't secured.

Priya challenges how the system in the UK relies on evidence, and states that when someone is in survival mode, they are not forward planning or thinking in advance what they should be recording or making sure they have evidence of.

'We escape, I don't think, OK, tomorrow I will leave my husband and then I will go to UK and then I will make asylum claim, I don't think, oh OK, my husband has slapped me, let me make a video – this is impossible for a person, you are just trying to survive. There is no evidence. This is frustrating to me. It is not possible to collect evidence and this and this...you are just scared for your life. [This evidence needed] is annoying. I can't prove it, not OK for the Home Office to ask about these things.'

The piece of paper that confirms a conclusive grounds decision is important to individuals, even when it may not give access to ongoing support, the right to work, or an automatic right to stay in the UK. It means that they have been heard, that they have been believed. The processes currently in place appear to start from a position of not believing survivors and work back from there, when what's needed to avoid people continuing to be exploited is the opposite.

Priya would also like to see people in the NRM (who are not from the UK) given the right to work. She described to me how she thought this could work, suggesting that people shouldn't automatically be given money by the government if they were able to contribute. Although this may not be for everyone, Priya was surprised by what she received each week from being in support and expressed that she would be happy to see a system in which she would be able to contribute via work or volunteering – almost as a quid pro quo mechanism. She certainly was not someone who agreed with playing the system; she was grateful for what she was receiving but wanted to also be given the opportunity to give back. This is far from the portrayal we are often given of those who come to the UK.

'What we take from the government, if we earn ourselves we will not be a burden on the government. Happy to earn the money... Self-respect, OK I can do, at the moment, at this time, we are paralysed [with no access to work and nothing to do]. [With work] your mind is occupied.'

She was realistic that her trauma meant she couldn't work full-time but that her previous education (masters level and a teaching degree) meant that she had skills that she wanted to use. She linked being able to use her skills and experience to restoring her dignity and self-respect, things she described as having been taken from her during her exploitation.

Roze told me how tiring it was to wait for four years and still not be believed. All she wants is clarity on her situation so that she can '*start to make plans and build a life for her and her child*'.

For all the people who wanted to share their thoughts with me on the system and what they would like to see change, the underlying principle was the need and desire for connection.

Stephen, **Roze**, **Nadia**, and **Priya** all wanted to:

- be believed
- have their story heard
- know where they fit
- feel safe
- know what was next
- contribute
- have the opportunity to work
- plan and prepare themselves for the next steps
- move forwards with their lives.

We need to ensure the systems in place and those who are involved in them offer this clarity for survivors; that they are treated as adults, their experiences heard, and alternative, viable options presented. Even if the only realistic option in the current systems of support is for someone to consider returning home, we should accept this reality and not offer false hope or promises we can't fulfil.

Rather than being overwhelmed by its enormity or frozen by our perceived powerlessness, the present reality of modern slavery just needs us to do what we can. As a friend of mine once told me, you just need to build the wall in front of you one brick at a time. We need to take the issue on board, appreciate the enormity of it, but not become paralysed by it – we all have a role to play in tackling it. It is like the starfish story. A young boy was once walking along a beach that was littered with starfish.

One by one, he started picking them up and throwing them back into the ocean, knowing they wouldn't survive until the tide came back in. A man was walking along the beach and stopped to ask the young boy why he was bothering to throw them back when there were so many of them. The boy responded, 'Well, I am making a difference for this one, and this one and this one...'

I do not know how things worked out for **Marios**, **Dung**, **Ly**, **Ling**, **Zhang Li**, **Olga**, or those who returned to the **car wash** and the **caravan site**. I don't know if they stayed in their situations, if they were able to find a way to leave them, if they were found and deported, found and arrested, found and supported. What I do know is that when I met them, what I and what the system was able to offer them, for a whole variety of reasons, some of which I have alluded to and some of which I will have been completely unaware of, meant that they couldn't leave in that moment. I am unaware of what has happened to **Matt** and **Sam** and whether they ended up serving prison sentences. I don't know what happened to all those who were referred to support – **Igor**, **Arfas**, **Mihaela**, and **Riso** – or if they had positive outcomes. I do know that **Elbina**, **Zara**, **Priya**, and **Roze** are all still waiting for decisions on their cases, prevented from moving forwards with their lives.

Media portrayals of desperate individuals leaving desperate situations behind them will tell us that everyone arriving on those dinghies are coming to take what's 'ours'. What if, instead of viewing people as a threat, we just met them where they were at, offered them help and support in their time of need?

When we connect, we are able to see beyond the labels people have been assigned. We are able to start seeing people as equal. We are able to work out how to establish connections. We are able to allow room for choice, for empowerment, and for people to discover their own agency. We are able to create simple, equitable, understandable, and accessible pathways, designed and developed with all involved in the process.

We are able to lower the hurdles people face.

We are able to learn from survivors and those with lived experience:

'I want to be part of society.' (Roze 2020)

Closing Thoughts

No man should judge unless he asks himself in absolute
honesty whether in a similar situation he might not have
done the same.
(VIKTOR FRANKL 2006, P.55)

The systems at play in our society rank people, attribute their value and
their worth to what they have achieved, how much they earn, how well
known they are in their sector, what they take and what they give. Are
they a net contributor or a net drain? Our opinion of someone changes
based on what we think we know about people. We judge, sometimes
without having the full picture.

We have opinions on people who claim benefits, on people who arrive
in dinghies or under lorries, on people who we think should have stayed
in Calais, on people who work in the sex industry, on young black men
who are caught with drugs on them. We all make assumptions.

It is the normal way of things and it bleeds into all we do.

Those who are on benefits, who have arrived in the UK clandestinely,
who work in the sex industry, who are arrested for moving drugs across
the country also have their own assumptions about what their available
options are, about what their journeys will bring, and hope that it will
offer them something different. They hope that life may be different,
that the arduous journey will have been worth it, that safety and choice

will be available. Alongside that hope will be elements of fear that they won't be believed, that they will be arrested again, that they will be left behind, and that what they are really going through won't be seen or understood. People hope that their burdens may be lifted. They place trust in the systems in place to help them.

Those identified as survivors of slavery are initially viewed as people needing help and support – rightfully so in some cases and if this is what they choose.

If they decline help, our approach to them often changes – they face potential deportation, arrest, or being left in the situations they were identified in. People move from potential victim to potential perpetrator in a matter of moments; it is the way the system is designed. Black and white, in or out.

What begins as a compassionate response, a response to the need seen, changes if the individual in question doesn't respond in the way we deem a 'victim' would or should.

As accounts are given to different agencies, at different times, as details change, as traumatic processes trigger, and as the impact of revealing all that has happened to them dawns on a survivor and they decide to not say any more, the system and those working within it become suspicious. Within these suspicions, what we are really questioning is whether or not we believe that this individual really deserves the help we are in a position to give. Do they fall into the deserving category or the undeserving category?

Human nature means we will use things that are not necessarily fair or accurate in our approach to determining if someone is deserving or not. Things like how a survivor presents and whether they look and act as if they are a victim, as if they are vulnerable, whether they answer questions posed or shut down and appear to ignore the person trying to engage with them, whether they seem feisty or demanding or ungrateful for what is on offer – these and many more assumptions we make will impact our abilities to offer what someone needs and will prevent connections from being formed.

I am not proposing that these things are conscious decisions that professionals make, but I am calling out the kinds of behaviours that inevitably feed into our decisions on whether or not we believe someone is a survivor or not and what they should and shouldn't be able to access. I am also aware that preventing connections from being formed is a way that people protect themselves, maintain professional boundaries, and are able to continue doing jobs in which they see and hear about some of the worst parts of humanity – but I do wonder what would happen if we began to remove the barriers we have put up and started to be real with each other.

We don't see people with the potential to be net contributors; we only see net drains.

I have often wondered about what could be different in the system, and one thing I always come back to is what if something else could be offered at that moment of identification. There are times I know that if I had been able to offer someone alternative decent work, they would have taken it. They didn't want the NRM, safe-house support, a support worker, or to work with the police on prosecuting a case. They wanted and needed to earn money; it was what they wanted to do initially – it was a catalyst for accepting the offer of work. We all need purpose and meaning. For many of us work provides this – it provides our contribution to society.

This would not work for everyone and there are times that I know that safe houses and support also offer lifelines that others need.

But what if we could offer multiple lifelines, based on what an individual needs?

The International Labour Organization (2021) summarises 'decent work' to mean taking account of the aspirations of people in their working lives:

> It involves opportunities for work that is productive and delivers a fair income, security in the workplace and social protection for families, better prospects for personal development and social integration, freedom for people to express their concerns, organize and participate

in the decisions that affect their lives and equality of opportunity and treatment for all women and men.

I like this. It could certainly provide a foundation for how we approach not just survivors of trafficking but our whole work force.

Standing on a car-wash forecourt being told that no support was needed – but if there were other options available for work and somewhere to live, this would be considered – highlights what I think I and many others already know: we haven't quite got what we are offering right yet, for all survivors along the far-reaching spectrum of slavery.

Offering the thing that the individual needs first up, creating that connection with them, beginning that relationship of trust, putting down that first marker of 'I see you and I hear you' may just allow for everything else that is needed to be worked out later.

With decent work opportunities comes empowerment and the chance to feel stable. From stability comes choice, and for some this may include choosing to accept support and help, at a time and in a way that they deem appropriate for them.

This is, of course, overly simplified and would have to be considered alongside a raft of other things, but it would be a start. What if we could work on giving people what it was they were looking for in the first place?

A sense of belonging the teenager so desperately wants or the fact that by earning money they can contribute to the household income. The opportunity presented of travel and working abroad that feels like it may only come around once in a lifetime. A journey taken to try to secure employment and income when there is no work at home.

These may be crass and stereotypical examples, but they help me make the point. We are all looking for something, we all want to be part of something, to protect those who mean something to us, to provide, and we all have hopes and dreams. What if the system could help survivors realise some of these? What if our systems provided pathways for them to become net contributors, valued by our society, the roles they perform seen as important and them seen as equal?

What if survivors could come forward and express what was happening of their own free will, in their own time, and be part of the process to determine what happens next for them? What if the fear of deportation, of penalty, of having no rights, of being arrested was removed?

For some survivors this will not be possible. Their situation of exploitation means they are isolated, unaware of their rights and entitlements, unable to leave their situation – these individuals arguably need an external intervention.

The support offered, from the moment of identification, has to take into account these differences and more.

We forget that they were people before they were trafficked and exploited; we forget that this was done to them, that burdens they were carrying meant someone saw an opportunity to use them, to make money from them.

What I have learned and am still learning is that we often don't know everything, we don't share all of ourselves with all people, we want to be able to wear different masks in different situations and with different people. Yet the system to support identified survivors of slavery expects them to share everything, in a set timeframe, if what they are saying is to be believed. We must be able to do better. To connect differently.

Society ranks people based on our attributes, what we can and can't have access to, what we deserve and what we don't deserve.

We categorise people – we tell ourselves that this is based on practically helping people to access appropriate support and on having finite resources.

We are scared of the unknown, scared of people who are different to us, scared of the 'other', and this fear seeps into the systems we develop and create to maintain distance, a safe separation so that those who are different can't encroach too much on what we have.

We assign them a label, we agree what that label allows access to – what services, what support. But, we forget, I think, the biggest label, the one we all share, the one we can all relate and connect to – we are all human. We all know what it means to laugh, to cry, to be hurt, to do the hurting. We will have all experienced pain, suffering, and loss in some way, shape, or form. This is not intended to oversimplify the issues being faced nor does it intend to rank people's experiences as comparable or similar, but it intends to remind us of, regardless of what has happened to us, what choices or lack of choices we have had, that we are inextricably linked, connected to other humans.

In my own mind, I can easily list those people I feel in no way, shape, or form able to connect to – people who seem fundamentally different to me in their approaches to life, their politics, their life experiences, who are seemingly just incomparable. What if, instead of making it about them and how different they are to me, I looked at the points where I can see similarity? I admit, for some people, I will have to dig deep to find commonality and this will require patience and a change of attitude on my part. I need to reflect that I have made assumptions, which may on occasion be accurate, but more often are not. I need to accept that I've come to these assumptions based on the minute amount of information I think I have about them. I haven't walked in their shoes. I haven't tried to understand the situation from their point of view.

As hard as this can be to do, when we do it, we do find out what we share. There is a dawning of realisation that the people we think are different to us are maybe not so different after all.

And the really tricky thing with this journey of discovery is that once we realise we are not so different, we start to question why we, why our politics, our legislation, our systems, our global economy, treat people so differently.

Why do we value some people more than others?

I think our whole system is based on stereotypes and assumptions. Stereotypes come from somewhere and they can assist how systems are designed, but they are only useful if the systems at play also allow for the outliers, the people who don't fit the stereotypes, and if they allow for development and change. As we learn more about ourselves and about others, we discover that the system favours some and disadvantages others.

Is it the systems at play that direct our assumptions about the values of others, or is it our opinion of others that creates the systems that proliferate disadvantage? One or the other, a combination of both, neither?

We are willing to share some of what we have, some of our resources, but not all of them – there has to be a limit, a cut-off, a point at which we can say we have done all we can, right? We have offered what is reasonably expected, we have played our part – we can do no more.

Civil society and political systems help to maintain the divide between us as individuals.

The labels we give ourselves or the labels we are assigned by others determine how we are viewed by professionals, by peers, and by society generally. Labels also impact how we view ourselves, what we come to believe of ourselves, and what we come to believe we are worth.

We have to change the narrative for individuals labelled as trafficked, survivors of modern slavery. We have to come alongside survivors to allow them this opportunity themselves.

Although the label of victim or survivor may initially be useful to access support services, it should not be where the story ends for people, or if it does end here, it is because this is what that individual has chosen, for themselves.

We are all changing, the whole time. We are all learning to cope, we are all learning to navigate an ever-changing world and our place within it. We are no different – we are humans trying to make sense of what has happened, what we need to do to survive our present, and what we dream and hope our future will look like.

If we continue to view people differently, if we continue to assign labels, if we continue to not connect, we will continue the current status quo – the haves, the have-nots, the believed, the not-believed, the deserving, the undeserving. We end up with arbitrary access to arbitrary services that individuals have not been able to decide for themselves, designed by people who have no lived experience, no understanding of the push and pull factors, the situations, and the origins that meant people ended up exploited, taken advantage of, promised the world only to be disappointed and hurt.

We contribute to and we facilitate the accepted norms of how people are treated, because we as civil society don't connect with people as equal. It is individuals who become politicians, members of law enforcement, staff our judiciary, our frontline support teams. If these biases exist in us, they are carried with us into our professional lives and into the systems we develop and instigate.

We aim to offer help but is it helpful?

Some of the people I've met have suffered more horrific ordeals than I can ever imagine, some have made choices that on the surface I would question, some have taken the only option they believed was available to them.

Every one of them carried with them the impact and the truths of their experiences, and these deserved to be heard, told by the individual they belong to, in a way they are happy to share them, and at a time that feels right to them.

The narrative of a victim ends when an individual decides it should. The labels assigned are ripped off and this is a cause for celebration. Celebrated because they are in control of the process of redefining themselves. We – as society, as professionals, as people – may be able to play a supporting role in their experience, but it is a supporting role. We should never play starring roles – we need to come alongside at the right moment, in the right way, to enable empowerment and connect with others as equals.

Acknowledgements

To those of you whose names I have not remembered, I do remember you, the places we met, your situations, your stories, and the look in your eyes, I hope this is enough. I think the loss of these names was an unconscious way for me to protect myself in some little way from the horrors you divulged and from what you shared of your experiences. I realise that sentence has me and my protection in the middle of it, and the irony is at the time it is most likely that it was you who needed protection. For this I am sorry.

I find some comfort in the fact that often your real name, the one given to you at birth, the one that you connect with, that is a part of you, would not be the name you had given me. I am aware that people give themselves names, labels if you will, that they can associate with certain parts of their life, being, and existence, and other labels and names that remain, for them, protected. We all wear masks that we chop and change, use and replace as the situation demands. Why should you have trusted the person who said they were there to help you? What gave me the right to expect you to share that part of yourself with me? Although your name may be missing from my memory, I hope I do you, your memory, and our interaction justice through the writing of this book. It is important that we educate people and expose what is going on behind closed doors, helping people to see what they are either unaware of or unwilling and unable to engage with. My hope is that by sharing some of my experiences of the issues, we can stop this happening to people in the future.

The impact you have had on me has been profound. To all those I have met, I offer my thanks – thank you for the connection. Even if it was the briefest of moments, thank you for taking the time, for sharing part of yourself. I hope you also felt that I shared part of me. Thank you for giving me your time and for voicing your opinions and thoughts on what needs to change in the systems that held you in situations of exploitation and then didn't offer you what you needed once this was behind you.

I am grateful to all those who have given of their time to help me explore how different people, professions, and systems interact with, support, and, in some cases, conspire against those who need supporting. They will not find their names in this book, nor will they find transcripts of their interviews and the time we spent together as I pulled together ideas, themes, and the chapters of this book. However, each and every one of them – and they know who they are – has contributed, and without them this would not have been possible. Every conversation I have had in the process of preparing for writing this book has shown me the complexity and interconnectedness of the issue of modern slavery. The passion, dedication, and tenacity of those who work on the frontline and interact with those who have experienced exploitation, trafficking, and slavery are inspirational and undeniable. The work that goes on behind the scenes, the extra hours put in, and the number of people who go above and beyond to ensure individuals are supported, advocated for, and given access to the help they need and deserve are often unseen.

References

African Commission on Human and Peoples' Rights (1981) *African Charter on Human and Peoples' Rights* (Chapter I: Human and Peoples' Rights). Accessed on 21/06/2021 at www.achpr.org/legalinstruments/detail?id=49

Anti-Trafficking Monitoring Group (2016) *Class Acts? Examining Modern Slavery Legislation across the UK*. Accessed on 25/03/2021 at www.antislavery.org/wp-content/uploads/2017/01/atmg_class_acts_report_web_final.pdf

Asylum and Immigration (Treatment of Claimants) Act (2004). London: HMSO.

BBC News (2016) 'Modern slavery: Theresa May vows to defeat "evil"'. Online, 31 July 2016. Accessed on 25/03/2021 at www.bbc.co.uk/news/uk-36934853

Bhoola, U. (2018) *Legislating against Modern Slavery, Human Trafficking and Forced Labour*. Commonwealth Parliamentary Association UK. Accessed on 25/03/2021 at www.uk-cpa.org/media/2375/e-handbook-legislating-against-modern-slavery-human-trafficking-and-forced-labour.pdf

Brown, B. (2020) 'Unlocking us: On being heard and being seen.' Podcast, 23 March 2020. Accessed on 25/03/2021 at https://brenebrown.com/unlockingus/?pg=4

Children's Act (1989). London: HMSO.

Cooper, C., Hesketh, O., Ellis, N., and Fair, A. (2017) *A Typology of Modern Slavery Offences in the UK*. London: Home Office. Accessed on 25/03/2021 at https://assets.publishing.service.gov.uk/government/uploads/system/uploads/attachment_data/file/652652/typology-modern-slavery-offences-horr93.pdf

Coroners and Justice Act (2009). London: HMSO.

Crown Prosecution Service (2020) 'Human trafficking, smuggling and slavery.' Updated 30 April 2020. Accessed on 25/03/2021 at www.cps.gov.uk/legal/h_to_k/human_trafficking_and_smuggling/#a20

Council of Europe (1950) *European Convention on Human Rights*. Strasbourg: European Court of Human Rights. Accessed on 25/03/2021 at www.echr.coe.int/Documents/Convention_ENG.pdf

Council of Europe (2005) *Council of Europe Convention on Action against Trafficking in Human Beings*. Warsaw: COE. Accessed on 25/03/2021 at https://ec.europa.eu/anti-trafficking/legislation-and-case-law-international-legislation-council-europe/council-europe-convention-action_en

Dias, D. (2017) *The Ten Types of Human: Who We Are and Who We Can Be*. London: Penguin.

Donoghue Solicitors (2021) 'Warrant definition.' Accessed on 20/05/2021 at www.donoghue-solicitors.co.uk/actions-against-the-police/police-warrant-claims/warrant-definition

European Parliament (2021) 'Fact sheets on the European Union: The European Economic Area (EEA), Switzerland and the North.' Accessed on 20/05/2021 at www.europarl.europa.eu/factsheets/en/sheet/169/the-european-economic-area-eea-switzerland-and-the-north

Fair Trade Fund Incorporated (2011) 'How many slaves work for you?' Accessed on 25/03/2021 at https://slaveryfootprint.org

Frankl, V.E. (2006) *Man's Search for Meaning*. Boston, MA: Beacon Press.

Free Movement (2019) 'What is the difference between refugee status and humanitarian protection?' Accessed on 20/05/2021 at www.freemovement.org.uk/what-is-the-difference-between-refugee-status-and-humanitarian-protection/#:~:text=An%20asylum%20seeker%20who%20does,from%20the%20EU%20Qualification%20Directive

Gallagher, A.T. (2010) *The International Law of Human Trafficking*. Cambridge: Cambridge University Press.

Gentleman, A. (2020) 'Essex lorry deaths: 39 Vietnamese migrants suffocated in container, court hears.' *The Guardian*, 7 October 2020. Accessed on 19/04/2021 at www.theguardian.com/uk-news/2020/oct/07/essex-lorry-deaths-39-vietnamese-migrants-suffocated-in-container-court-hears

GOV.UK (2021) 'Countries in the EU and EEA.' Accessed on 20/05/2021 at www.gov.uk/eu-eea

HM Government (2018) *Serious Violence Strategy*. Accessed on 21/07/2021 at https://assets.publishing.service.gov.uk/government/uploads/system/uploads/attachment_data/file/698009/serious-violence-strategy.pdf

HM Government (2020) *2020 UK Annual Report on Modern Slavery*. Accessed on 22/07/2021 at https://assets.publishing.service.gov.uk/government/uploads/system/uploads/attachment_data/file/927111/FINAL-_2020_Modern_Slavery_Report_14-10-20.pdf

HMSO (2015) *Explanatory Notes*, Modern Slavery Act 2015, Chapter 30. Accessed on 23/06/2021 at www.legislation.gov.uk/ukpga/2015/30/pdfs/ukpgaen_20150030_en.pdf

Home Office (2017) *A Home Office Guide to Living in Asylum Accommodation*. London: UK Visas and Immigration. Accessed on 25/03/2021 at https://assets.publishing.service.gov.uk/government/uploads/system/uploads/attachment_data/file/821324/Pack_A_-_English_-_Web.pdf

Home Office (2020) 'Discretionary leave considerations for victims of modern slavery.' Accessed on 25/03/2021 at https://assets.publishing.service.gov.uk/government/uploads/system/uploads/attachment_data/file/941844/dl-for-victims-of-modern-slavery-v4.0ext.pdf

Home Office (2021) *Modern Slavery: Statutory Guidance for England and Wales (under s49 of Modern Slavery Act 2015) and Non-Statutory Guidance for Scotland and Northern Ireland*. Accessed on 25/03/2021 at https://assets.publishing.service.gov.uk/government/uploads/system/uploads/attachment_data/file/974794/March_2021_-_Modern_Slavery_Statutory_Guidance__EW__Non-Statutory_Guidance__SNI__v2.1_.pdf

Hope and Homes for Children (2019) 'Dismantling Ukraine's orphanage-based care system: A challenging national reform.' 31 May 2019. Accessed on 25/03/2021 at www.hopeandhomes.org/blog-article/dismantling-ukraines-orphanage-based-care-system-a-challenging-national-reform

Human Rights Act (1998). London: HMSO.

Human Trafficking and Exploitation (Criminal Justice and Support for Victims) Act (Northern Ireland) (2015). London: HMSO.

Human Trafficking and Exploitation (Scotland) Act (2015). London: HMSO.

Human Trafficking Foundation (2015) *Trafficking Survivor Care Standards.* Accessed on 25/03/2021 at www.antislaverycommissioner.co.uk/media/1067/ trafficking-survivor-care-standards-2015.pdf

Humphrey, H. (1976) 'Senator Humphrey's address to Democratic National Convention' (New York City), 13 July 1976. Accessed on 25/03/2021 at www2.mnhs.org/library/findaids/00442/pdfa/00442-04021.pdf

IHH Humanitarian Relief Foundation (2014) *Report on World's Orphans.* Turkey: IHH. Accessed on 25/03/2021 at https://reliefweb.int/sites/reliefweb.int/files/ resources/REPORT%20ON%20WORLD%27S%20ORPHANS.pdf

Independent Anti-Slavery Commissioner (2017) 'Supporting adult survivors of slavery to facilitate recovery and reintegration and prevent re-exploitation.' Accessed on 20/05/2021 at www.antislaverycommissioner.co.uk/media/1261/ long-term-support-recommendations.pdf

International Labour Organization (1930) *Forced Labour Convention, 1930.* Geneva: ILO. Accessed on 25/03/2021 at www.ilo.org/dyn/normlex/ en/f?p=NORMLEXPUB:12100:0::NO::P12100_ILO_CODE:C029

International Labour Organization (1957) *Abolition of Forced Labour Convention, 1957.* Geneva: ILO. Accessed on 25/03/2021 at www.ilo.org/dyn/normlex/ en/f?p=1000:12100:0::NO::P12100_ILO_CODE:C105

International Labour Organization (1999) *Worst Forms of Child Labour Convention, 1999.* Geneva: ILO. Accessed on 25/03/2021 at www.ilo.org/dyn/normlex/ en/f?p=NORMLEXPUB:12100:0::NO::P12100_ILO_CODE:C182

International Labour Organization (2014) *Profits and Poverty: The Economics of Forced Labour.* Geneva: ILO. Accessed on 25/03/2021 at www.ilo.org/wcmsp5/groups/ public/---ed_norm/---declaration/documents/publication/wcms_243391.pdf

International Labour Organization (2021) 'Decent work.' Accessed on 19/04/2021 at www.ilo.org/global/topics/decent-work/lang--en/index.htm

Kara, S. (2021) 'Panel discussion: Modern slavery.' 23 February 2021. Accessed on 25/03/2021 at www.youtube.com/watch?v=sLMq8uEB8is&list=PL-wj4-Geqxth_ww5LTXKFgscoVjoVK-CeK&index=1.

Kohli, R.K.S., Connolly, H., Stott, H., Roe, S., *et al.* (2019) *An Evaluation of Independent Child Trafficking Guardians – Early Adopter Sites: Final Report.* London: Home Office. Accessed on 25/03/2021 at www.gov.uk/government/ publications/an-evaluation-of-independent-child-trafficking-guardians-early-adopter-sites-final-report

Lee, H. (1960) *To Kill a Mockingbird*. London: William Heinemann.

Maslow, A. (1943) 'A theory of human motivation.' *Psychological Review* 50, 4, 370–396.

May, T (2016) 'Defeating modern slavery: article by Theresa May.' Accessed on 22/07/2021 at https://www.gov.uk/government/speeches/defeating-modern-slavery-theresa-may-article

Modern Slavery Act (2015). London: HMSO.

Official Journal of the European Union (2011) Directive 2011/36/EU of the European Parliament and of the Council of 5 April 2011 on preventing and combating trafficking in human beings and protecting its victims, and replacing Council Framework Decision 2002/629/JHA. Accessed on 25/03/2021 at https://eur-lex.europa.eu/legal-content/en/TXT/?uri=CELEX%3A32011L0036

Official Journal of the European Union (2012) *Charter of Fundamental Rights of the European Union* (2012/C 326/02). Accessed on 21/06/2021 at https://ec.europa.eu/info/aid-development-cooperation-fundamental-rights/your-rights-eu/eu-charter-fundamental-rights_en

Reed, S., Roe, S., Grimshaw, J., and Oliver, R. (2018) *The Economic and Social Costs of Modern Slavery*. London: Home Office. Accessed on 25/03/2021 at www.antislaverycommissioner.co.uk/media/1258/the-economic-and-social-costs-of-modern-slavery.pdf

Refugee Council (2021) 'The truth about asylum: Asylum seekers and refugees – who's who?' Accessed on 20/05/2021 at www.refugeecouncil.org.uk/information/refugee-asylum-facts/the-truth-about-asylum

Reuters (2019) 'Five years on, is the UK's landmark anti-slavery law fit for purpose?' Accessed on 25/03/2021 at www.reuters.com/article/us-britain-slavery-expertviews-trfn-idUSKBN1WX02J

Rights Lab and Office of the Independent Anti-Slavery Commissioner (2021) 'The benefits and the barriers to accessing employment: Considerations for survivors of Modern Slavery.' Accessed on 21/07/2021 at https://www.antislaverycommissioner.co.uk/media/1599/rights_lab_access-to-work-pathways_final.pdf

Rittel, H.W.J. and Webber, M.M. (1973) 'Dilemmas in a general theory of planning.' *Policy Science* 4, 155–169.

Sandel, M.J. (2009) *Justice: What's the Right Thing to Do?* London: Penguin.

Sen, A. (1999) *Development as Freedom*. Oxford: Oxford University Press.

Sexual Offences Act (2003). London: HMSO.

Sigmon, J.N. (2008) 'Combating modern day slavery issues in identifying and assisting victims of human trafficking worldwide.' *Victims & Offenders 3*, 2–3, 245–257.

Singer, P. (2015) *The Most Good You Can Do: How Effective Altruism Is Changing Ideas About Living Ethically*. New Haven, CT: Yale University Press.

Slave Trade Act (1807). London: HMSO.

Slave Trade Felony Act (1811). London: HMSO.

Slavery Abolition Act (1833). London: HMSO.

UK Visas and Immigration (2021) 'What UK Visas and Immigration does.' Accessed on 20/05/2021 at www.gov.uk/government/organisations/uk-visas-and-immigration#:~:text=UK%20Visas%20and%20Immigration%20is,part%20of%20the%20Home%20Office

UNHCR (1951) *Convention and Protocol Relating to the Status of Refugees*. Accessed on 20/05/2021 at www.unhcr.org/uk/3b66c2aa10

United Kingdom Border Force (UKBF) (2021) 'About us.' Accessed on 20/05/2021 at www.gov.uk/government/organisations/border-force/about

United Nations (1926) *Slavery Convention*. Geneva: OHCHR. Accessed on 25/03/2021 at www.ohchr.org/en/professionalinterest/pages/slaveryconvention.aspx

United Nations (1948) *Universal Declaration of Human Rights*. Geneva: UN. Accessed on 25/03/2021 at www.ohchr.org/EN/UDHR/Documents/UDHR_Translations/eng.pdf

United Nations (1951) *Convention relating to the Status of Refugees*. Accessed on 25/03/2021 at www.ohchr.org/Documents/ProfessionalInterest/refugees.pdf

United Nations (1966) *International Covenant of Civil and Political Rights*. Geneva: OHCHR. Accessed on 25/03/2021 at www.ohchr.org/EN/ProfessionalInterest/Pages/CCPR.aspx

United Nations (1966) *International Covenant on Economic, Social and Cultural Rights*. Geneva: OHCHR. Accessed on 25/03/2021 at www.ohchr.org/EN/ProfessionalInterest/Pages/CESCR.aspx

United Nations (2000) *Protocol to Prevent, Suppress and Punish Trafficking in Persons, Especially Women and Children, supplementing the United Nations Convention against Transnational Crime.* Vienna: UNODC. Accessed on 25/03/2021 at www.ohchr.org/en/professionalinterest/pages/protocoltraffickinginpersons.aspx

United Nations Office on Drugs and Crime (2009) *Anti-Human Trafficking Manual for Criminal Justice Practitioners Module 3.* Vienna: UNODC. Accessed on 25/03/2021 at www.unodc.org/documents/human-trafficking/TIP_module3_Ebook.pdf

United Nations Office on Drugs and Crime (2010) 'Human trafficking indicators.' Accessed on 25/03/2021 at www.unodc.org/pdf/HT_indicators_E_LOWRES.pdf

United Nations Office on Drugs and Crime (2015) *Trafficking in Persons for the Purpose of Organ Removal: Assessment Toolkit.* Vienna: United Nations. Accessed on 25/03/2021 at www.unodc.org/documents/human-trafficking/2015/UNODC_Assessment_Toolkit_TIP_for_the_Purpose_of_Organ_Removal.pdf

Unseen (2020) *Missing Home: Providing Safety to Trafficked Children.* Bristol: Unseen. Accessed on 25/03/2021 at www.unseenuk.org/resources/unseen_childrens_report.pdf

Unseen (2021) 'Modern slavery explained: Spot the signs of modern slavery.' Accessed on 25/03/2021 at www.unseenuk.org/modern-slavery/spot-the-signs

Glossary of Terms

Anti-Slavery Partnership (ASP)

www.aspartnership.org.uk

The ASP framework was developed to promote and develop effective multi-agency partnership working across the South-West region to bring human trafficking and modern slavery to an end. The model consists of localised partnerships and an overarching regional board.

Asylum accommodation

Asylum accommodation is split into initial and dispersal accommodation. There is no choice available as to the location or type of accommodation offered.

- **Initial accommodation** is short-term housing, usually in a hostel-type environment. It is used as emergency and temporary accommodation in advance of support applications being fully assessed.
- **Dispersal accommodation** is longer-term temporary accommodation managed by accommodation providers on behalf of the Home Office. People stay in this form of accommodation until their asylum claim is determined.

(Home Office 2017)

Asylum process

A person seeking asylum is someone who has left their country of origin because they feel they are unable to live safely in any part of their own country because they fear persecution. In the UK, someone who is determined to require asylum protection will be granted refugee status or humanitarian protection. (Refugee Council 2021)

Asylum support
Asylum support, including accommodation, is provided to asylum seekers who do not have any other way of supporting themselves. (Home Office 2017)

Cannabis cultivation
Production of cannabis (usually on a large scale). In the UK, this has been found to occur in residential houses, warehouses, farm buildings, and in underground bunkers (known as 'grow houses'). The usual mode of operation is for 'gardeners' to be locked into grow houses and expected to tend to the plants.

Competent Authority
Refers to the UK's decision-making body responsible for making reasonable grounds (RG) decisions and conclusive grounds (CG) decisions regarding individuals referred as potential victims of modern slavery. It is known as the Single Competent Authority (SCA), replacing the two competent authorities that existed prior to April 2019. (Home Office 2021)

Conclusive grounds (CG) decision
A CG decision is taken by the Single Competent Authority as to whether, on the balance of probabilities, there are sufficient grounds to decide that the individual being considered is a victim of modern slavery (human trafficking or slavery, servitude, or forced or compulsory labour). (Home Office 2021)

County lines
Is defined in the Serious Violence Strategy (Home Office 2018, p.48) as follows: 'County lines is a term used to describe gangs and organised criminal networks involved in exporting illegal drugs into one or more importing areas [within the UK], using dedicated mobile phone lines or other form of "deal line". They are likely to exploit children and vulnerable adults to move [and store] the drugs

and money and they will often use coercion, intimidation, violence (including sexual violence) and weapons.'

Discretionary leave (DL)

Refers to leave granted outside of the Immigration Rules. Discretionary leave is based on the individual circumstances of the victim. A positive conclusive grounds (CG) decision does not result in an automatic grant of immigration leave. However, unless the confirmed victim has an outstanding asylum claim at the time the positive CG decision is made, automatic consideration (for non-EEA [European Economic Area] victims) should normally be given at the same time, or as soon as possible afterwards, to whether a grant of DL is appropriate under this policy. If the confirmed victim has an outstanding asylum claim and the deferral of a decision on whether to grant discretionary leave would not itself result in the withdrawal of any NRM support which the victim receives and still needs, then the asylum claim should normally be decided before any consideration is given to whether the victim is eligible for DL under the DL policy. Discretionary leave may be considered under this specific policy where the SCA has made a positive CG decision that an individual is a victim of modern slavery and they satisfy one of the following criteria:

- leave is necessary owing to personal circumstances
- leave is necessary to pursue compensation
- victims who are helping police with their enquiries.

(Home Office 2020)

European Economic Area (EEA)

The EEA includes EU countries as well as Iceland, Liechtenstein, and Norway. It allowed these countries to be part of the EU's single market (European Parliament 2021).

Switzerland is not an EU or EEA member but it is part of the single market. This means Swiss nationals have the same rights as other EEA nationals. Nationals from the EU and EEA countries pre-Brexit were able to exercise their rights and live and work in the UK.

European Union

The EU is an economic and political union of 27 countries. It operates under a single market which allows free movement of goods, capital, services, and people between member states. (GOV.UK 2021)

First responders

An authority that is authorised to refer a potential victim of modern slavery into the National Referral Mechanism. There are different cohorts of first responders in Scotland and Northern Ireland: Police, UK Visas and Immigration, Border Force, Immigration Enforcement, National Crime Agency, local authorities, Gangmasters and Labour Abuse Authority, non-governmental organisations. (Home Office 2021)

Gangmasters and Labour Abuse Authority (GLAA)

www.gla.gov.uk

The GLAA is responsible for protecting vulnerable and exploited workers in the sectors it is responsible for. They investigate reports of worker exploitation and illegal activity such as human trafficking, forced labour, and illegal labour provision. The GLAA runs a licensing scheme for specific sectors to ensure employers meet the legal standards required.

Humanitarian protection

If an asylum seeker does not meet the criteria for refugee status, they will be considered for humanitarian protection. To be granted humanitarian protection, there must be evidence that they would face a real risk of serious harm if returned to their country of origin. Upon a grant of humanitarian protection, an individual receives five years of limited leave to remain in the UK. (Free Movement 2019)

Independent Child Trafficking Guardians (ICTGs)

ICTGs are individuals appointed to provide an independent service through a contract with the Home Office. They are appointed based on their experiences relevant to child trafficking, criminal justice, social care, asylum and immigration by the service provider and offer a source of advice for trafficked children. The

ICTG service provides somebody who can speak up on behalf of, and act in the best interests of, the child. The ICTG service model provides two discrete services to children who have been trafficked: ICTG Direct Worker to support children for whom there is no one with parental responsibility for them in the UK, and ICTG Regional Practice Coordinator whose role is to focus on children who do have a figure with parental responsibility for them in the UK; 'Independent Child Trafficking Guardian Direct Worker ("ICTG Direct Worker")' provides one-to-one support to a child who has been trafficked and help them navigate, as appropriate, the respective local authority children's services and the immigration and criminal justice systems, as well as ensuring that their educational and health needs are met through liaison with the appropriate statutory agencies and public authorities. (Home Office 2021)

Modern slavery
Unless otherwise specified, modern slavery refers to both human trafficking and slavery, servitude, and forced or compulsory labour.

Modern Slavery Unit (MSU)
Home Office team responsible for policy, legislation, and the Modern Slavery Victim Care Contract (MSVCC).

Modern Slavery Victim Care Contract (MSVCC)
The Home Office contract to provide care to adult victims of modern slavery in England and Wales. (Home Office 2021)

National Referral Mechanism (NRM)
The UK's framework for identifying and supporting victims of modern slavery. It is one means of ensuring that adult victims receive the necessary support and assistance in the period immediately after their identification as a potential victim. (Home Office 2021)

The process – an overview of how it works
The NRM process has several stages and involves a variety of different frontline agencies and practitioners at different stages in the process.

Step 1: Identify: Potential victim identified and consents to enter the NRM.

Step 2: Refer: A referral to enter the NRM is made with the information available. The referral will be made by a first responder agency – these agencies can be law enforcement, government departments and agencies, and non-governmental organisations. This referral goes to the competent authority (a Home Office team that makes NRM decisions).

Step 3: Decision 1 – reasonable grounds: 'I suspect but I can't prove': Based on the NRM referral form information, the competent authority will consider if there are reasonable grounds (RG) to believe that the individual is a victim of modern slavery, forced or compulsory labour, or human trafficking. This is based on the threshold of 'I suspect but cannot prove'.

- Negative RG – not deemed to be a victim of modern slavery: no further progress through the NRM or the support systems attached to this.
- Positive RG – offered access to support known as the 'reflection and recovery' period.

Step 4: Supported: Victims are offered access to a range of support for the duration between a positive RG decision and a CG decision being made.

Step 5: Decision 2 – conclusive grounds: 'on the balance of probabilities': At the CG stage, the competent authority is considering if there are grounds to decide that the individual is a victim of modern slavery or not.

- Negative CG – not deemed to be a victim of modern slavery: need to exit the support system.
- Positive CG – confirmed as a victim of modern slavery: still offered support but this is focused on planning to move on and exit the support system as needs are met.

Step 6: Move on and exit support: A support worker will carry out an assessment to determine ongoing needs and how and when these will be met, by which agency, and agree a pathway to exit support.

Note: At the time of writing the Nationality and Borders Bill is reviewing the decision thresholds for the RG and CG decisions, and these look set to change if the Bill passes in its current format.

Non-governmental organisation (NGO)

An organisation that is independent of government – in a UK context, such organisations are also referred to as charities, the charity sector, or the third sector.

Potential victim

An individual who is suspected of being a victim of modern slavery. They may have received a positive reasonable grounds (RG) decision but will not yet have received a conclusive grounds (CG) decision from the Single Competent Authority. (Home Office 2021)

Reasonable grounds decision

A reasonable grounds (RG) decision is a decision taken by the Single Competent Authority; the decision maker suspects but cannot prove that the individual being considered is a victim of modern slavery (human trafficking or slavery, servitude, or forced or compulsory labour). (Home Office 2021)

Reception centre

A temporary safe place that survivors of human trafficking and exploitation can be taken to for immediate care and support (usually following law enforcement operational activity).

Reflection and recovery period

Refers to the period between the date of a positive RG decision and a CG decision; this will usually be at least 45 days. (Home Office 2021)

Refugee

Article 1 of the 1951 United Nations Convention relating to the Status of Refugees states that a refugee is a person who:

> owing to a well-founded fear of being persecuted for reasons of race, religion, nationality, membership of a particular social group or political opinion, is outside the country of his nationality and is unable or, owing to such fear,

is unwilling to avail himself of the protection of that country; or who, not having a nationality and being outside the country of his former habitual residence as a result of such events, is unable or, owing to such fear, is unwilling to return to it. (UNHCR 1951)

Refugee status is granted by the government when it determines that an individual who has applied for asylum meets the United Nations definition. This determination usually comes with being granted status to initially live in the UK for five years.

Smuggling

The UN Protocol against the Smuggling of Migrants by Land, Sea and Air, adopted in 2000 defines human smuggling as 'the procurement, in order to obtain, directly or indirectly, a financial or other material benefit, of the illegal entry of a person into a state party of which the person is not a national'. (Crown Prosecution Service 2020)

Support provider

A body employed or engaged pursuant to the Modern Slavery Victim Care Contract (MSVCC) to provide care and coordination services for victims, including by way of a sub-contract. (Home Office 2021)

Survivor

The term survivor is used by the anti-slavery sector. It is often preferred over the term 'victim'. It is, however, another label assigned to an individual. I usually refer to someone as a victim during their situation of exploitation and a survivor after this time. This is not wholly accurate as arguably during exploitation people are also surviving. The sector is not yet getting the language right, and it is usually best to ask the person in question about the terminology they are comfortable using to describe themselves.

United Kingdom Border Force (UKBF)

UKBF is responsible for securing the UK's borders (land, sea, and air). It aims to facilitate the legitimate movement of individuals and goods, while preventing those who would cause harm from entering the UK. UKBF is part of the Home Office. (UKBF 2021)

United Kingdom Visas and Immigration (UKVI)

UKVI is responsible for making the decision about who has the right to visit or stay in the UK. UKVI is part of the Home Office. (UKVI 2021)

Voluntary Returns Service

A Home Office service supporting individuals to return to their country of origin through financial means or support in kind. (Home Office 2021)

Warrant

A warrant is a legal document, issued by a court, allowing police, or other permitted authority, to make an arrest, seize property, conduct a search, or execute a judgment.

A search warrant is a type of warrant issued by a court that allows the police to conduct searches of a specific location or vehicle. A court will only grant a warrant if there are reasonable grounds to suspect that an offence has been committed, and that the premises need to be searched as it may contain evidence that will be of benefit or importance to a trial. (Donoghue Solicitors 2021)

Welfare visits

Welfare visits and checks have become established as common practice in UK policing and refer to police conducting visits to a location or person where someone is believed to be vulnerable or at risk for a wide variety of reasons.

Young offenders institute (YOI)

A YOI is a custody setting for young people (aged 15–18) run by the prison service or private companies.

Types of criminal exploitation

As described in *A Typology of Modern Slavery Offences* (Cooper *et al.* 2017), p.3.

Financial fraud (including benefit fraud)
Victims are exploited financially; most commonly, their identity documents are taken and used to claim benefits. This type often occurs alongside other types.

Forced gang-related criminality
Victims are forced to undertake gang-related criminal activities, most commonly relating to drug networks. Victims are often children who are forced by gangs to transport drugs and money between urban areas and suburban areas and market and coastal towns.

Forced labour in illegal activities
Victims are forced to provide labour to offenders for illegal purposes. The most common example is victims forced to cultivate cannabis in private residences.

Trafficking for forced sham marriage
Traffickers transport EU national victims to the UK and sell these victims to an exploiter in a oneoff transaction. Exploiters marry victims to gain immigration advantages and often sexually abuse them.

Professional approaches

Trafficking Survivor Care Standards (2015)
Accessibility: the service needs to be equally accessible to all survivors. You should check before accepting new referrals that survivors meet your service criteria to ensure that you can assess and address their needs. Your service should be welcoming and promote equality of access and engagement.

Confidentiality: you should ensure that survivors are made aware at the outset of the duty of confidentiality which applies to all persons employed by the support agency, so that they are clear and have a choice regarding disclosure. Any personal information shared by survivors should not be disclosed to any third party or agency without their prior informed consent. Respecting confidentiality is crucial to promoting their trust in the service and encouraging their engagement.

Culturally sensitive approach: you should actively promote equality and diversity, making sure that survivors are treated fairly and with dignity, on the basis of their individual needs and with full respect for their gender (including gender reassignment), race, nationality, ethnic or national origin, disability, religion, beliefs, sexual orientation or age. Your service provision should be diverse, inclusive and flexible to meet the different requirements of each survivor.

Empowering approach: you should support survivors to regain trust in their own ability to control their lives as this is a crucial step towards reducing their vulnerability and preventing re-victimisation. Be aware, however, that the ability of survivors to rebuild a sense of self-worth, confidence and empowerment will very much depend on their own resources, general and mental health. In order to promote empowerment you should:

- Recognise that survivors are, despite their vulnerability, individuals with goals, dreams and aspirations.
- Give back control and restore the decision-making power of survivors as quickly and supportively as possible, by recognising that they are the experts of their own needs and are responsible for their own recovery.
- Provide support in a way that recognises their strength, resourcefulness and resilience.

Gender-sensitive approach: you should recognise that the needs of women and men are different and that, in order to treat them equally, their gender identity in relation to their needs and circumstances ought to be understood and acknowledged. Also, the impact of trafficking upon survivors may be different depending on their gender and/or type of exploitation. Your service should also strive to offer tailor-made support that takes into account the specific needs of survivors with due regard to other factors such as their age and their trafficking history.

Holistic and victim-centred approach: you should strive to provide integrated, holistic and survivor-led support that considers all aspects of each individual – including their physical, emotional, mental, spiritual, financial, legal and social well-being. You should place survivors at the centre of the decision-making process and provide support based on their individual needs.

Human rights-based approach: you should recognise that trafficking is a severe form of exploitation that violates survivors' basic human rights. Therefore, your support should never be contingent upon their ability or willingness to cooperate with the authorities and should always be offered on an informed and consensual basis, with a view to respecting their human dignity and promoting their rights.

Multi-agency approach: you should adopt a multi-disciplinary approach and support the work of the Government and law enforcement agencies in a way that is respectful of your service users' human rights. You should work in partnership with mainstream providers to ensure that survivors are able to access all their entitlements, including access to health care, legal and financial help, and psychological support.

Professional boundaries: you should bear in mind that trafficked survivors are vulnerable persons (whether adults or children) and that their vulnerability may not be obvious. Therefore, you should have policies and procedures in place that set limits for safe, acceptable and effective behaviour by workers. Fostering positive attachments and healthy relationships within boundaries is a crucial step to keeping both survivors and workers emotionally safe. Breaches may lead to survivors feeling betrayed and/or dependent on individual workers.

Safe working approach: you should prioritise the safety of survivors, staff and volunteers by adopting adequate policies and procedures, and monitoring implementation across all your organisational activities.

Trauma-informed approach: you should recognise the impact of traumatic experiences upon survivors' lives and behaviours and always strive to do no further harm by ensuring that support is provided in a way that is respectful of their need for safety, respect, and acceptance.

www.antislaverycommissioner.co.uk/media/1067/trafficking-survivor-care-standards-2015.pdf (pp.32–34)

Legal Appendix

Throughout the book, I have referred to international, European, and domestic legal instruments, legislation, and directives pertinent to modern slavery.

As I didn't want the book to become too focused on legislation because I am not a legal practitioner or expert and although the law forms an important basis for the approaches used to tackle and criminalise slavery, this book was not intended to be a legal summary of how we have got to where we are. In the text, I have referenced the legal sources briefly and below you will find an overview of each of the ones I have mentioned – their full titles, the dates they were written, the articles they contain relevant to slavery and trafficking, and a link to them. This section is for those who are interested in learning more about the legal frameworks and structures in place – it comes with the caveat that these are the ones I have referenced in the book (mainly in Chapter 3) and may not, from a legal perspective, cover all instruments lawyers would call upon or consider relevant. Modern slavery is a complex crime that interacts with multiple layers of international, European, and domestic instruments.

References to the prohibition of slavery in key international human rights instruments

Universal Declaration of Human Rights (United Nations 1948)

Article 4 of the declaration states:

No one shall be held in slavery or servitude; slavery and the slave trade shall be prohibited in all their forms.

www.un.org/en/universal-declaration-human-rights

International Covenant on Civil and Political Rights (Office of the High Commissioner for Human Rights, United Nations (OHCHR) 1966)

Article 8 of the covenant states:

1. No one shall be held in slavery; slavery and the slave-trade in all their forms shall be prohibited.
2. No one shall be held in servitude.
3.
    (a) No one shall be required to perform forced or compulsory labour;
    (b) Paragraph 3 (a) shall not be held to preclude, in countries where imprisonment with hard labour may be imposed as a punishment for a crime, the performance of hard labour in pursuance of a sentence to such punishment by a competent court;
    (c) For the purpose of this paragraph the term "forced or compulsory labour" shall not include:
        (i)   Any work or service, not referred to in subparagraph (b), normally required of a person who is under detention in consequence of a lawful order of a court, or of a person during conditional release from such detention;
        (ii) Any service of a military character and, in countries where conscientious objection is recognized, any national service required by law of conscientious objectors;

(iii) Any service exacted in cases of emergency or calamity threatening the life or well-being of the community;

(iv) Any work or service which forms part of normal civil obligations.

www.ohchr.org/en/professionalinterest/pages/ccpr.aspx

International Covenant on Economic, Social and Cultural Rights (OHCHR 1966), Articles 6 (1) and 7

Article 6 (1) of the covenant states:

1. The States Parties to the present Covenant recognize the right to work, which includes the right of everyone to the opportunity to gain his living by work which he freely chooses or accepts, and will take appropriate steps to safeguard this right.

Article 7 of the covenant states:

The States Parties to the present Covenant recognize the right of everyone to the enjoyment of just and favourable conditions of work which ensure, in particular:

(a) Remuneration which provides all workers, as a minimum, with:

(i)   Fair wages and equal remuneration for work of equal value without distinction of any kind, in particular women being guaranteed conditions of work not inferior to those enjoyed by men, with equal pay for equal work;

(ii) A decent living for themselves and their families in accordance with the provisions of the present Covenant;

(b) Safe and healthy working conditions;

(c) Equal opportunity for everyone to be promoted in his employment to an appropriate higher level, subject to no considerations other than those of seniority and competence;

(d) Rest, leisure and reasonable limitation of working hours and periodic holidays with pay, as well as remuneration for public holidays.

www.ohchr.org/EN/ProfessionalInterest/Pages/CESCR.aspx

African Charter on Human and Peoples' Rights (Chapter I: Human and Peoples' Rights) (African Commission on Human and Peoples' Rights 1981)

Article 5 of the charter states:

Every individual shall have the right to the respect of the dignity inherent in a human being and to the recognition of his legal status. All forms of exploitation and degradation of man, particularly slavery, slave trade, torture, cruel, inhuman or degrading punishment and treatment, shall be prohibited.

www.achpr.org/legalinstruments/detail?id=49

International Labour Organization

The ILO presents expected and minimum labour standards within international conventions which include the International Labour Organization Forced Labour Convention 1930 (No. 29), the International Labour Organization Abolition of Forced Labour Convention 1957 (No. 105), and the International Labour Organization Worst Forms of Child Labour 1999 Convention (No. 182).

International Labour Organization Forced Labour Convention, 1930 (No. 29)

Article 2 of the convention states:

1. For the purposes of this Convention the term *forced or compulsory labour* shall mean all work or service which is exacted from any person under the menace of any penalty and for which the said person has not offered himself voluntarily.

*www.ilo.org/dyn/normlex/en/f?p=1000:12100:0::NO::P12100_*
ILO_CODE:C029

International Labour Organization Abolition of Forced Labour Convention, 1957 (No. 105)

Article 1 of the convention states:

Each Member of the International Labour Organisation which ratifies this Convention undertakes to suppress and not to make use of any form of forced or compulsory labour—

(a) as a means of political coercion or education or as a punishment for holding or expressing political views or views ideologically opposed to the established political, social or economic system;

(b) as a method of mobilising and using labour for purposes of economic development;

(c) as a means of labour discipline;

(d) as a punishment for having participated in strikes;

(e) as a means of racial, social, national or religious discrimination.

Article 2 of the convention states:

Each Member of the International Labour Organisation which ratifies this Convention undertakes to take effective measures to secure the immediate and complete abolition of forced or compulsory labour as specified in Article 1 of this Convention.

www.ilo.org/dyn/normlex/en/f?p=1000:12100:0::NO::P12100_ILO_CODE:C105

International Labour Organization Worst Forms of Child Labour Convention, 1999 (No. 182)

Article 3 of the convention states:

For the purposes of this Convention, the term **the worst forms of child labour** comprises:

(a) all forms of slavery or practices similar to slavery, such as the sale and trafficking of children, debt bondage and serfdom and forced or compulsory labour, including forced or compulsory recruitment of children for use in armed conflict;

(b) the use, procuring or offering of a child for prostitution, for the production of pornography or for pornographic performances;

(c) the use, procuring or offering of a child for illicit activities, in particular for the production and trafficking of drugs as defined in the relevant international treaties;

(d) work which, by its nature or the circumstances in which it is carried out, is likely to harm the health, safety or morals of children.

www.ilo.org/dyn/normlex/en/f?p=NORMLEXPUB:12100:0::NO::
P12100_ILO_CODE:C182

Office of the United Nations High Commissioner for Human Rights

Protocol to Prevent, Suppress and Punish Trafficking in Persons Especially Women and Children, supplementing the United Nations Convention against Transnational Organized Crime (United Nations 2000)

Known as the Palermo Protocol, it provides the first internationally recognised definition of human trafficking:

Article 3

For the purposes of this Protocol:

(a) "Trafficking in persons" shall mean the recruitment, transportation, transfer, harbouring or receipt of persons, by means of the threat or use of force or other forms of coercion, of abduction, of fraud, of deception, of the abuse of power or of a position of vulnerability or of the giving or receiving of payments or benefits to achieve the consent of a person having control over another person, for the purpose of exploitation. Exploitation shall include, at a minimum, the exploitation of the prostitution of others or other forms of sexual exploitation, forced labour or services, slavery or practices similar to slavery, servitude or the removal of organs;

(b) The consent of a victim of trafficking in persons to the intended exploitation set forth in subparagraph (a) of this article shall be irrelevant where any of the means set forth in subparagraph (a) have been used;

(c) The recruitment, transportation, transfer, harbouring or receipt of a child for the purpose of exploitation shall be considered "trafficking in persons" even if this does not involve any of the means set forth in subparagraph (a) of this article.

www.ohchr.org/en/professionalinterest/pages/protocoltraffickinginpersons.aspx

References to slavery in European Conventions and Directives

European Convention on Human Rights (Council of Europe 1950)

Article 4 of the Convention – Prohibition of slavery and forced labour

1. No one shall be held in slavery or servitude.
2. No one shall be required to perform forced or compulsory labour.
3. For the purpose of this article the term "forced or compulsory labour" shall not include:
   (a) any work required to be done in the ordinary course of detention imposed according to the provisions of Article 5 of this Convention or during conditional release from such detention;
   (b) any service of a military character or, in case of conscientious objectors in countries where they are recognised, service exacted instead of compulsory military service;
   (c) any service exacted in case of an emergency or calamity threatening the life or well-being of the community;
   (d) any work or service which forms part of normal civic obligations.

www.echr.coe.int/documents/convention_eng.pdf

Charter of Fundamental Rights of the European Union (2012/ C326/02) (Official Journal of the European Union 2012)

Article 5 – Prohibition of slavery and forced labour

1. No one shall be held in slavery or servitude.
2. No one shall be required to perform forced or compulsory labour.
3. Trafficking in human beings is prohibited.

Council of Europe Convention on Action against Trafficking in Human Beings (Council of Europe 2005)

Article 1 – Purposes of the Convention

The purposes of this Convention are:

(a) to prevent and combat trafficking in human beings, while guaranteeing gender equality;

(b) to protect the human rights of the victims of trafficking, design a comprehensive framework for the protection and assistance of victims and witnesses, while guaranteeing gender equality, as well as to ensure effective investigation and prosecution;

(c) to promote international cooperation on action against trafficking in human beings.

Chapter III – Measures to protect and promote the rights of victims, guaranteeing gender equality
Article 10 – Identification of the victims

1. Each Party shall provide its competent authorities with persons who are trained and qualified in preventing and combating trafficking in human beings, in identifying and helping victims, including children, and shall ensure that the different authorities collaborate with each other as well as with relevant support organisations, so that victims can be identified in a procedure duly taking into account the special situation of women and child victims and, in appropriate cases, issued with residence permits under the conditions provided for in Article 14 of the present Convention.

2. Each Party shall adopt such legislative or other measures as may be necessary to identify victims as appropriate in collaboration with other Parties and

relevant support organisations. Each Party shall ensure that, if the competent authorities have reasonable grounds to believe that a person has been victim of trafficking in human beings, that person shall not be removed from its territory until the identification process as victim of an offence provided for in Article 18 of this Convention has been completed by the competent authorities and shall likewise ensure that that person receives the assistance provided for in Article 12, paragraphs 1 and 2.

3. When the age of the victim is uncertain and there are reasons to believe that the victim is a child, he or she shall be presumed to be a child and shall be accorded special protection measures pending verification of his/her age.

4. As soon as an unaccompanied child is identified as a victim, each Party shall:
    (a) provide for representation of the child by a legal guardian, organisation or authority which shall act in the best interests of that child;
    (b) take the necessary steps to establish his/her identity and nationality;
    (c) make every effort to locate his/her family when this is in the best interests of the child.

Article 12 – Assistance to victims

1. Each Party shall adopt such legislative or other measures as may be necessary to assist victims in their physical, psychological and social recovery. Such assistance shall include at least:
    (a) standards of living capable of ensuring their subsistence, through such measures as: appropriate and secure accommodation, psychological and material assistance;
    (b) access to emergency medical treatment;
    (c) translation and interpretation services, when appropriate;
    (d) counselling and information, in particular as regards their legal rights and the services available to them, in a language that they can understand;
    (e) assistance to enable their rights and interests to be presented and considered at appropriate stages of criminal proceedings against offenders;
    (f) access to education for children.

2. Each Party shall take due account of the victim's safety and protection needs.

3. In addition, each Party shall provide necessary medical or other assistance to victims lawfully resident within its territory who do not have adequate resources and need such help.

4. Each Party shall adopt the rules under which victims lawfully resident within its territory shall be authorised to have access to the labour market, to vocational training and education.

5. Each Party shall take measures, where appropriate and under the conditions provided for by its internal law, to co-operate with non-governmental organisations, other relevant organisations or other elements of civil society engaged in assistance to victims.

6. Each Party shall adopt such legislative or other measures as may be necessary to ensure that assistance to a victim is not made conditional on his or her willingness to act as a witness.

7. For the implementation of the provisions set out in this article, each Party shall ensure that services are provided on a consensual and informed basis, taking due account of the special needs of persons in a vulnerable position and the rights of children in terms of accommodation, education and appropriate health care.

Article 13 – Recovery and reflection period

1. Each Party shall provide in its internal law a recovery and reflection period of at least 30 days, when there are reasonable grounds to believe that the person concerned is a victim. Such a period shall be sufficient for the person concerned to recover and escape the influence of traffickers and/or to take an informed decision on cooperating with the competent authorities. During this period it shall not be possible to enforce any expulsion order against him or her. This provision is without prejudice to the activities carried out by the competent authorities in all phases of the relevant national proceedings, and in particular when investigating and prosecuting the offences concerned. During this period, the Parties shall authorise the persons concerned to stay in their territory.

2. During this period, the persons referred to in paragraph 1 of this Article shall be entitled to the measures contained in Article 12, paragraphs 1 and 2.

3. The Parties are not bound to observe this period if grounds of public order prevent it or if it is found that victim status is being claimed improperly.

Article 14 – Residence permit

1. Each Party shall issue a renewable residence permit to victims, in one or other of the two following situations or in both:

    (a) the competent authority considers that their stay is necessary owing to their personal situation;

    (b) the competent authority considers that their stay is necessary for the purpose of their cooperation with the competent authorities in investigation or criminal proceedings.

2. The residence permit for child victims, when legally necessary, shall be issued in accordance with the best interests of the child and, where appropriate, renewed under the same conditions.

3. The non-renewal or withdrawal of a residence permit is subject to the conditions provided for by the internal law of the Party.

4. If a victim submits an application for another kind of residence permit, the Party concerned shall take into account that he or she holds, or has held, a residence permit in conformity with paragraph 1.

5. Having regard to the obligations of Parties to which Article 40 of this Convention refers, each Party shall ensure that granting of a permit according to this provision shall be without prejudice to the right to seek and enjoy asylum.

Article 15 – Compensation and legal redress

1. Each Party shall ensure that victims have access, as from their first contact with the competent authorities, to information on relevant judicial and administrative proceedings in a language which they can understand.

2. Each Party shall provide, in its internal law, for the right to legal assistance and to free legal aid for victims under the conditions provided by its internal law.

3. Each Party shall provide, in its internal law, for the right of victims to compensation from the perpetrators.

4. Each Party shall adopt such legislative or other measures as may be necessary to guarantee compensation for victims in accordance with the conditions under its internal law, for instance through the establishment of a fund for victim compensation or measures or programmes aimed at social assistance and social integration of victims, which could be funded by the assets resulting from the application of measures provided in Article 23.

Article 16 – Repatriation and return of victims

1. The Party of which a victim is a national or in which that person had the right of permanent residence at the time of entry into the territory of the receiving Party shall, with due regard for his or her rights, safety and dignity, facilitate and accept his or her return without undue or unreasonable delay.

2. When a Party returns a victim to another State, such return shall be with due regard for the rights, safety and dignity of that person and for the status of any legal proceedings related to the fact that the person is a victim, and shall preferably be voluntary.

3. At the request of a receiving Party, a requested Party shall verify whether a person is its national or had the right of permanent residence in its territory at the time of entry into the territory of the receiving Party.

4. In order to facilitate the return of a victim who is without proper documentation, the Party of which that person is a national or in which he or she had the right of permanent residence at the time of entry into the territory of the receiving Party shall agree to issue, at the request of the receiving Party, such travel documents or other authorisation as may be necessary to enable the person to travel to and re-enter its territory.

5. Each Party shall adopt such legislative or other measures as may be necessary to establish repatriation programmes, involving relevant national or international institutions and non-governmental organisations. These programmes aim at avoiding re-victimisation. Each Party should make its best effort to favour the reintegration of victims into the society of the State of return, including reintegration into the education system and the labour market, in particular through the acquisition and improvement of their professional skills. With regard to children, these programmes should include enjoyment of the right to education and measures to secure adequate care or receipt by the family or appropriate care structures.

6. Each Party shall adopt such legislative or other measures as may be necessary to make available to victims, where appropriate in cooperation with any other Party concerned, contact information of structures that can assist them in the country where they are returned or repatriated, such as law enforcement offices, non-governmental organisations, legal professions able to provide counselling and social welfare agencies.

7. Child victims shall not be returned to a State, if there is indication, following a risk and security assessment, that such return would not be in the best interests of the child.

https://rm.coe.int/168008371d

EU Anti-Trafficking Directive (European Parliament and the Council of Europe 2011)

The Directive provides binding legislation to prevent trafficking, to prosecute criminals effectively and better to protect the victims, in line with the highest European standards. The Directive takes a victim-centred approach, including a gender perspective, to cover actions in different areas such as criminal law provisions, prosecution of offenders, victims' support and victims' rights in criminal proceedings, prevention and monitoring of the implementation.

Article 14 of the Directive states:

> Victims of trafficking in human beings should, in accordance with the basic principles of the legal systems of the relevant Member States, be protected from prosecution or punishment for criminal activities such as the use of false documents, or offences under legislation on prostitution or immigration, that they have been compelled to commit as a direct consequence of being subject to trafficking. The aim of such protection is to safeguard the human rights of victims, to avoid further victimisation and to encourage them to act as witnesses in criminal proceedings against the perpetrators. This safeguard should not exclude prosecution or punishment for offences that a person has voluntarily committed or participated in.

Article 18 of the Directive states:

> It is necessary for victims of trafficking in human beings to be able to exercise their rights effectively. Therefore assistance and support should be available to them before, during and for an appropriate time after criminal proceedings. Member States should provide for resources to support victim assistance, support and protection. The assistance and support provided should include at least a minimum set of measures that are necessary to enable the victim to recover and escape from their traffickers. The practical

implementation of such measures should, on the basis of an individual assessment carried out in accordance with national procedures, take into account the circumstances, cultural context and needs of the person concerned. A person should be provided with assistance and support as soon as there is a reasonable grounds indication for believing that he or she might have been trafficked and irrespective of his or her willingness to act as a witness. In cases where the victim does not reside lawfully in the Member State concerned, assistance and support should be provided unconditionally at least during the reflection period. If, after completion of the identification process or expiry of the reflection period, the victim is not considered eligible for a residence permit or does not otherwise have lawful residence in that Member State, or if the victim has left the territory of that Member State, the Member State concerned is not obliged to continue providing assistance and support to that person on the basis of this Directive. Where necessary, assistance and support should continue for an appropriate period after the criminal proceedings have ended, for example if medical treatment is ongoing due to the severe physical or psychological consequences of the crime, or if the victim's safety is at risk due to the victim's statements in those criminal proceedings.

https://eur-lex.europa.eu/LexUriServ/LexUriServ.
do?uri=OJ:L:2011:101:0001:0011:EN:PDF

Relevant domestic legislation

Human Rights Act (1998)

Article 4 of the act states:

Prohibition of slavery and forced labour

1. No one shall be held in slavery or servitude.
2. No one shall be required to perform forced or compulsory labour.
3. For the purpose of this Article the term "forced or compulsory labour" shall not include:
   (a) any work required to be done in the ordinary course of detention imposed according to the provisions of Article 5 of this Convention or during conditional release from such detention;

(b) any service of a military character or, in case of conscientious objectors in countries where they are recognised, service exacted instead of compulsory military service;

(c) any service exacted in case of an emergency or calamity threatening the life or well-being of the community;

(d) any work or service which forms part of normal civic obligations.

www.legislation.gov.uk/ukpga/1998/42/schedule/1/part/I/chapter/3

Asylum and Immigration (Treatment of Claimants) Act (2004)

Section 4 of the act states:

Trafficking people for exploitation

(1) A person commits an offence if he arranges or facilitates the arrival in the United Kingdom of an individual (the "passenger") and—

    (a) he intends to exploit the passenger in the United Kingdom or elsewhere, or

    (b) he believes that another person is likely to exploit the passenger in the United Kingdom or elsewhere.

(2) A person commits an offence if he arranges or facilitates travel within the United Kingdom by an individual (the "passenger") in respect of whom he believes that an offence under subsection (1) may have been committed and—

    (a) he intends to exploit the passenger in the United Kingdom or elsewhere, or

    (b) he believes that another person is likely to exploit the passenger in the United Kingdom or elsewhere.

(3) A person commits an offence if he arranges or facilitates the departure from the United Kingdom of an individual (the "passenger") and—

    (a) he intends to exploit the passenger outside the United Kingdom, or

    (b) he believes that another person is likely to exploit the passenger outside the United Kingdom.

(4) For the purposes of this section a person is exploited if (and only if)—

    (a) he is the victim of behaviour that contravenes Article 4 of the Human Rights Convention (slavery and forced labour),

(b) he is encouraged, required or expected to do anything as a result of which he or another person would commit an offence under the Human Organ Transplants Act 1989 (c. 31) or [under section 32 or 33 of the Human Tissue Act 2004],

(c) he is subjected to force, threats or deception designed to induce him—

   (i)   to provide services of any kind,

   (ii) to provide another person with benefits of any kind, or

   (iii) to enable another person to acquire benefits of any kind, or

(d) he is requested or induced to undertake any activity, having been chosen as the subject of the request or inducement on the grounds that—

   (i)   he is mentally or physically ill or disabled, he is young or he has a family relationship with a person, and

   (ii) a person without the illness, disability, youth or family relationship would be likely to refuse the request or resist the inducement.

(5) A person guilty of an offence under this section shall be liable—

(a) on conviction on indictment, to imprisonment for a term not exceeding 14 years, to a fine or to both, or

(b) on summary conviction, to imprisonment for a term not exceeding twelve months, to a fine not exceeding the statutory maximum or to both.

Section 4 is now omitted from the Asylum and Immigration (Treatment of Claimants) Act since 2016 on account of the Modern Slavery Act (2015), Human Trafficking and Exploitation (Criminal Justice and Support for Victims) Act (Northern Ireland) 2015, and Human Trafficking and Exploitation (Scotland) Act 2015 being enacted.

www.legislation.gov.uk/ukpga/2004/19/section/4

Sexual Offences Act (2003)

Section 59 (A) of the act states:
Trafficking people for sexual exploitation

(1) A person ("A") commits an offence if A intentionally arranges or facilitates—

    (a) the arrival in, or entry into, the United Kingdom or another country of another person ("B"),

    (b) the travel of B within the United Kingdom or another country, or

    (c) the departure of B from the United Kingdom or another country,

(2) with a view to the sexual exploitation of B.

(3) For the purposes of subsection (1)(a) and (c) A's arranging or facilitating is with a view to the sexual exploitation of B if, and only if—

    (a) A intends to do anything to or in respect of B, after B's arrival, entry or (as the case may be) departure but in any part of the world, which if done will involve the commission of a relevant offence, or

    (b) A believes that another person is likely to do something to or in respect of B, after B's arrival, entry or (as the case may be) departure but in any part of the world, which if done will involve the commission of a relevant offence.

(4) For the purposes of subsection (1)(b) A's arranging or facilitating is with a view to the sexual exploitation of B if, and only if—

    (a) A intends to do anything to or in respect of B, during or after the journey and in any part of the world, which if done will involve the commission of a relevant offence, or

    (b) A believes that another person is likely to do something to or in respect of B, during or after the journey and in any part of the world, which if done will involve the commission of a relevant offence.

(5) A person who is a UK national commits an offence under this section regardless of—

    (a) where the arranging or facilitating takes place, or

    (b) which country is the country of arrival, entry, travel or (as the case may be) departure.

(6) A person who is not a UK national commits an offence under this section if—

    (a) any part of the arranging or facilitating takes place in the United Kingdom, or

    (b) the United Kingdom is the country of arrival, entry, travel or (as the case may be) departure.

(7) A person guilty of an offence under this section is liable—

(a) on summary conviction, to imprisonment for a term not exceeding 12 months or a fine not exceeding the statutory maximum or both;

(b) on conviction on indictment, to imprisonment for a term not exceeding 14 years.

(8) In relation to an offence committed before the commencement of section 154(1) of the Criminal Justice Act 2003, the reference in subsection (6)(a) to 12 months is to be read as a reference to 6 months.

Section 59(A) is now omitted from the Sexual Offences Act on account of the Modern Slavery Act (2015), Human Trafficking and Exploitation (Criminal Justice and Support for Victims) Act (Northern Ireland) 2015, and Human Trafficking and Exploitation (Scotland) Act 2015 being enacted.

www.legislation.gov.uk/ukpga/2003/42/section/59A/2015-07-31

Coroners and Justice Act (2009)

Section 71 of the act states:

Slavery, servitude and forced or compulsory labour

(1) A person (D) commits an offence if—

(a) D holds another person in slavery or servitude and the circumstances are such that D knows or ought to know that the person is so held, or

(b) D requires another person to perform forced or compulsory labour and the circumstances are such that D knows or ought to know that the person is being required to perform such labour.

(2) In subsection (1) the references to holding a person in slavery or servitude or requiring a person to perform forced or compulsory labour are to be construed in accordance with Article 4 of the Human Rights Convention (which prohibits a person from being held in slavery or servitude or being required to perform forced or compulsory labour).

(3) A person guilty of an offence under this section is liable—

(a) on summary conviction, to imprisonment for a term not exceeding the relevant period or a fine not exceeding the statutory maximum, or both;

(b) on conviction on indictment, to imprisonment for a term not exceeding 14 years or a fine, or both.

(4) In this section—
- "Human Rights Convention" means the Convention for the Protection of Human Rights and Fundamental Freedoms agreed by the Council of Europe at Rome on 4 November 1950;
- "the relevant period" means—
(a) in relation to England and Wales, 12 months;
(b) in relation to Northern Ireland, 6 months.

Section 59(A) is now omitted from the Coroners and Justice Act on account of the Modern Slavery Act (2015), Human Trafficking and Exploitation (Criminal Justice and Support for Victims) Act (Northern Ireland) 2015 and Human Trafficking and Exploitation (Scotland) Act 2015 being enacted.

www.legislation.gov.uk/ukpga/2009/25/section/71

The Modern Slavery Act (2015)

The Modern Slavery Act 2015 is an Act of Parliament and reached Royal Assent in March 2015. It is designed to tackle slavery in the UK and consolidates previous offences relating to trafficking and slavery. Modern slavery includes human trafficking but also encompasses cases of slavery, servitude, and compulsory labour. (For explanatory notes on the Act, see HMSO (2015).)

Part 1 Offences Section 1: Slavery, servitude and forced or compulsory labour

(1) A person commits an offence if—
(a) the person holds another person in slavery or servitude and the circumstances are such that the person knows or ought to know that the other person is held in slavery or servitude, or
(b) the person requires another person to perform forced or compulsory labour and the circumstances are such that the person knows or ought to know that the other person is being required to perform forced or compulsory labour.
(2) In subsection (1) the references to holding a person in slavery or servitude or requiring a person to perform forced or compulsory labour are to be construed in accordance with Article 4 of the Human Rights Convention.

(3) In determining whether a person is being held in slavery or servitude or required to perform forced or compulsory labour, regard may be had to all the circumstances.

(4) For example, regard may be had—

    (a) to any of the person's personal circumstances (such as the person being a child, the person's family relationships, and any mental or physical illness) which may make the person more vulnerable than other persons;

    (b) to any work or services provided by the person, including work or services provided in circumstances which constitute exploitation within section 3(3) to (6).

(5) The consent of a person (whether an adult or a child) to any of the acts alleged to constitute holding the person in slavery or servitude, or requiring the person to perform forced or compulsory labour, does not preclude a determination that the person is being held in slavery or servitude, or required to perform forced or compulsory labour.

Part 1 Offences Section 2: Human trafficking

(1) A person commits an offence if the person arranges or facilitates the travel of another person ("V") with a view to V being exploited.

(2) It is irrelevant whether V consents to the travel (whether V is an adult or a child).

(3) A person may in particular arrange or facilitate V's travel by recruiting V, transporting or transferring V, harbouring or receiving V, or transferring or exchanging control over V.

(4) A person arranges or facilitates V's travel with a view to V being exploited only if—

    (a) the person intends to exploit V (in any part of the world) during or after the travel, or

    (b) the person knows or ought to know that another person is likely to exploit V (in any part of the world) during or after the travel.

(5) "Travel" means—

    (a) arriving in, or entering, any country,

    (b) departing from any country,

    (c) travelling within any country.

(6) A person who is a UK national commits an offence under this section regardless of—

(a) whose the arranging or facilitating takes place, or

(b) whose the travel takes place.

(7) A person who is not a UK national commits an offence under this section if—

(a) any part of the arranging or facilitating takes place in the United Kingdom, or

(b) the travel consists of arrival in or entry into, departure from, or travel within, the United Kingdom.

Part 1 Offences Section 3: Meaning of exploitation

(1) For the purposes of section 2 a person is exploited only if one or more of the following subsections apply in relation to the person.

Slavery, servitude and forced or compulsory labour

(2) The person is the victim of behaviour—

(a) which involves the commission of an offence under section 1, or

(b) which would involve the commission of an offence under that section if it took place in England and Wales.

Sexual exploitation

(3) Something is done to or in respect of the person—

(a) which involves the commission of an offence under—

(i)   section 1(1)(a) of the Protection of Children Act 1978 (indecent photographs of children), or

(ii) Part 1 of the Sexual Offences Act 2003 (sexual offences), as it has effect in England and Wales, or

(b) which would involve the commission of such an offence if it were done in England and Wales.

Removal of organs etc

(4) The person is encouraged, required or expected to do anything—

(a) which involves the commission, by him or her or another person, of an offence under section 32 or 33 of the Human Tissue Act 2004 (prohibition of commercial dealings in organs and restrictions on use of live donors) as it has effect in England and Wales, or

(b) which would involve the commission of such an offence, by him or her or another person, if it were done in England and Wales.

Securing services etc by force, threats or deception

(5) The person is subjected to force, threats or deception designed to induce him or her—

(a) to provide services of any kind,

(b) to provide another person with benefits of any kind, or

(c) to enable another person to acquire benefits of any kind.

Securing services etc from children and vulnerable persons

(6) Another person uses or attempts to use the person for a purpose within paragraph (a), (b) or (c) of subsection (5), having chosen him or her for that purpose on the grounds that—

(a) he or she is a child, is mentally or physically ill or disabled, or has a family relationship with a particular person, and

(b) an adult, or a person without the illness, disability, or family relationship, would be likely to refuse to be used for that purpose.

www.legislation.gov.uk/ukpga/2015/30/part/1

Section 45 of the Modern Slavery Act (2015) provides:

Defence for slavery or trafficking victims who commit an offence

(1) A person is not guilty of an offence if—

(a) the person is aged 18 or over when the person does the act which constitutes the offence,

(b) the person does that act because the person is compelled to do it,

(c) the compulsion is attributable to slavery or to relevant exploitation, and

(d) a reasonable person in the same situation as the person and having the person's relevant characteristics would have no realistic alternative to doing that act.

(2) A person may be compelled to do something by another person or by the person's circumstances.

(3) Compulsion is attributable to slavery or to relevant exploitation only if—

(a) it is, or is part of, conduct which constitutes an offence under section 1 or conduct which constitutes relevant exploitation, or

(b) it is a direct consequence of a person being, or having been, a victim of slavery or a victim of relevant exploitation.

(4) A person is not guilty of an offence if—

(a) the person is under the age of 18 when the person does the act which constitutes the offence;

(b) the person does that act as a direct consequence of the person being, or having been, a victim of slavery or a victim of relevant exploitation, and

(c) a reasonable person in the same situation as the person and having the person's relevant characteristics would do that act.

(5) For the purposes of this section—

"Relevant characteristics" means age, sex and any physical or mental illness or disability

"Relevant exploitation" is exploitation (within the meaning of section 3) that is attributable to the exploited person being, or having been, a victim of human trafficking.

(6) In this section references to an act include an omission.

(7) Subsections (1) and (4) do not apply to an offence listed in Schedule 4.

(8) The Secretary of State may by regulations amend Schedule 4.

www.legislation.gov.uk/ukpga/2015/30/section/45/enacted

Section 48 of the Modern Slavery Act (2015) provides:

Independent child trafficking advocates

(1) The Secretary of State must make such arrangements as the Secretary of State considers reasonable to enable persons ("independent child trafficking advocates") to be available to represent and support children who there are reasonable grounds to believe may be victims of human trafficking.

(2) In making arrangements under subsection (1) the Secretary of State must have regard to the principle that, so far as practicable, a child should be represented and supported by someone who is independent of any person who will be responsible for making decisions about the child.

(3) The arrangements may include provision for payments to be made to,

or in relation to, persons carrying out functions in accordance with the arrangements.

(4) A person appointed as an independent child trafficking advocate for a child must promote the child's well-being and act in the child's best interests.

(5) The advocate may (where appropriate) assist the child to obtain legal or other advice, assistance and representation, including (where necessary) by appointing and instructing legal representatives to act on the child's behalf.

(6) The Secretary of State must make regulations about independent child trafficking advocates, and the regulations must in particular make provision—

   (a) about the circumstances in which, and any conditions subject to which, a person may act as an independent child trafficking advocate;

   (b) for the appointment of a person as an independent child trafficking advocate to be subject to approval in accordance with the regulations;

   (c) requiring an independent child trafficking advocate to be appointed for a child as soon as reasonably practicable, where there are reasonable grounds to believe a child may be a victim of human trafficking;

   (d) about the functions of independent child trafficking advocates;

   (e) requiring public authorities which provide services or take decisions in relation to a child for whom an independent child trafficking advocate has been appointed to—

      (i) recognise, and pay due regard to, the advocate's functions, and

      (ii) provide the advocate with access to such information relating to the child as will enable the advocate to carry out those functions effectively (so far as the authority may do so without contravening a restriction on disclosure of the information).

(7) The Secretary of State must, no later than 9 months after the day on which this Act is passed, lay before Parliament a report on the steps the Secretary of State proposes to take in relation to the powers conferred by this section.

www.legislation.gov.uk/ukpga/2015/30/section/48/enacted

Section 52 of the Modern Slavery Act (2015) provides:

Duty to notify Secretary of State about suspected
victims of slavery or human trafficking

(1) If a public authority to which this section applies has reasonable grounds to believe that a person may be a victim of slavery or human trafficking it must notify—

    (a) the Secretary of State, or

    (b) if regulations made by the Secretary of State require it to notify a public authority other than the Secretary of State, that public authority.

(2) The Secretary of State may by regulations make provision about the information to be included in a notification.

(3) Regulations under subsection (2) must provide that a notification relating to a person aged 18 or over may not include information that—

    (a) identifies the person, or

    (b) enables the person to be identified (either by itself or in combination with other information),

    (c) unless the person consents to the inclusion of the information.

(4) Regulations under subsection (2)—

    (a) may provide that a public authority which includes information in a notification in accordance with the regulations does not breach any obligation of confidence owed by the public authority in relation to that information;

    (b) may not require or authorise the inclusion of information which contravenes any other restriction on the disclosure of information (however imposed).

(5) This section applies to—

    (a) a chief officer of police for a police area,

    (b) the chief constable of the British Transport Police Force,

    (c) the National Crime Agency,

    (d) a county council,

    (e) a county borough council,

    (f) a district council,

    (g) a London borough council,

    (h) the Greater London Authority,

(i) the Common Council of the City of London,

(j) the Council of the Isles of Scilly,

(k) the Gangmasters Licensing Authority.

(6) The Secretary of State may by regulations amend subsection (5) so as to—

(a) add or remove a public authority;

(b) amend the entry for a public authority.

The Modern Slavery Act 2015 improved support and protection for victims, helped law enforcement target perpetrators, and made sure those involved can be punished. The Act covers England and Wales, but some parts apply in Scotland and Northern Ireland.

The differences in the legislation are outlined in a report produced by the Anti-Trafficking Monitoring Group (2016). The report states that laws in both Scotland and Northern Ireland include the minimum international standards of support and assistance for victims, placing a duty on the authorities to provide this support. The Modern Slavery Act does not include minimum standards of support, setting entitlements out in statutory guidance rather than law.

www.legislation.gov.uk/ukpga/2015/30/section/52/enacted

Human Trafficking and Exploitation (Criminal Justice and Support for Victims) Act (Northern Ireland) (2015)

www.legislation.gov.uk/nia/2015/2/enacted

Human Trafficking and Exploitation (Scotland) Act (2015)

www.legislation.gov.uk/asp/2015/12/enacted

Children's Act (1989)

Section 17 of the Children's Act (1989) provides:

Provision of services for children in need, their families and others.

(1) It shall be the general duty of every local authority (in addition to the other duties imposed on them by this Part)—

(a) to safeguard and promote the welfare of children within their area who are in need; and

(b) so far as is consistent with that duty, to promote the upbringing of such children by their families,

(2) by providing a range and level of services appropriate to those children's needs.

www.legislation.gov.uk/ukpga/1989/41/section/17

United Nations

United Nations Convention of the Right of the Child (1989)

Article 39 states:

States Parties shall take all appropriate measures to promote physical and psychological recovery and social reintegration of a child victim of: any form of neglect, exploitation, or abuse; torture or any other form of cruel, inhuman or degrading treatment or punishment; or armed conflicts. Such recovery and reintegration shall take place in an environment which fosters the health, self-respect and dignity of the child.

www.unicef.org.uk/wp-content/uploads/2010/05/UNCRC_united_nations_convention_on_the_rights_of_the_child.pdf

Overview of Unseen

www.unseenuk.org

Unseen is a national UK-wide modern slavery charity with one mission: to end slavery.

Unseen does this by empowering survivors, equipping stakeholders, and influencing systemic change.

- Unseen provides direct survivor support services to men, women, and children through safe-house accommodation and outreach services, as well as free advice and support to victims, frontline professionals, and the general public via the UK's Modern Slavery Helpline available 24/7, 365 days a year.
- Unseen equips stakeholders through the provision of training, advice, and resources, training around 2000 frontline personnel per year.
- Unseen influences systemic change by working closely with the UK and overseas governments.

By buying this book you are also donating to Unseen and helping to keep vital survivor support services running.

The author has decided that all proceeds from the sale of this book will be donated to Unseen.

Subject Index

Author Index